Best wishes
from Heath

Francis M. Heath
"Partners in Progress" by Linda Richardson

Produced in Co-operation with the
Sault Ste. Marie Chamber of Commerce

Windsor Publications (Canada) Ltd.
Burlington, Ontario

# Sault Ste. Marie

## CITY BY THE RAPIDS

### An Illustrated History

Frances M. Heath

Windsor Publications (Canada) Ltd.—
History Book Division
Managing Editor: Karen Story
Design Director: Alexander D'Anca

Staff for *Sault Ste. Marie*
Manuscript Editor: Lane A. Powell
Photo Editor: Loren Prostano
Editor, Corporate Biographies: Brenda
    Berryhill
Production Editor, Corporate Biographies:
    Alyson Gould
Senior Proofreader: Susan J. Muhler
Editorial Assistants: Didier Beauvoir, Thelma
    Fleischer, Kim Kievman, Kathy B.
    Peyser, Pat Pittman, Theresa Solis
Sales Representative, Corporate Biographies:
    Elsie Savoir
Layout Artist, Corporate Biographies: Bonnie
    Felt
Layout Artist: Mari Catherine Preimesberger
Designer: Tanya Maiboroda

Elliot Martin, Chairman of the Board
James L. Fish III, Chief Operating Officer

# CONTENTS

During winter months the Great Lakes are transformed into magnificent ice-scapes. Photo by Colin Shaw. Courtesy, Westfile Inc.

# FOREWORD

It has been more than 80 years since the publication of *The Story of Bawating Being the Annals of Sault Ste. Marie,* by Edward H. Capp, the last thematically and chronologically developed history of Sault Ste. Marie. During the years between 1904 and 1988 an increasing number of excellent books have been written on topics of specific interest, but the general history of the community has remained largely untouched. Fortunately, the Sault Ste. Marie Chamber of Commerce recognized the gap and opted to mark its Centennial with the publication of an illustrated history book.

Co-operation has long been regarded as a hallmark of the spirit of Sault Ste. Marie. The ability to work together in peace and harmony has enabled everyone, from the earliest residents, to survive in an environment naturally fraught with hardship.

This willingness to help others still prevails, and simplified the preparation of this book. The staff of the Reference Department at the Sault Ste. Marie Public Library provided help above and beyond the call of duty. Staff members at the Algoma University College Library, the Bayliss Public Library, and the Sault Ste. Marie Museum provided immeasurable support and assistance. Thanks go as well to the Public Archives of Canada, the Archives of Ontario, and the state historical societies and archives of Michigan, Wisconsin, and Minnesota.

Photographs are an integral component of this book. The provincial and public archives, Parks Canada, Bayliss Public Library, the Sault Public Library, and Local Union 2251 United Steelworkers of America all generously loaned photos for reproduction purposes. Special thanks go to the Sault Ste. Marie Museum and to Betsy Allaway for allowing access to the Museum's photographic resources, and to private collector Lillian M. (Sel) Quinn. Kevin and Anna Dobble, Frank Calvano, Walter Materna, and Pat and Henry Speer accepted the challenge of reproducing the photographs for publication.

In the mid-1970s Sault native Morley Torgov wrote a book about growing up in Sault Ste. Marie, entitled *A Good Place to Come From.* Mr. Torgov was right—Sault Ste. Marie is a good place to come from. It is also a great place to be.

# INTRODUCTION

Sault Ste. Marie has enjoyed a long and colourful history. Although circumstances have changed with the times, two things have remained constant—the St. Mary's River and the rapids.

The river, and the St. Mary's rapids located in mid-channel, were created as a result of early glacial activity. Initially, although the river served as a natural east-west conduit, the rapids seriously impeded the flow of traffic. The first native peoples, their westward travels across Canada temporarily slowed by the rapids, made the best of the situation. With no small amount of perseverance they turned a potentially negative presence to their benefit. Bawating, the native community on the shore of the St. Mary's River, quickly gained renown as an important fishing and meeting place.

The river that brought native peoples from the west also brought European missionaries, explorers, and later fur traders from the east. Like the natives, the Europeans were frustrated in their movements by the rapids. They, too, took advantage of the naturally occurring stopping-place by constructing missions and posts, the rudiments of permanent settlement.

As commercial activity accelerated, the need to circumvent the hindrance created by the rapids became evident. The North West Company constructed a canoe lock in an attempt to resolve the problem, but it operated for less than 15 years before being destroyed by American troops during the War of 1812. The area was once again without a lock, a circumstance that remained until the construction of a canal and lock at Sault Ste. Marie, Michigan. The Canadian canal opened to traffic in 1895, creating an all-Canadian water route from the head of Lake Superior to the Atlantic Ocean. The canals on both sides of the St. Mary's River eliminated the need to maintain separate fleets on the upper and lower Great Lakes. The locks soon became the busiest in the world.

Because of its strategic location on the St. Mary's River, Sault Ste. Marie flourished. Industrial and commercial activity evolved rapidly, followed closely by the growth of social services.

The river continues to play an important role in the community. Its shores remain the meeting place they were so many generations ago.

*Scenic St. Joseph's Island National Historic Park is located 28 miles east of Sault Ste. Marie along Highway 17. It is noted for sponsoring maple syrup festivals, and for its 100 miles of exceptionally well-groomed snowmobile trails. Photo by Colin Shaw. Courtesy, Westfile Inc.*

# Chapter One

*Glaciers gouged the St. Mary's Rapids from the red sandstone bedrock. Indian legends and lore, however, presented a much more colourful explanation for the occurrence. Courtesy, Sault Ste. Marie Museum*

# RENDEZVOUS AT THE RAPIDS

Sault Ste. Marie is located along the edge of the Canadian Shield, one of the oldest landforms of the continent of North America. About a million years ago continental glaciers were formed. One glacier, perhaps thousands of feet thick and weighing millions of tons, spread across the region. As the ice sheet moved in a southwesterly direction, the immense size and weight modified the topographical features: bedrock was stripped of its mantle; some surfaces were scratched and gouged and others were smoothed. Elevated areas were abraded. Old river valleys that ran parallel to the direction of the glacier's movement were widened, deepened, and lengthened.

Gradually, the climate moderated. Tempered by a warming trend, the glaciers retreated northward and relieved the earth of the pressure exerted by the ice. Glacial till was again gathered up, this time by the receding sheets, and deposited in new locations. Masses of sterile rock formations were left behind in rugged ridges interspersed with a myriad of channels, lakes, and bogs. The result was a formidable and seemingly barren landscape.

Sault Ste. Marie and the surrounding areas are situated on two levels of land—the Upper and Lower Algonquin Lowlands. The lower plain level is only a few feet above the level of the river. The upper plain level is separated from the river by a sixty-foot escarpment. The region, from its vantage point along the southern fringe of the Shield, displays diverse formations of rock, sand and gravel deposits, and clay belts, as well as agriculturally rich land.

*Right: The encampment of Colonel Wolseley, (when the Chicora was refused permission to pass through the American lock system) is depicted in this watercolour, painted by William Armstrong in 1901. Courtesy, City of Sault Ste. Marie, Armstrong Collection*

*Below right: William Armstrong painted this portage road which was used by travellers before the construction of the batteau lock by the North West Company in 1796. Courtesy, City of Sault Ste. Marie, Armstrong Collection*

*Above: The first Anglican church in Sault Ste. Marie was established in 1832. St. Luke's Church depicted in this 1945 painting, was built in 1870. Courtesy, Anglican Diocese of Algoma*

*Left: William Armstrong painted this Indian hut in the style of Paul Kane, an artist known for his interpretations of early Indian life in Canada and the United States. Courtesy, City of Sault Ste. Marie, Armstrong Collection.*

*Below: The home of Charles Oakes Ermatinger was constructed along the banks of the St. Mary's River, and illustrated here by William Armstrong. Courtesy, City of Sault Ste. Marie, Armstrong Collection*

The Great Lakes are very young, having achieved their modern form and appearance some 13,000 years ago. Lake Superior is the wildest and most turbulent of the five Great Lakes. It is one of the largest and deepest inland bodies of water in the world, second only to the Caspian Sea. Lake Superior is connected to the more placid Lake Huron by means of the St. Mary's River. The 20-foot difference in the water levels of the two lakes is equalized at the rapids in the river. Father Dablon, an early Jesuit missionary, described the rapids as ". . . a very violent current of waters from Lake Superior, which, finding themselves checked by a great number of rocks that dispute this passage, form a dangerous cascade half a league in width, all these waters descending and plunging headlong together, as if by a flight of stairs . . . "

Ojibway oral tradition offers an interpretation slightly more fanciful than the geological explanation for the creation of the river and the rapids. According to legend, an Indian hunter built a dam across the narrows in an attempt to trap an elusive beaver. He hoped that by holding back the waters he would be able to force the beaver from his lodge. Leaving his wife to watch the dam, the hunter went off in search of other game. Suddenly, Manabosho, the great uncle of the Ojibway, appeared chasing a deer. When the deer leaped into the water above the dam, Manabosho called to the woman to help him. As she left the dam site, the beaver surfaced, breaking through the dam and scattering the stones down the channel, thus creating the rapids. When the brave returned, he was consumed with anger and killed his wife for her carelessness. According to legend the rushing water is her unheeded explanation being cried out to her husband; the bubbles are her tears.

It is not known precisely when the first inhabitants settled in this area. Indian archeological explorations indicate, however, that the earliest inhabitants may have arrived as early as 10,000 years ago. Archeological records indicate that there were numerous cultural movements in and out of the Great Lakes Basin before a permanent settlement took place. The first nomadic visitors were probably members of the Plano culture, whose ancestors had come from Asia across the ancient land bridge. They spread westward across North America east of the Rocky Mountains and across the plains. The Plano culture was followed by the Shield Archaic culture and then by the Laurel culture. Archeological records indicate that as these cultural movements came and went, so too did the area's inhabitants.

The nomadic tribesmen were transient, but the impediment to water travel created by the rapids in the St. Mary's River remained constant. From the time of the earliest travellers, the shores of the rapids became a natural stopping point on any journey either eastward or westward. The strategic location of the settlement provided a natural defense system by affording an excellent view of all movement along the St. Mary's River. The turbulent, fast-moving waters of the rapids created a unique and enticing ecosystem which encouraged the settlement of the area. Wild game and fowl were abundant; fruits, berries, and other foodstuffs to supplement the native diet were readily available, and materials for the construction of shelter was plentiful. Perhaps most importantly, though, the rapids provided a natural habitat for whitefish.

Whitefish quickly became a vital component in both the dietary and economic facets of settlement life. Fishing was a year-round activity—sturgeon was especially plentiful in the spring and whitefish in the fall. The natives called the whitefish Attikamak, or "caribou of the water". The most common method of catching the fish involved the use of a dipnet—a pole about 10 feet long with a net attached to the end. Fishing was a two-man operation. The man in the stern would steer the canoe in among the rocks and lodge it there. The man in the bow would stand and wield the dipnet. Alexander Henry, the British fur trader and explorer, noted that as late as 1760 ". . . a skillful fisherman, in autumn, will take upwards of 500 fish in two hours . . ."

Word of the abundance of the whitefish spread rapidly throughout the Algonkian nation. Within a short time, the fishing village on the shores of the St. Mary's River had evolved into a seasonal meeting place for other native groups anxious to share in the food wealth. The permanent settlement, thought to have some 150 to 200 residents, burgeoned to an estimated 2,000 in the fall. It was a simple matter to distinguish the residents from the visitors on the basis of their fishing skills; the local fishermen were much more adept and technologically advanced in their techniques than were the transients.

Bawating, as the settlement came to be known, assumed additional social,

cultural, and economic significance as a meeting place. The easy accessibility by water and the fact that the rapids created a natural impediment to travel made the settlement a natural stopping point. The Algonkian peoples who congregated seasonally at Bawating were related in language and culture. They did not recognize territorial boundaries and exhibited friendly relations with one another. These genial relationships were often solidified and cemented at the meetings at Bawating. Defense alliances and trade agreements were often negotiated. It was not uncommon to cement a deal with a marriage between young men and women from the various congregated tribes. Since marriage between members of the same band was a taboo, these deals served a dual purpose.

The economic importance of the meeting place soon superseded the social. The bands were largely self-sufficient, but frequent social interaction led to the establishment of strong trading bonds. Bartering became an integral part of the meeting place activities. Hides were exchanged for maple sugar, fish for tobacco, and copper nuggets for corn.

*The seasonal settlement at Bawating was much larger than the permanent one. Thousands of native people travelled to Bawating and established their camps on the shores of the St. Mary's River. Courtesy, Sault Ste. Marie Museum*

The interaction between the permanent residents and the seasonal visitors resulted in an exchange of ideas. The clan system indigenous to the agricultural Indians of the southern regions was adopted by the native people of this area.

The Ojibway residents at Bawating lived in small, highly integrated groups. Each member of the community had tasks to carry out. The men were traditionally hunters and fishermen responsible for ensuring a steady supply of food, while the women cared for the home and family. With the influx of agricultural concepts and know-how from the regions south of the lakes, the women gained the extra responsibility for the growing and harvesting of foodstuffs.

The residents lived in dome-shaped dwellings known as wigwams or wickiups. The homes could be of any size or shape but the dome roof was a constant characteristic. The framework consisted of saplings anchored in the ground and then bent and lashed together to form arches. The exterior was covered with birch bark, animal hides, or any other available materials. This made for a lightweight and portable home. The coverings could be removed and the poles dislodged with a minimum of effort.

Nature was a guiding force in the lives of these early residents. In the flora and fauna they found their gods. The stellar constellations served as their calendars reminding them of the changing seasons. The appearance of Orion, for example, heralded the approach of fall, and with it the annual whitefish run. As the stars foretold the approach of spring, the male residents of the settlement prepared to spend a month in the sugar bush. The maple trees would be tapped and the sap gathered to produce maple sugar, a dietary staple as well as an important trade item.

Traditionally, the local Ojibway were hunters. In addition to small game like squirrels, rabbits, and wolverines,

*The homes of the Chippewa Indians were made of birch bark and saplings and were often constructed by the women and children of the tribe. The wigwam pictured here was large enough to house more than six family members and was at least partially portable. Courtesy, State Historical Society of Wisonsin*

larger game like moose were pursued. Generally, dogs were used to herd the moose. In mating season, calls would be fashioned from rolled birch bark. Once the moose was attracted and cornered, it would be speared or beaten by a group of hunters. Beaver was another popular prey. There were two predominant methods of trapping the beaver, and both dated back to prehistoric times. One method, known as trenching, entailed sealing off both entrances to the beaver's lodge to trap the animals within. The hunters would then dig through the roof of the lodge and spear or club the beavers. The second method was used in the spring during the runoff; a dam would be constructed in a swollen channel to flood the lodge and force the beavers out. As they surfaced, they would be speared or clubbed.

The Ojibway Indians were, in effect, the area's first miners. They first mined pure copper ore from surface outcrops, and later, as it became more difficult to find above ground, they followed ore veins and dug it out of the ground. In the native copper workshops, the copper was removed from the rocks by first heating the rocks in a fire pit and then dousing them with cold water, causing the rock to crack. The copper could then be removed by hammering it out of the rock.

The copper was used to produce weapons and tools as well as ornaments. Initially, the items were large and required vast amounts of the metal in their production. As it became increasingly difficult to obtain the copper, however, the manufactured items became smaller.

There was a mythology or superstition surrounding the discovery and mining of copper, which prevailed long after the Indians' contact with Europeans. One legend was recounted by explorer Jonathan Carver in 1796:

*One of the Chippewa chiefs told me that some of their people being once driven on the island of Maurepas, which lies on the north east part of the lake, found on it large quantities of heavy, shining yellow sand and that from their description must have been copper dust. Being struck with the beautiful appearance of it, in the morning when they re-entered their canoe, they attempted to bring some of it away; but a spirit of an amazing size, according to their account sixty feet in height, strode after them and commanded them to deliver back what they had taken away. Terrified at his gigantic stature, and seeing that he had nearly overtaken them, they were glad to restore their shining treasure; on which they were suffered to depart without further molestation. Since this incident no Indian has heard it will venture near the same haunted coast.*

The location of the copper was a closely guarded secret that was never willingly divulged. According to a letter written by Antoine Denis Raudot in 1710, disclosure was forbidden:

*All Indians believe that, if they were to point out a mine to anyone else, they would die within the year; they are so convinced of this that it is almost impossible to get them to reveal where they are, and this is why we know only those the knowledge of which they cannot possibly conceal.*

# Chapter Two

The Missionary, *an engraving copied from a painting by Frederick Remington, was a memorial to the many French missionaries who sought to bring Christianity to the North American Indians. Life in the New World was difficult for missionaries who were often scorned by natives for denouncing tribal traditions.* Courtesy, State Historical Society of Wisconsin

# THE SAULT AND
# THE FUR TRADE

When the first French explorers sailed to North America in the early sixteenth century, they were searching for a northwest passage to Asia, a means of avoiding the treacherous sea voyage around the Cape of Good Hope. As they travelled toward the interior of North America along the St. Lawrence River, they were certain that they had located the long-sought route to the silks, spices, and precious gems and minerals readily found in China, India, and other parts of Asia. But rather than the eagerly anticipated easy route to instant wealth, they encountered a rugged, inhospitable land with seemingly little to offer but vast expanses of forest and fresh water.

Although Jacques Cartier had explored the eastern coast of modern-day Canada as far as the Gaspe Peninsula in 1534 and a year later became the first of the French explorers to sail up the St. Lawrence River, it was not until 1610 that the French penetrated the North American continent to reach what is now Ontario. Another eight years passed before the first Europeans arrived at the settlement at Bawating.

With the extensive trade and communications network maintained by native peoples, the residents of Bawating would have been aware of the impending arrival of the Europeans long before they reached the settlement. The arrival of Etienne Brûlé, then, would have been met with a high degree of curiosity tempered with suspicion and possibly some fear.

*Above: Samuel de Champlain, regarded as the Father of New France, was responsible for sending Etienne Brule in search of a water route to the Orient. Based on Brule's reports, Champlain prepared a map in 1632 showing not only the "Grans Lac" (Lake Superior) and its connection with "Mer Douce" (Lake Huron) by means of the yet unnamed St. Mary's River, but also the settlement at the Sault. Courtesy, Archives of Ontario*

Etienne Brûlé was a protégé of the French explorer and cartographer Samuel de Champlain. In 1610, when he had been at Quebec for only two years, Champlain sent Brûlé into the wilderness to familiarize himself with the language and customs of the native peoples. Brûlé returned to Quebec only to set out once more in 1617, this time to explore the " Mer Douce", Lake Huron. Upon his return to Quebec, Brûlé reported that he had reached Bawating. He returned to Bawating in 1622, this time accompanied by Grenoble. They renamed the settlement Sault du Gas-

ton in honour of Gaston, brother of King Louis of France. To support their claim that they had reached Bawating, Brûlé and Grenoble produced a piece of the copper indigenous to the area.

It is generally acknowledged that Champlain used the information provided by Brûlé to create his 1632 map of New France. Since Champlain himself travelled no further west than the French River, Brûlé must have supplied him with a relatively accurate description of the size and location of the permanent settlement as well as the size and configuration of Lake Superior. Champlain referred to the area as "Sault" in keeping with the name change applied by Etienne Brûlé.

Following Brûlé's departure, no Europeans visited this area until Jean Nicolet arrived in 1634. Like Brûlé, Nicolet had been sent out by Champlain to live among the Indians. Nicolet became so proficient in the dialects of the native peoples and so familiar with their customs that he was a readily welcomed visitor in the villages and encampments throughout the region. His acceptance by the native populace permitted Nicolet to forge a strong, lasting alliance with the Indians.

Nicolet apparently never abandoned the hope that he would one day find the Northwest Passage. As he neared the straits at the Sault for the first time he concluded that the channel would empty into the long-sought western sea. He donned the damask robe that he carried with him in anticipation of this momentous event, and after firing a volley of shots to announce his arrival, he advanced to make the acquaintance of the "Asians". Imagine his chagrin and disappointment (to say nothing of the amusement of the native spectators) when he found that he was still among the Indian people with whom he had been living for some 16 years!

Christianity followed close on the heels of the exploration of the North American wilderness. The Roman Catholic Church in France was the driving force behind the surge of missionary zeal that dispatched a number of priests to contact and Christianize the Indians. The Jesuits, who ultimately came to dominate the religious life of New France, were the most avid missionaries working amongst the Indians.

The fact that the Ojibway at Bawating greeted the Jesuits without hostility did not mean that they accepted the teachings of the "black robes" or that they were prepared to surrender their

traditional religions. Ojibway mythology accorded Bawating a sacred significance and the annual gatherings on the shores of the River bore strong religious significance. Several religious groups existed within the confines of the native community. The most intricate of these was the sacred Medewin society, which was based on myth, ritual, and tradition. Another was the Mashkike, a group composed predominantly of women. They practiced the art of herbalism. The Walones were a highly elusive group who presided over mystic ceremonies such as night-long feasts, and performed dangerous fire tricks. The final native religious group was the Jessakkids. They were seers with the power to isolate and destroy fire spirits. The Jessakkids, more than any other of the Ojibway religious groups, resisted the teachings of the Jesuit priests.

The first Jesuits to travel to the area were Fathers Isaac Jogues and Charles Raymbault, who arrived in 1642. The two priests, if not necessarily their teachings, were accepted by the Ojibway. Jogues and Raymbault were invited to live among the Indians at Bawating, an invitation they declined because of the isolation of the community, according to the *Jesuit Relations* of 1642:

*The captains of this Nation of the Sault invited our Fathers to take up their abode among them. They were given to understand that this was not impossible, provided that they were well disposed to receive our instruction. After having held a council, they replied that they greatly desired this great fortune, that they would embrace us as their brothers, and would profit by our*

*Facing page: Based on information provided by Etienne Brule, Samuel de Champlain created his famed 1632 map of New France. Note that the cartographer located an Indian settlement at the site of Sault Ste. Marie. Courtesy, Gordon Daun Collection, Judge Stere Room, Bayliss Public Library*

*words. But we need Labourers for that pur-
pose; we must first try to win the Peoples
that are nearest to us, and meanwhile pray
Heaven to hasten the moment of their conversion.*

Even though this degree of acceptance left the Ojibway on the brink of conversion, 19 years lapsed between the departure of the Fathers Jogues and Raymbault and the arrival of the next priest, Father Rene Menard. Menard, in turn, was followed by Father Claude Allouez in 1665. Father Allouez provided an interesting and invaluable description of the Ojibway religion, which was recorded in the *Jesuit Relations* for that year:

*The Savages regard this Lake Superior as
a Divinity, and offer its sacrifices whether
on account of its size, for its length is two
hundred leagues, and its greatest width
eighty,—or because of its goodness in furnishing fish for the sustenance of all these
tribes, in default of game, which is scarce
in the neighbourhood. One often finds at
the bottom of the water pieces of pure copper
. . . I have seen such pieces several times
in the Savages hands; and since they are
superstitious, they keep them as so many
divinities . . .*

As a result of Father Allouez's reports to the Jesuit superiors in New France, it was decided that a permanent mission should be constructed at the Sault. According to the recollections of Father Mercier, again recorded in the *Jesuit Relations*, the Sault was selected as

the site for the mission because ". . . it was the place where the natives were first encountered in the upper country and it was the rendezvous of all the natives who composed the great trading fleets which annually went down to Montreal."

Father Jacques Marquette was dispatched to the Sault in 1668. As Apostle for the District, his job was to assist Father Claude Dablon in ministering to the spiritual needs of the natives of the Algonkian nation. It was Marquette who was responsible for the construction of the mission. It consisted of a residence for the missionaries as well as several outbuildings. The entire site was surrounded by a 12-foot palisade. The location of the mission on the shores of the St. Mary's River was deemed to be ". . . very advantageous in which to perform apostles functions since it is the greatest resort of most of the Savages of these region . . ." Marquette remained at the Sault until 1669, when he was transferred to La Pointe du Saint Esprit at Chequogemon Bay. He did, however, leave one lasting reminder of his stay: he changed the name of the settlement from Sault du Gaston to Sault de Sainte Marie in honour of the Virgin Mary.

Following the departure of Father Marquette, the mission remained operational. When Father Galinee, a superior missionary, and his travelling companion de Casson undertook a voyage to the upper lakes in 1670, they found the mission to be a thriving hub of activity:

*At last we arrived . . . at the Sainte-Marie
of the Sault, the place where the Jesuit*

*Fathers have made their principal establishment for the mission of the Ottawas and their neighbouring tribes. They have two men in their service since last year, who have built them a pretty fort, that is to say, a square of cedar posts twelve feet high, with a chapel and house inside the fort so that they now see themselves in the condition of not being dependent in any way on the Indians. They have a large clearing well planted, from which they ought to gather a good part of their sustenance . . . The fruit these fathers are producing here is more for the French who are often here to the number of twenty or twenty-five than for the Indians; for although there are some who are baptized, there are none yet that are good enough Catholics to be able to attend divine service . . . I saw no particular sign of Christianity amongst the Indians of this place . . .*

The *Jesuit Relations* of 1669-1670 emphasize the physical features of the area:

*What is commonly called the Sault is not properly a Sault, or a very high water fall, but a very violent current of waters from Lake Superior, which, finding themselves checked by a great number of rocks that dispute their passage, form a dangerous cascade half a league in width, all these waters descending and plunging headlong together, as if by a flight of stairs, over the rocks which bar the whole river.*

The *Relations* indicated that the whitefish was important to the area:

*It is at the foot of these rapids, and even amid these boiling waters, that extensive fishing is carried on, from spring until winter, of a kind of fish found usually only in Lake Superior and Lake Huron. It is called in the Native language "Atticameg" and in ours "Whitefish" because in Truth it is very white; and it is most excellent, so that it furnishes food almost by itself to the greater part of all these peoples.*

The narrator of the *Relations* enumerated the presence of 19 nations at the Sault when he visited. He attributed the number of visitors to the readily available food supplies: "This convenience of having fish in such quantities that one has only to go to and draw them out of the water, attracts the surrounding nations to the spot during the summer."

Until 1671 no formal claim to the land surrounding Sault St. Marie had been made. Then, on June 4 of that year, the French asserted title at a colourful pageant. Simon-François Daumont, Sieur de St. Lusson, took possession of all of North America west of Montreal in the name of King Louis XIV of France. St. Lusson had been sent out in 1670 to find the copper mines in the Lake Superior region and to locate, if possible, the still-sought Northwest Passage. This action was taken by the French in retaliation against British expansion and fur trade activity in the area surrounding Hudson Bay. At a pageant at Sault de Ste. Marie, St. Lusson "caused the greatest portion possible of the other neighbouring tribes to be assembled there, who attended to the number of fourteen nations . . ."

Through his interpreter, Nicolas Perrot, St. Lusson informed the natives of the new sovereignty of all the territory, both discovered and as yet unexplored. After informing the Indians of his intentions, St. Lusson erected ". . . a cross . . . in order that the fruits of Christianity be produced there, and near it a cedar pole to which he later affixed the arms of France . . ." Father Claude Dablon, who witnessed the pageant as a representative of the Roman Catholic Church, reported that the declarations of St. Lusson were accepted by the natives ". . . with the delight and astonishment of all these people who had never seen anything of this kind." Although the cross and the pole were soon uprooted by the Ojibway, they were unable in any way to alter the far-ranging implications of the pageant. In effect it marked the introduction of explorations that saw the French expand north to James Bay, west to the Rocky Mountains, and south to the Gulf of Mexico.

The Pageant of St. Lusson provided the impetus for the development of the mission at Sault de Ste. Marie. In a letter dated October 1683, the Superior of the Jesuit Missions described the work being done at this northern locale. The Superior, like many of his contemporaries, noted that the Indian tribes used the settlement as a meeting place:

*We have houses with chapels at Sault de Ste. Marie . . . wherein we perform with entire freedom all the exercises of Religion . . . Father Charles Albiane . . . has now entire charge of the entire mission at the Sault. There he works for the Instruction*

*not only of the Saulteurs, but also of the Crees and of many savages who dwell to the North of Lake Superior, and who come to Sault Ste. Marie.*

The small mission at the Sault was plagued by disaster. In 1671 the original mission was burned to the ground. A second mission was constructed in 1674 but it, too, was doomed. It was destroyed in the course of an Indian war that took the lives of 230 people.

The mission was reconstructed once more, but by 1689 the Iroquois had advanced as far northward as Sault Ste. Marie, which threatened its existence still another time. The ensuing wars between the Ojibway and the Iroquois led to the closure of the mission and to a temporary cessation of attempts to explore and Christianize the area. As a consequence, the European factor passed from the local scene. When European movement in the area resumed, the focus had changed; although the missionaries remained active, the compelling force behind the French incursion was commercial. The region surrounding Sault Ste. Marie, which had originally appeared to offer so little, had yielded something as valuable as the exotic riches of the Orient sought by the early explorers—furs.

The relationship that evolved between the European visitors to Sault Ste. Marie and the Ojibway residents of the community was based upon the European desire for furs and the ability of the local native people to fulfill this need.

In an attempt to capitalize on the potential wealth of North America, King

Charles II of England in 1670 granted a charter to Prince Rupert authorizing the formation of a fur trading enterprise, the Hudson's Bay Company. This company was given exclusive control of all territory that drained directly or indirectly into Hudson Bay. Outposts were established at numerous strategic points throughout the region in order to facilitate the fur trading operations with the natives.

The impetus behind the creation of the Hudson's Bay Company had been the discoveries of Pierre Esprit Radisson and his brother-in-law and travelling companion, Medard Chouart des Groseilliers. In 1659, Radisson and Groseilliers set out from Montreal and travelled westward to Chequogemon Bay. These early explorers passed through Sault Ste. Marie en route and they pitched camp near the St. Mary's rapids. Radisson, who maintained a journal of his travels, recorded that

*The Rapids was formerly the dwelling of those with whom we wear and consequently we must not ask them if they knew where they have layed. We made cottages at our advantages and found the truth of what those men have often [said], that if once we could come to that place we should make good cheare of a fish they call assignack, wch signifieth a whitefish. The bears, the castors and ye orinack sheweth often but to their cost; indeed it was to us like a terrestrial paradise.*

This "terrestrial paradise" proved to be a highly lucrative locale for Radisson and Groseilliers. They discovered the immense natural wealth of the area and before embarking on their return voyage to Montreal they loaded all available canoes with furs.

Upon their return to New France, the governor of the colony seized the furs and fined the two men on the pretext that they had not secured his permission before embarking on their explorations. Groseilliers, according to some reports, was jailed for his actions. Radisson and Groseilliers applied to the Governor of New France for a hearing and when their appeal was rejected they submitted their petition for justice to the government of France. Their pleas were ignored yet again; in retaliation for this lack of hearing, Radisson and Groseilliers approached English officials and offered to share with them the invaluable information they had gathered regarding the geography and natural resources of the interior of North America. The English were most anxious to acquire the information the two French explorers possessed. It was on the basis of this information that the Hudson's Bay Company was formed.

For many years the agents of the Hudson's Bay Company carried out their tasks undisturbed. Although the French had formally claimed the region surrounding Sault Ste. Marie at the Pageant of St. Lusson in 1671, the British traders enforced their ownership of the territory and only occasionally did independent French traders infringe in an attempt to broaden their sphere in the never-ending quest for furs.

The attitude of the French government toward their land claim changed in 1750. In that year, Louis de Bonne, Sieur de Miselle, and Louis de Gardeur,

In 1750 the French en-
forced their claim to New
France. Louis le Gardeur,
Sieur de Repentigny (pic-
tured here) and Louis de
Bonne, Sieur de Miselle,
were granted a tract of
land along the St. Mary's
River. The grant recip-
ients informed the King
of France of their inten-
tion to construct a resting
spot for voyageurs. Cour-
tesy, Gordon Daun Collec-
tion, Judge Stere Room,
Bayliss Public Library

Sieur de Repentigny, were granted a tract of land along the rapids of the St. Mary's River. The grant fronted six leagues along the river and extended six leagues inland. It also included exclusive rights to the fur trade privileges and control of this vital outlet point on Lake Superior. In the petition presented to the King of France, the grant recipients stated that a post would be constructed on the land to provide a safe haven for voyageurs, "especially those who trade in the northern region", and to destroy the trade relations between the Indians and the British.

De Repentigny travelled to Sault Ste. Marie in the autumn of 1750. Immediately upon arrival, he and his men began construction of a fort. Work continued throughout the winter of 1750-1751, when trees were cut to provide the stakes for a palisade. By the summer of 1751 the enclosure, which measured 110 feet square and included three timber houses, was completed.

Once the construction work was finished, de Repentigny turned his hand to yet another practical matter: the provision of food for the inhabitants of the post as well as its many visitors. He transported livestock, including a bull, a horse, and a pair of oxen, from Mackinac, and then he hired Jean-Baptiste Cadotte, a French voyageur "married to an Indian women at Sault Ste. Marie", to begin cultivating the land.

The nature of the area and its role in the fur trade changed in 1763 with the negotiation of the Treaty of Paris at the conclusion of the Seven Years' War. According to the terms of the treaty, French territories in Canada were ceded to the British, and French garrisons and posts in the upper country fell under British jurisdiction. British traders eagerly moved into the area, anxious to share in the Indian trade which the French had dominated from the early days of the fur trade.

One of the earliest British traders to travel to Sault Ste. Marie was Alexander Henry. In 1765 the commander at Mackinac granted the monopoly in the Lake Superior fur trade to Henry. Immediately upon issuance of the monopoly, Henry left Mackinac for Sault Ste.

Marie, where he took Jean Baptist Cadotte as his partner. Jonathan Carver, who visited the Sault Ste. Marie area in 1766, reported that there was a fort at the Sault and that it was occupied by Cadotte, inferring that Henry and Cadotte had assumed ownership of the palisaded fort constructed by de Repentigny and previously farmed by Cadotte. Henry apparently remained at Sault Ste. Marie as an independent trader until the winter of 1770-1771.

The Hudson's Bay Company tried to ignore the independents such as Henry. As their numbers grew, however, and as the volume of business they transacted increased, the company was forced to expand the number of posts they maintained in order to remain competitive.

The independent fur trade continued to grow in strength and prosperity until, in 1779-1780, the North West Company was formed by a group of free traders. Although the company was most active in the northwest, it also conducted business in the area south and west of the Great Lakes known to the traders as the Fond du Lac.

The North West Company was composed of experienced and enthusiastic traders, many of whom had been wintering in the northwest even before the 1763 peace treaty. Their energy and enthusiasm were generated largely by the desire to generate a profit from the new business venture. Their zeal was evidenced by their treatment of the French independents who continued to operate within the territorial confines of the North West Company. By 1787 the Company had bought out as many of the independents as possible. Those

who refused to relinquish their independent status were subjected to such duress and harassment that they had little option except to move to new trading areas or to abandon the trading enterprise completely. Independents reluctant to leave the area often joined the North West Company so that they could continue to live and work in their chosen regions. Within a relatively short time, the North West Company came to dominate the fur trade activity of the Lake Superior region.

The North West Company post at Sault Ste. Marie was originally located on the south shore of the St. Mary's River. Following the signing of the Treaty of Utrecht, which was negotiated in 1794 and became effective in 1796, the British were legally obligated to vacate all forts and posts located in American territory. In compliance with this legislation, the North West Company transferred its post to the north shore of the river and obtained rights from the Ojibway chiefs and tribal elders to occupy a site not far from the foot of the St. Mary's rapids. The post the Company constructed consisted of several buildings, including living quarters, storage houses, and numerous outbuildings, as well as a sawmill. Then, in 1797 they began construction of a canoe lock. The completion of the lock in 1798 greatly facilitated the movement of men, supplies, furs, and canoes around the natural barrier created by the rapids. The lock eliminated the need to portage heavy loads at Sault Ste. Marie.

The westward expansion of the fur trade and the construction of Fort St. Joseph ensured British domination of the upper Great Lakes in the late-eighteenth century. In an attempt to ameliorate the effects of the British influence and at the same time assert their own authority, the Americans established garrisons at both Detroit and Mackinac. The only other jarring note in this otherwise pastoral scene was the dissension within the North West Company that led to the formation of the rival XY Company. Regardless, however, the fur trade seems to have continued uninterrupted.

It was during this period of relative stability and tranquility in the economic and social history of Sault Ste. Marie that Charles Oakes Ermatinger, the noted local fur trader, arrived in the settlement.

Ermatinger entered the fur trade in 1797 as an independent, following a family tradition established by his father Laurenz and his uncle Forrest Oakes, two original partners in the North West Company. Ermatinger set out from Montreal in the spring of that year, and by the fall he had travelled as far west as Sandy Lake, near the headwaters of the Mississippi River. While wintering at Sandy Lake, Ermatinger took as his wife Mananowe, the daughter of Katawabeda, an influential Indian chief. In the spring of 1798 Charles and Charlotte (as Mananowe came to be known) continued the journey westward begun by Charles; they arrived at Fort George on the Fraser River late in the fall of 1798.

Charles relinquished his status as an independent trader shortly after reaching the western post. Much to the chagrin of the Nor' Westers, he joined ranks with the XY Company. Although he was apparently very successful during his years with the XY Company, he severed his ties with that organization in 1800 and joined the North West Company, with the understanding that if he served the company well for five years he would be admitted as a partner. Obviously his work measured up to the standards established by the proprietors since the minutes of their annual meeting for 1805 stated in part that it was unanimously resolved that "C.O. Ermatinger should be [one of] the first clerks provided for . . ." In consideration of his past service and as an inducement to maintain the quality of his work, Charles was assigned ". . . one share or hundredth part of the North West Company for the outfit of the year 1808 . . ."

The following year, 1806, Ermatinger wintered at Lake Winnipeg with George Nelson. According to the journal maintained by Nelson, Ermatinger was an extremely prudent and farsighted man who was capable of providing a good living for his family in an area where most men would have been hard pressed to even survive. It came as a shock to Nelson to learn in September 1807 that his friend Ermatinger had, in his words, ". . . gone to Montreal, an equivalent in our vocabulary to disgrace, which he certainly, for many reasons, did not deserve." Although Nelson did not elaborate on the nature of the "disgrace" to which he referred, he fuelled the mystery by adding that Ermatinger had ". . . severely writhed under the pressure and nature of slander . . ."

It was following this clouded departure from the North West Company that Charles moved Charlotte and their children to Sault Ste. Marie. As a site for their new home he selected a heavily wooded lot on the north side of the St. Mary's River about a mile and a half below the rapids. Ermatinger resumed his status as an independent trader and constructed a residence which doubled as a headquarters for his trading operations, complete with a post and store.

Ermatinger began to make plans for the replacement of his temporary log buildings in 1812. Before his plans had advanced to the construction stage, however, war was declared against Great Britain by the United States, and men and materials from the Sault were pressed into action.

As a benefit of advance notification, Captain Charles Roberts, commander of Fort St. Joseph, was prepared for the war prior to the formal declaration on June 18, 1812. John Jacob Astor, the proprietor of the American Fur Company, had informed Roberts and other British officials of the impending war. Although Astor probably orchestrated the information leak in an attempt to protect his furs on Mackinac Island, he later denied his participation and placed the blame on "Mr. Carp who attended to my business in my absence. He while I was in Washington sent an express to Montreal to the pepol who are engaged with me on the Indian trade informing them of the declaration of war also one to St. Joseph's to the agent there."

From the outset, the capture of Fort Michilimackinac topped the British list of priorities. Sir Isaac Brock, commander of the British forces in Upper Canada, ordered Captain Roberts to take "the most prompt and effective

measures" to possess himself of Michilimackinac.

Fur traders, both company men and independents, together with their employees and the Indians under their influence, gathered at Fort St. Joseph to prepare for the attack on Mackinac Island. Among the traders who gathered were John Johnston and Jean-Baptist Nolin of Sault Ste. Marie, Michigan, and Charles Oakes Ermatinger of Sault Ste. Marie, Upper Canada. Robert Dickson travelled from the headwaters of

*The American Fur Company, owned by John Jacob Astor (1763-1848), offered serious competition to both the North West and Hudson's Bay companies. At one time or another, many of the important area fur traders including Charles Oakes Ermatinger and John Johnston were in the employ of the American Fur Company. Courtesy, Sault Ste. Marie Museum*

the Mississippi River with some 110 Indians. Ojibway from the area also gathered at the fort. Altogether, in addition to the regular force stationed at the fort, there were 180 traders and their men and 400 Indians prepared to launch the attack on Fort Michilimackinac.

Under the command of Captain Roberts, Fort Michilimackinac on Mackinac Island was captured on July 17, 1812, without any bloodshed.

Peace returned to the region following this brief but strategically vital skirmish. It was during this lull in the storm that Ermatinger actually began construction of his stone house. The work continued through 1813, and by 1814 the exterior was virtually complete.

The 1814 attack on the communities on both sides of the St. Mary's River marked the return of war to the area and resulted in the destruction of vital segments of each settlement. The American forces, under the command of Major Holmes, completely destroyed the North West Company post on the north shore of the river. Dwelling houses, warehouses, stables with livestock, the sawmill, and the canoe lock were all burned.

Once the holdings of the North West Company had been destroyed, the troops crossed the river to the home of John Johnston. Johnston, a fur trader living in Sault Ste. Marie, Michigan, had been born in Ireland but was a long-time resident of the United States. During the various campaigns of the war he fought on the side of the British, which led the Americans to regard him as a traitor and "a thorough British sympathizer." In retaliation for his role in the sei-

zure and later protection of Fort Michilimackinac, the soldiers burned his home and outbuildings, forcing his wife and children to flee to safety.

Curiously enough, although Charles Ermatinger had been a key participant in the capture of Fort Michilimackinac in 1812, unlike John Johnston, he did not take part in its defense in 1814. He was seized and questioned by the American commander, the only man on either side of the river to suffer such an indignity, but he was released after a couple of hours. As the American troops departed, they left his extensive cache of furs intact and his impressive stone house untouched.

The amalgamation of the North West and Hudson's Bay companies in 1821 terminated Sault Ste. Marie's importance as a key post on the express route between Montreal and the posts in the northwest and beyond. The canoe brigades which had previously travelled westward in the spring and then travelled back to Montreal in September laden with furs no longer passed through the Sault. Instead, supplies were transported by way of the much shorter and less expensive Hudson Bay route. They were landed at York Factory and distributed from there to the various western posts.

Like the post at Sault Ste. Marie, those posts at Batchewana and Michipicoten were adversely affected by the amalgamation of the companies. The Batchewana post, which also served as a fishing station, was operated by the North West Company for a short period of time in the early nineteenth century. The Michipicoten post had a longer and more colourful history. The first sub-

stantial post at Michipicoten had been constructed in 1725. It had been built by the French and was retained by them until the arrival of Alexander Henry. In 1780 the post was purchased by two independent traders who in turn sold it to the North West Company. By this time, Michipicoten House consisted of residences for the factor and his employees as well as a trading house. The North West Company continued to exercise control over the mouth of the Michipicoten River until 1797. In that year, however, the Hudson's Bay Company challenged their authority by constructing a post on the opposite shore of the river. The Hudson's Bay Company abandoned their post in 1803 but returned to it in 1816 following the hostilities that developed between the fur trading companies in the aftermath of the Seven Oakes Massacre at Lord Selkirk's Red River Settlement.

With the amalgamation of the Hudson's Bay and North West companies and the altered express routes, the fortunes of the fur trade in the area surrounding Sault Ste. Marie slipped into a state of decline from which it never recovered. The Hudson's Bay Company continued to operate a trading post at the Sault but because of the meager profit it generated it was regarded as a gesture of good will. It also served to protect the business ties the company cultivated with the Ojibway, and to prevent the American Fur Company from monopolizing the local Indian trade. It was evident to everyone involved in the fur trade, however, that Sault Ste. Marie's days of glory as a fur trading post would never be regained.

*Following the merger between the North West and Hudson's Bay fur companies in 1821, the Hudson's Bay Company took possesion of the post at Sault Ste. Marie. Although it was not financially viable, the HBC maintained the post in order to prevent monopolization of the trade with the Indians by the American Fur Company. Courtesy, Sault Ste. Marie Public Library*

# Chapter Three

*The old Hudson's Bay post was trans-
formed into a boarding house during
the construction of the canal.
Courtesy, Sault Ste. Marie Museum*

# ON THE BRINK
# OF SETTLEMENT

T he amalgamation of the North West and Hudson's Bay companies in 1821 symbolized the end of an era in Sault Ste. Marie
history. Although the Hudson's Bay Company continued to
operate a post at the foot of the St. Mary's rapids, it was simply to
maintain a presence in the area. The post was not a profitable enterprise
but it did serve to remind the American Fur Company that the Hudson's Bay Company was a rival to be reckoned with even in an area
where the fur trade had dramatically dwindled.

The fur trade had inhibited settlement of the region in the early
years of the venture. In fact, the fur trade companies had actively dis-
couraged settlement. They feared that the physical development of
settled areas, and the naturally ensuing home ties, would make the voyageurs and traders reluctant to travel and to remain away from home
and family for the duration of the fur trading season. The companies
also feared that the growth of populated settlements would destroy the
natural habitats of the animals and drive them farther and farther into
the wilderness.

In an early collaborative effort, Canadian historians Arthur Lower
and Harold Innis wrote that from the outset there were two separate
and distinct motives behind the settlement of Canada. The first motive
was purely exploitive: to plunder the natural wealth of this new country

for financial gain. The second motive was more complex. In the opinion of Lower and Innis, it centered on the basic human need and desire to possess land and to build new societies. The fur trade is a prime example of the exploitation motive at work in Sault Ste. Marie. It was not until the 1830s that the community embarked on the second phase: settlement building.

Anna Jameson, the noted traveller and diarist, made Sault Ste. Marie her last stop on her tour of the lower lakes and Lake Huron in 1837. Although stretches of her voyage from York were made in sailing ships, portions such as that from Manitoulin Island to Mackinac Island to Sault Ste. Marie were made in batteaux and canoes. Mrs. Jameson was struck by the desolate appearance of the area and by the rough frontier living conditions. In *Sketches in Canada and Rambles among the Redmen* (also known as *Winter Studies and Summer Rambles*), the published account of her adventures in Upper Canada, Mrs. Jameson wrote: ". . . the whole country around us is in its primitive state, covered with the interminable swamp and forest where the bear and the moose roam—and the lakes and living streams where the beaver builds his hut. The cariboo, or rein-deer, is still found on the northern shores." According to her recollections, the difference between the north and south shores of the river at the Sault was striking:

*On the American side there is a settlement of whites, as well as a large village of Chippewas; there is also a mission (I believe of the Methodists), for the conversion*

*of the Indians. The fort, which had been lately strengthened, is merely a strong and high enclosure, surrounded with pickets of cedar-wood, within the stockade are the barracks and the principal trading store . . . The village is increasing into a town and the commercial advantage of its situation must raise it ere long to a place of importance.*

By way of comparison, however,

*On the Canadian side, we have not even those demonstrations of power or prosperity. Nearly opposite to the American fort is a small fort belonging to the North West Fur Company; below this, a few miserable log huts occupied by some French Canadians and voyageurs in the service of the company, a set of lawless "mauvais sujets" from all I can learn. Lower down stands the house of Mr. and Mrs. MacMurray, with the Chippewa village under their care and tuition . . . A lofty eminence, partly clothed with forest, rises behind the house on which stands the little missionary church and school-house for the use of the Indian converts.*

Anna Jameson was greatly impressed by the mission operated by the Reverend and Mrs. William MacMurray. MacMurray spent time in Sault Ste. Marie in 1832 and returned to the settlement in 1833 under the auspices of the Society for Converting and Civilizing the Indians of Upper Canada and Propagating the Gospel among Destitute Settlers, the missionary branch of the Anglican Church.

Left: According to the
terms of the 1850 Robin-
son Treaty, the Batche-
wana band of Ojibway
retained various lands including a fishing station
on Whitefish Island.
They maintained owner-
ship of Whitefish Island
even after they sold other
reserved lands in 1859.
Courtesy, Sault Ste.
Marie Museum

William MacMurray quickly earned the confidence and respect of the native population. His influence with the Ojibway increased further when, soon after his arrival in Sault Ste. Marie, MacMurray married Charlotte Johnston, the daughter of John Johnston and his Chippewa wife. Charlotte acted as his interpreter and cultural intermediary, enabling him to deal with his parishioners in their own language and in terms appropriate to their cultural milieu. In addition to his church-related duties, MacMurray served as the headmaster at the school he established for the instruction of the Ojibway children. It was MacMurray's goal to provide the children not only with book-learning skills but also with life skills. He taught them agricultural techniques, which enabled them to maintain gardens planted with potatoes and Indian corn. Not only did he teach them how to supplement their diets through the addition of vegetables, but he ensured that the female students were taught to cook and to sew. MacMurray was subtly attempting to transform the native culture into one more European in outlook and appearance. By shaping the minds of the 30 children attending his school, MacMurray sought to leave an indelible impression on the native community. He was zealous in his attempts to "convert and civilize" the Indians by helping them to overcome the growing alcohol problem within the community, by introducing a European style of dress, and by discouraging the "wild and restless" habit of travelling annually to the winter hunting grounds.

The year 1838 was a watershed year for MacMurray's fledgling mission. In the five years that passed from the time the mission opened, MacMurray had conducted 145 baptisms, 7 burials, and 13 marriages, and he had gathered 66 communicants. A change in government in 1838, together with the ensuing policy changes, meant that funds for missions and schools such as those at Sault Ste. Marie were discontinued. Whereas Sir John Colbourne had taken a strong interest in the Indian missions and promised to expand the village and build log huts for the residents, his successor, Sir Francis Bond Head, as Governor of Upper Canada, felt no such compunction toward the native people of Upper Canada. Under the direction of Bond Head, the focus of government policy shifted and the commitments made by Colbourne were never honoured.

Quite naturally, the Indians felt that they had been deceived and ill-treated. Rather than forever be regarded as the person who reneged on a promise, William MacMurray left Sault Ste. Marie. But the Indian people did not let the matter drop with MacMurray's departure. Chief Shingwaukonce, or Little Pine, petitioned Bond Head on behalf of the local Ojibway:

*My Father, you have made promises to me and to my children. You promised me houses, but as yet nothing has been performed, although five years are past. I am now growing very old, and to judge by the way you have used me, I shall be laid in my grave before I see any of your promises fulfilled. Many of your children address you and tell you they are poor, and they are much better off than I am in everything. I can say, in sincerity, that I am poor. I am like the beast of the forest that has no shelter. I lie down on the snow and cover myself with the boughs of trees. If the promises had been made by a person of no standing, I should not be astonished to see his promises fail. But you who are so great in riches and power, I am astonished that I do not see your promises fulfilled! I would have been better pleased if you had never made such promises to me, than that you should have made them and not performed them.*

*But, my Father, perhaps I do not see clearly; I am old and perhaps I have lost my eyesight; and if you should come to visit us, you might discover these promises already performed! I have heard that you have visited all parts of the country around. This is the only place you have not yet seen, if you will promise to come I will have my little fish ready drawn from the water, that you may taste of the food that sustains me.*

MacMurray was succeeded by the Reverend F.A. O'Meara, who stayed in Sault Ste. Marie only two years before moving on to Manitouwaning.

This decline in the Anglican mission was an indication that the community was stagnating rather than growing and prospering in a manner similar to settlements in the southern portions of the province or even those on the opposite shore of the St. Mary's River. The situation baffled both local residents and government officials at York. Unfortunately for the community, it continued along this lacklustre path for several years.

The spirits and fortunes of the area rallied briefly in the 1840s. In 1842 W.E. (later Sir William) Logan was appointed Geologist for the United Provinces. His appointment, coupled with the important geological discoveries of Dr. Douglass Houghton in Northern Michigan, stimulated an interest in the presumed mineral potential of what is now northern Ontario. In this particular region, the sudden interest led to a run on applications to explore the northern shores of lakes Superior and Huron. Thirty-one applications were filed in 1845, 30 of which were for the Superior region. The number of applications jumped to 133 the following year: 100 on Superior and the remaining 33 on Huron. Ironically, although the largest number of claims was staked along Lake Superior, the first lucrative mineral discoveries were made on Lake Huron.

Although the presence of native copper had been known to the Ojibway from very early times, Radisson and Groseilliers were among the first Europeans to actually see and touch the copper. The event was so momentous that Radisson recorded it in his diary. According to the entry, they travelled along the St. Mary's River to Lake Superior, where they made camp.

*Here we found a small river. I was so curious that I enquired my dearest friends the name of this streame. They named me it Pauabickkomesibs wch signifieth a small river of copper. I asked him the reason. He told me, "come I shall shew ye thee reason why," I was in a place which was not 200 paces in ye woods, where many peeces of copper weare uncovered. Further he told me*

John Prince arrived in Sault Ste. Marie in 1860 to assume his appointment as first judge for the newly created Judicial District of Algoma. He served in this capacity until his death in 1870. Courtesy, Sault Ste. Marie Museum

*that the mountaine I saw was of nothing else. Seeing it so faire and pure, I had in mind to take a peece of it, but they hindered me, telling my brother there was more where we weare to goe. In this Great Lake with mine own eyes I have seene which are admirable, and can maintine of a hundred pounds . . .*

Regardless of this spectacular discovery, the copper veins along Lake Superior did not prove to be fruitful or financially viable. The veins along Lake Huron, however, particularly those at Bruce Mines, were both. The discovery at Bruce Mines stemmed from prospecting activity begun in 1845. The years between 1846 and 1850 witnessed widespread growth in the mining industry.

By the early 1850s, the settlement at Bruce Mines had a "thriving look". There were about 75 homes and 500 residents, 300 of whom worked in the mines. In addition, the settlement boasted a Methodist chapel, a public house, a store, and a store house.

The mines were located in close proximity to the settlement. There were 10 shafts from which the ore was removed from the ground in its raw state. Once the copper was removed from the ground, it was crushed by steam-driven machinery and then water washed in puddling troughs. The ore was shipped in this unrefined state to Wales. Louis Agassiz visited the area in 1850 and was struck by the appearance of the ore: "The long pier to which we moored was heaped with the most brilliant ore of the kinds the miners call 'horseflesh' and 'peacock ore', having every hue of blue, purple and golden."

The idyllic early days of mining rapidly dissipated. The Bruce Mines, once one of the most important world producers of copper, began to decline in output, until by 1865 production had dropped to a mere fraction of initial levels. The veins were not as good in depth as they had been on the surface, which made them both difficult and costly to mine. To compound the problem, the price of copper had dropped to 14 cents per pound from 24 cents in 1850.

The slowdown in the mines had widespread social ramifications. Judge John Prince very melodramatically described the potential plight of Sault Ste. Marie in the event of the closure of the mines in a letter to the Honourable Alexander Campbell:

*A few days ago I addressed a letter to your colleague, the Secretary of State for Canada [Sir Hector Louis Langevin], informing him that I have good grounds for believing that on the opening of the navigation a set of brigands, and ruffians, and others from the mines above this place—fellows who are about to be discharged because the copper mines do not "pay"—will invade us and plunder us of everything moveable, and not only us but everybody else in the district whose personal property they can consume, or carry away, etc. They are represented to me to number at least five hundred; and against such a force, any resistance by us would be utterly useless—for we have neither men, nor arms nor ammunition . . . to prevent their outrages.*

Other, smaller mines along Lake Huron, as well as those along Lake Superior, met a similar fate. Curiously

enough, all of this activity, however transient, skirted Sault Ste. Marie, leaving the community untouched. Mining in the area was not the long-sought road to prosperity and settlement.

Although the first sawmill in Sault Ste. Marie dated back to the late eighteenth century, lumbering as a commercial enterprise did not surface in the area until after 1850. Lumbering operations were confined to the Ottawa and Trent waterway systems during the first half of the nineteenth century, although mills were built at places such as Blind River and Milford Haven on St. Joseph Island. These mills mainly supplied the lumber needs of the few settlers who established farms on the fertile strip of

*By the late 1880s the entire shoreline from Blind River to Sault Ste. Marie had been attacked by lumbering interests from the United States and portions of the province of Ontario. Of the 221 million feet of lumber supplied by the entire Georgian Bay area, the North Shore alone contributed 82 million feet. Courtesy, Sault Ste. Marie Museum*

land along the north shore of Lake Huron.

Lake Huron's north shore possessed the most extensive stands of trees, and consequently the wealthiest timber stands. Until the readily accessible timber stands in the southern and eastern portions of the province had been depleted, however, it was not feasible to begin forestry operations. The lack of transportation, the distance from the markets, and the fact that the cut timber could only be moved to markets during the summer months all contributed to the reluctance of loggers to work in the area.

By 1881 it was noted that Muskoka was "thinning out", thus signifying the beginning of large-scale lumbering in Algoma. Mills sprang up at the mouth of virtually every river emptying into Lake Huron, and towns such as Spragge, Spanish River, and Thessalon were born.

To the early lumbermen, white pine was the only kind of lumber worthy of consideration. The virgin stands of the trees were so extensive that it was naively assumed that they would last indefinitely, an attitude that resulted in wasteful and extravagant consumption. As cutting operations extended inland from the shore, and as the supplies of pine were exhausted, loggers resorted to spruce, maple, birch, hemlock, and poplar. Some oak was also cut but it was not regularly harvested since it did not float. Unfortunately, the forested-over area was not replanted. The thin soil sheet was exposed to the elements and eroded away, leaving nothing but a barren rock surface.

Like mining, lumbering created a

temporary boom in the area's economy. But once again, the effects of this industrial spurt left Sault Ste. Marie untouched. It provided seasonal employment for miners and farmers but did little for the village's residents.

Farming has been practiced at Sault Ste. Marie from the earliest days of European settlement. The Jesuits introduced farming to the native people and the practice continued. Charles Oakes Ermatinger maintained a very large vegetable garden and also grew fields of grain, which he processed in his grist mill. On the opposite side of the river, John Johnston kept ". . . plenty of cattle, hogs, sheep and domestic fowl . . ." He also had ". . . extensive plantations of corn and potatoes, with a beautifully arranged and well stocked fruit and flower garden."

Later attempts at farming did not meet with the same degree of success as those of the earlier settlers. The lack of progress in the development of farming

stemmed from a variety of problems. Farming methods successful in Europe and in other parts of Canada did not produce the same results in northern Ontario. Climatic variances, irregular soil conditions, a lack of seed hardy enough to germinate and grow during a shortened growing season, a lack of accessible markets, and a lack of roads or railroads on which to transport and distribute agricultural produce all contributed to the retarded development.

The prospect of land ownership had succeeded in attracting many immigrants to the southern portion of the province. By 1860, however, much of the prime agricultural land had been settled, forcing prospective farmers to move in a northwesterly direction in search of arable land. The government fostered settlement through a land-grant system, following a settlement study by the Commissioner of Agriculture and Public Works.

As would be expected, farmers were more readily attracted to the area during the periods of industrial expansion. Mining and lumbering both had served to lure settlers: the industries provided employment for farmers during the off season and a market during the summer and fall. When the industries slumped, markets and employment potential dried up, and farmers moved westward in search of both.

In keeping with Joseph Wilson's dire prediction that a key stumbling block to the settlement of Sault Ste. Marie and the surrounding area was the fact that settlers were not permitted to buy their land, a surveyor was sent to lay out the park lot for the town. Alexander Vidal was dispatched to Sault Ste. Marie in the spring of 1846 to conduct a survey in anticipation of the negotiation of the Indian treaties. These treaties would see the land previously owned by the Indians ceded to the Crown through a nominal purchase agreement. The land would then be purchasable by the residents and by potential settlers. Neither group would be in the awkward position of being squatters.

The government of Upper Canada

may have looked upon the survey as a positive step, and the decision to proceed with it was undoubtedly applauded by local residents, but the native population was deeply distressed by the action.

Upon his arrival at Sault Ste. Marie, Alexander Vidal was met by Chief Shingwaukonce. In a letter to the honourable D.B. Papineau, the minister responsible for Crown lands, Vidal described his meeting with the Indian Chief:

*I consider it my duty . . . to inform you that the Indian chief residing in the neighbourhood and called Shing-gwak waited upon me this morning in the company with the young hereditary chief Nab-na-gu-ghing and several other Indians for the purpose of claiming all the land here as their own,—*

*They say that the government have never purchased the land from them and expressed their indignation at my having been sent to survey it . . . I said little to them but promised to make known to the government through you that they claimed the land as their own and stated my belief that on receipt of my letter they would either be written to on the subject or an agent sent here to enquire into it. With this they appeared satisfied and said they would offer no impediment to my going on with the survey.*

True to his word, the chief permitted Vidal to carry out his survey without interference.

But the survey was only the first step in the process that would allow settlers to purchase their land. The Robinson Treaties, so named for W.B.

Robinson, the chief negotiator, were land agreements: the native people were given reserves and annuities in return for the rights to the land.

Once arrangements had been made with the Indians, it was essential that the survey work initiated by Vidal be continued. For this reason, Joseph Wilson indicated he was prepared to take up the survey where Vidal had stopped. In May 1851 he wrote to the Honourable J.H. Price, requesting permission:

*I beg leave to commence the survey of the following lands: that tract of land east of Mr. Vidal's survey and so far as the Indian Reservation at "Garden River" and back as far as "Root River". Also the land between Pointe aux Pins (West) and the West end of Mr. Vidal's survey, say 1 mile back, on the latter tracts there are at present 8 settlers.*

Wilson also urged that the surveyed lands be sold at reasonable prices to enable settlers to purchase the land they lived on and farmed or gardened:

*In order to encourage the settlement of the Sault, I would respectfully urge [on] the government the expediency of selling the Sault at a low price say those on the river at 4/-, inland at 2/6 and the village lots not higher than 2/-, each.*

*As the first step towards the improvement of the Sault, I would urge [on] the government the necessity of immediate adjustments of the claims of the present occu-*

*pants. There are only three or four conflicting ones which will require examination.*

Permission was denied to Wilson.

Another surveyor did not arrive until 1855, when Albert Salter was hired to survey the arable land between Lake Nipissing and Sault Ste. Marie. The following year, he returned to run the base line for a proposed road from Lake Nipissing to Lake Superior. Subsequent surveyors drew the median lines at 18-mile intervals, which formed the township boundaries.

By ordering the survey work, the government of Upper Canada had taken another step toward the settlement of Sault Ste. Marie.

According to Joseph Wilson, there was yet another reason for the lack of settlement in Sault Ste. Marie—the lack of a formal government structure. In response to this perceived need, Wilson proposed the establishment of a district judiciary as the first step toward the solution. The suggestion was acted upon by the Dominion Government in 1858 with the creation of the Judicial District of Algoma. John A. Macdonald, who was at that time the attorney general, was not convinced that the experiment would succeed in enticing settlers northward; in a letter to Sanfield MacDonald, he explained that "Our legislation with respect to Algoma was altogether experimental. It was represented to us that the country would not be sited until it had judicial institutions and tribunals which would protect life and liberty."

The Judicial District of Algoma, as created in 1858, encompassed a vast territory, stretching as it did from the

French River in the east, to James Bay in the north, to a then undefined point in the west, which now constitutes the Ontario/Manitoba border. The immense size of the district made it cumbersome and difficult to administer. Once the district had been defined, people were appointed to fill the newly created legal and judicial positions. Richard Carney was named the stipendiary magistrate and remained as the chief judicial officer until the appointment of Colonel John Prince as the first judge for the District of Algoma. Other positions filled included: sheriff, clerk of the

Richard's wife, Mary.

Prince had settled in the Sandwich area of southwestern Ontario following his emigration to Canada. He had been called to the bar prior to leaving England and he resumed his legal career in Canada. Shortly after his arrival in 1833, Prince was appointed to the Panel of Judges for the Western District, an event that marked his entry into public life in Canada. His foray into the political arena began in 1836. His political career, both as a candidate and as an elected representative, followed an erratic up-and-down path.

As a military officer, Prince was an active participant in the 1837 Rebellion of Upper Canada. Unfortunately, in military circles he is best remembered for a single instance of over-zealousness in the performance of his duties. Following a skirmish at Windsor, Prince ordered the execution of four men whom he had taken as prisoners. Whether the demonstration was in response to his personal distaste for the republican ideals espoused by the prisoners or whether it stemmed from his fear that the judiciary of Upper Canada would fail to take action against the rebels will never be known, but the vengeful manner in which the executions were carried out resulted in considerable public outcry. Although Prince suffered both personally and professionally as a result of his actions, the effects were not permanent.

By the early 1850s Prince had grown dissatisfied with life in Sandwich, a restlessness that led him to begin looking for an alternative place to live and work. His searching brought him to Sault Ste. Marie in 1853 but he rejected

peace, crown attorney, registrar of deeds, gaoler (jailer), and constable.

John Prince had led an exciting, if somewhat checkered, life before moving to Sault Ste. Marie to assume the position of district judge. He had been born in Hereford, England, in 1796. Contrary to popular belief, John Prince was not the illegitimate son of the King of England; he was the son of Richard Prince, a miller and grain dealer, and

it as a potential home. In his estimation, the community was ". . . a wild and horrid and inhospitable place. I should not like to live there." Regardless of this initial negative reaction, the following year he again considered moving to the Sault. In a letter to Joseph Wilson, whom he had met on his first trip, he broached the topic of a possible judgeship. Buoyed by Wilson's response and by his desire to leave Sandwich, Prince wrote to Sir Alan McNabb in 1855 formally requesting appointment to the "Northern Judgeship".

Prince stepped up his campaign for appointment outside Sandwich following the unsatisfactory outcome of the election of 1857. Beginning in 1858 he entered into a prolonged series of discussions with Attorney General John A. Macdonald regarding the political appointment. The initial meetings progressed well according to Prince, but the Minister's indecision soon caused him to change his mind. "How difficult these ministers are to deal with and how negligent and careless towards their supporters!" he lamented. Although Macdonald assured Prince that his appointment to the Northern Judgeship was imminent, it was not until February 1859 that he received a letter from Sir Edmund Head formally offering him the position.

After lobbying long and hard for the position of Judge of Algoma, Prince did not move to Sault Ste. Marie, the district seat, until 1860. He probably had second thoughts about relocating once the decision regarding the judgeship had been made, since his second visit to the Sault had proved to be no more fruitful than the first. As on his

previous trip, he paid a visit to Joseph Wilson, and together they ". . . tramped until 2 o clock over rocks, morasses and up hills and down gullies looking at the land in the rear of the Sault on our side, and was much disappointed in the character of the soil. There is very little farming land, and they ask unreasonable prices for it." He went on to indicate that he was ". . . much disappointed with the land etc. as well as present appearances of the Sault etc. etc. I fear that farming there is out of the question for the want of roads, servants, etc., and I doubt, therefore whether it would be worth my while to take the Judgeship."

Ultimately Prince accepted the appointment, moved to Sault Ste. Marie, and took up residence in a boarding house run by Maria Hetherington, the woman who had been his landlady during his years in Toronto as a politician. The new judge was warmly received by the people of Sault Ste. Marie, and although he was initially flattered by all of the attention, he soon tired of it. Within a few days of his arrival he declared himself to be "Bored as usual, by a great many people calling upon me, and taking up my time. I fear I shall be as much annoyed here by visitors and intruders as I was at Sandwich . . ."

■

The St. Mary's River, and the proximity of Sault Ste. Marie to the river, are key elements in the evolution of a local transportation infrastructure and the growth of a settlement at this location.

Water transportation was the primary method used by the Ojibway. They required a craft that was sufficiently durable to withstand the rough waters and high winds common to the Great Lakes, but at the same time light enough to be easily portaged. The birch bark canoe, because it met those criteria and because the materials to produce it were readily available, became the principal means of transportation.

The earliest Europeans to reach the northern Ontario wilderness recognized the inherent value of the canoe. Gradu-

On August 25, 1852, President Millard Fillmore signed a bill that granted 750,000 acres for the construction of a canal in the American Sault. The St. Mary's Ship Canal Company was contracted to construct the canal. The work was completed in two years and the canal opened in May 1855. Courtesy, Public Archives of Canada

ally, however, the craft was modified to serve a wider range of functions. It was enlarged to permit the ready movement of more people and larger cargoes. The first adaptation was the batteau. Like the canoe, it was pointed at either end, but the bottom was flat. The design made it ideal for travelling in open water. A later modification, known as the Mackinaw boat, was much larger; each was constructed to carry 20 people plus baggage and supplies. Unlike the canoe and the batteau, the Mackinaw was a keel boat equipped with a mast and a sail that could be hoisted when strong winds prevailed.

The first decked vessel to sail on

Lake Superior was built at Point aux Pins by Louis Denis, Sieur de la Ronde, in 1734, but it was not until 1760 that the British began to construct similar vessels on the Upper Great Lakes. By the 1770s these decked sailing ships were a common sight on Lake Superior. Once they entered the St. Mary's River they could travel as far as Sault Ste. Marie before the rapids made further movement impossible.

As the wilderness opened up in response to the demands of the fur trade, and later as a result of mining and lumbering operations, the number and the size of ships plying the Great Lakes rapidly increased. The first commercial fleets consisted of sailing ships, which were slow. And because of their total susceptibility to the vagaries of nature, they were not reliable. Their dependence upon wind for propulsion created difficulties for ships negotiating the channel between lakes Superior and Huron. It was not uncommon for ships to be stranded for days or even weeks waiting for favourable winds. This precarious situation led to the development of a fleet of steam-propelled tugs to guide, or even tow, the sailing ships through the channel.

In a commercial sense, the last half of the nineteenth century was the period of greatest success for the sailing ship; ironically, it was also the time that witnessed its decline in popularity. As late as 1851, two-thirds of the Great Lakes vessels were sailing ships, and although by 1869 steamships were gradually taking over the passenger and package freight business, sailing ships still carried virtually all bulk freight.

The first steam-powered wooden

vessels on the Great Lakes were introduced in 1816. Prior to 1841, steamers were of the side-paddle variety, but there were numerous hazards associated with this type of ship. They tended to be small and poorly constructed. The engines were weak, and as a result the ships were incapable of making headway through heavy winds or rough waters. More seriously, however, was the danger this type of ship presented to the lives of the crew and passengers. Their lack of stability meant that they frequently capsized, and the installation of a steam engine into a wooden ship made it a potential firetrap.

The first steel ship built for the Great Lakes, the *Spokane*, was launched in 1886. At 249 feet in length, it would have been insignificant by today's standards, but nevertheless it did revolution-

ize shipping trends on the Lakes.

In 1798 the North West Company completed construction of a canal and lock system to facilitate the movement of men and furs between lakes Superior and Huron. The lock, which had a lift of nine feet, was large enough to accommodate canoes and batteaux. It replaced

*In 1870 Louis Riel and his Metis followers occupied the Hudson's Bay post Fort Garry to protest the company's unilateral decision to surrender the lucrative Rupert's Land to Canada. A small army under the command of Colonel Garnet Wolseley was dispatched to the Red River to restore peace. When one of Wolseley's ships, the Chicora, was denied passage through the American lock, the colonel and his troops set up camp on the Canadian side of the river below the canal. Courtesy, Archives of Ontario*

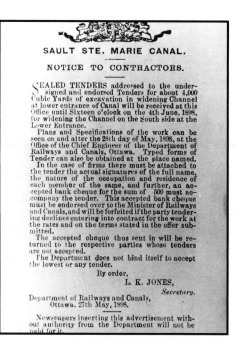

the portage road, which ran in a roughly east-west direction just north of the rapids.

This original lock system was in operation until 1814, when the lock, as well as the adjoining North West Company trading complex, was destroyed by American troops en route to Fort Michilimackinac. The communities on both sides of the St. Mary's River were once again deprived of a lock system. While transporters on the British side of the border reverted to the use of a portage road, a tow road was constructed on the American side.

The question of rebuilding the lock resurfaced periodically. It was not until 1837, however, that the first official steps were taken in this direction. In that year, the first session of the Michigan state legislature commissioned a study to investigate the feasibility of a canal at Sault Ste. Marie. Although a report recommending construction was submitted to the legislature in 1839, no

action was taken to begin construction. Then, when the potential mineral wealth of the area was developed in the 1840s, it was proposed that a canal be constructed on the north side of the border. Several plans for the construction of a British canal were submitted, but enthusiasm for the project waned in January 1853 with the passage of a Michigan bill authorizing construction of an American canal with a lock measuring 350 feet by 70 feet. The St. Mary's Falls Ship Canal Company was chartered, paving the way for construction of the canal to begin in June 1853. Although the work was beset with problems ranging from labour strikes to epidemics to a scarcity of labourers, the canal was operational on schedule in 1855. It opened Lake Superior to traffic and to shipping fleets that had, of necessity, operated only on the lower lakes. This eliminated the need for separate fleets on the upper and lower lakes.

The opening of the American canal lock system made possible new prospects for the communities on both sides of the St. Mary's River. Prior to the construction of the canal, the size of the vessels travelling to the area and the types and sizes of the cargoes they carried were arbitrarily restricted. The canal and lock system brought the two Saults abreast of technological advancements in the transportation field.

The American ship canal was freely used by both Canadian and American ships for many years. The political implications of the "*Chicora* Incident" of 1870, however, led to renewed demands for the construction of a lock on the Canadian side of the river. In that year the steamer *Chicora*, laden with men, munitions, and supplies, and en route to Fort Garry (Winnipeg) to help quell the Red River Rebellion, was refused permission to pass through the lock system because of the military nature of the expedition. Since the similarly laden steamer *Algoma* had passed through the American canal without any problem, Colonel Garnet Wolseley, commander of the *Chicora*, had no reason to anticipate that he would be refused passage through the system.

H.P. Baldwin, the governor of Michigan, had learned of the westward movement of these ships and had immediately notified the Department of State in Washington. In response, Hamilton

NOTICE

TO CONTRACTORS.

Plans and Specifications of the work to be done at the
UPPER and LOWER ENTRANCES OF THE

Sault Ste. Marie Canal

Can be seen at this office and at Sault Ste. Marie, Ont., on and after

FRIDAY, THE 23rd DAY OF NOVEMBER, NEXT,

Where forms of tender may be obtained.

Tenders for the execution of the works, addressed to the undersigned, and endorsed, "Tender for Sault Ste. Marie Canal," will be received until the arrival of the eastern and western mails on

FRIDAY, THE 7th DAY OF DECEMBER, NEXT.

By order
A. P. BRADLEY,
Secretary.

Department of Railways and Canals,
Ottawa, 26th Oct., 1888.

*Left: The Canadian government was prepared to proceed with a canal at Sault Ste. Marie in the spring of 1888, but according to a report prepared for J.H. Pope, Minister of Railways and Canals, the precise nature of the canal had not yet been decided. Once the decision was made, tenders were called. Courtesy, Sault Ste. Marie Museum*

*The inspectors, engineers, and contractors responsible for the construction of the Sault Ste. Marie Canal posed for a celebratory photograph upon completion of the project in 1894. Courtesy, Parks Canada, Sault Ste. Marie*

Fish, secretary of the Department of State, wrote:

*The President desires me to say that the granting of transit through or over any part of the territory of the United States of America to the Military Force of a Foreign Power is actually within the control and discretion of the Federal Government. And he desires me to say therefore that no military expedition of any foreign power whether of troops or of boats intended for this purpose is taking part in any military or warlike material be allowed to pass through the Sault Ste. Marie canal without express instructions from the Government at Washington.*

The instructions were received in time to prevent the passage of the *Chicora*. In an attempt to remove the military stigma, the troops and munitions were offloaded in Lake Huron and moved along the old portage road to Lake

*The contractors and engineers engaged to construct the canal were required to live on-site. Consequently, special accommodations were built for this purpose. Courtesy, Parks Canada, Sault Ste. Marie*

Superior. The empty ship was again presented for passage; again permission was refused.

The ship was held in abeyance for two weeks before the matter was resolved. The British ambassador intervened with the Department of State to explain the situation in Manitoba, and eventually permission to pass through the canal was granted.

The decision to build a Canadian canal and lock system, which would provide an all-Canadian water route from the Atlantic Ocean to the head of Lake Superior, followed hard on the heels of the *Chicora* incident. Construction did

not begin, however, until 1887. Coincidentally, it had become apparent to the Dominion government by this time that the steadily increasing wheat trade in the west and the potential of the steel and mining industries in other parts of Canada loomed on the horizon.

The canal officially opened in 1895. The entire canal measured 7,294 feet in length, with a lock 900 feet long and 60 feet wide. It was capable of handling ships with a maximum length of 777 feet and width of 59 feet.

Although the St. Mary's River has been a mainstay in the development of Sault Ste. Marie, it has also been largely

*Work on the Canadian lock was finally completed in 1894. Water was let into the lower level of the canal on September 27, 1894. Courtesy, Public Archives of Canada*

*Below: Some thirty docks dotted the Sault Ste. Marie waterfront by 1910. Each commercial enterprise had its own pier. Algoma Central's train tracks parallelled its docking facilities. Courtesy, Sault Ste. Marie Museum*

responsible for the isolation experienced by the community during its formative years. From a modern perspective, it is difficult to imagine the overwhelming sense of desolation that would have blanketed the area during the months of freeze-up. The 1881 de-

cision, then, to build the Canadian Pacific Railway (C.P.R.) appeared, at least intially, to be the boost Sault Ste. Marie needed. Perhaps the railroad would improve the Sault's fortunes by attracting both industry and settlers, but regardless, there was no doubt that the months of winter seclusion would end. A syndicate was organized to oversee the construction of the railroad. Several members suggested that in order to avoid the engineering difficulties that would be encountered in northern Ontario, the rail line should follow the old fur trade route along Lake Nipissing, across to Lake Huron and on to Sault Ste. Marie. At Sault Ste. Marie the line would cross into the United States and travel along the south shore of Lake Superior to Duluth, Minnesota. The proposal was rejected because other, more influential, members of the syndicate were of the opinion that the railway

should be constructed entirely on Canadian soil. As a result, the C.P.R. was built north of Sault Ste. Marie, skirting the community completely. It was not until 1887 that a spur line was built linking Sault Ste. Marie with the main C.P.R. line in Sudbury. With the construction of a bascule bridge that joined the C.P.R. with railroads in the United States, Sault Ste. Marie became a popular and well-used junction linking Canada with the markets of the vast hinterland of the American Midwest.

The growing awareness that land transportation was a key element in the settlement of the area also led to early efforts at road building. Albert Salter carried out the initial road survey in 1859. The result of his survey, the Great Northern Road, was to extend from the Spanish River in a northwesterly direction to the mouth of the Goulais River. Work began on the road in 1860. Although the original plan called for a road some 150 miles long, only about one half of it was completed.

By the mid-1880s all the prerequisites for the settlement of Sault Ste. Marie were in place. Government officials were permanently stationed at Sault Ste. Marie; the land had been surveyed and a Crown Lands agent appointed to oversee all land transactions; the Judicial District of Algoma was created and a legal system put in place; a land transport system was introduced and a canal was constructed to move vessels around the rapids. The community was once again teetering on the brink of settlement.

*Facing page, bottom: "Whalebacks" appeared on the Great Lakes in 1889. These early steel vessels resembled huge floating cigars. Although they fell into disuse after World War I, there was at least one that regularly plied the St. Mary's River up until the mid-1950s. Courtesy, Parks Canada, Sault Ste. Marie*

*Below: Icy conditions in the St. Mary's River made transit impossible. River travel came to an end with the fall freeze-up and did not resume until the spring thaw. Courtesy, Public Archives of Canada*

# Chapter Four

*The mill begun by Francis H.
Clergue was a groundwood pulp
mill. Spruce pulp was cut in the
area north of Sault Ste. Marie and
then shipped for processing. Courtesy,
Public Archives of Canada*

# CLERGUE'S INDUSTRIAL EMPIRE

I n the years preceding the birth of Sault Ste. Marie's heavy industrial base, local industry consisted principally of lumbering and subsistence farming. Construction of the ship canal and the extension of the Canadian Pacific Railway spurline from Sudbury to Sault Ste. Marie created sudden boom conditions: the population increased as local ranks were swelled by the influx of workmen, many of whom brought their families; there was a run on residential property as workers sought accommodations; the number of reasonably well-paying jobs naturally led to an increase in discretionary spending. The feeling of wealth and well-being that prevailed in the community had widespread ramifications as commercial enterprises prospered and long-sought social services finally appeared. In 1887, the village of Sault Ste. Marie was incorporated as a town.

Also incorporated in that year was the Sault Ste. Marie Water, Gas and Light Company. The principal officers of this newly formed company—W.J. Thompson, H.C. Hamilton, James Conmee, J.J. Kehoe, N.N. Neeld, and W.H. Plummer—realized the hydro-electric potential of the drop between lakes Superior and Huron at the St. Mary's River rapids. It was their intention to turn Lake Superior into the world's largest mill pond and to provide the town with power in the form of hydro-electricity. Perhaps more importantly, however, they foresaw that the community's ability to provide hydro-electricity would serve as a powerful inducement in its attempts to attract industry.

The company worked diligently throughout the summer of 1888 doing the spade work that would permit them to begin excavating the power canal and ultimately begin generating electricity. Once the land had been purchased for the generating facility, the town worked quickly to pass by-laws exempting the company from municipal taxes. To further ease the financial burden incurred by the company and its investors, municipal financial support was assured should it ever be needed. No sooner had the offer been made than the company turned to the town: by February 1889 the company had exhausted its capital and requested that the town of Sault Ste. Marie undertake to guarantee the payment of interest on 20-year debentures to be issued by the company.

In 1889 the name of the company was changed; it became the Ontario and Sault Ste. Marie Water, Light and Power Company. In keeping with the longer name, the company's mandate was also expanded. It was granted the right and authority to do whatever it deemed necessary to generate hydroelectric power from the rapids. To this end, it used the moneys generated from the sale of the debentures to purchase previously unattainable land north of the ship canal from the federal and provincial governments as well as from the Hudson's Bay Company and various individuals.

By the end of 1889 the company had once again run headlong into serious financial difficulties. Short of the purchase of the land, nothing had been done to develop a hydro-electric generating facility, and since all of the debenture money had been spent on the acqui-

sition of land they were once again financially embarrassed.

The situation gravely concerned the townspeople. Hydro-electricity had been touted, and accepted, as the means by which Sault Ste. Marie would be launched on the road to industrialization. Now, the company which had made the promises was unable to fulfill them. In return for its trust and for the monopoly it granted the company, the town had received nothing. Further negotiations between the town and the company led to the decision that partial public ownership would assure the project of a fresh influx of capital and would permit the actual construction work to begin. An agreement dated December 9, 1889, assigned to the town a 50 percent share of all paid-up stock in the company. According to the terms of the agreement, the town was to be represented on the company's board by four directors elected by the townspeople, and by one member appointed from the town council.

Since the agreement between the town and the power company also provided for further subscriptions from private investors, this, as well as the sale of further debentures, was carried out. With the necessary financing in place, excavation of the power canal was finally begun. The first sod was turned on July 30, 1892. Despite the initial optimism, work was sporadic. Digging was done as the sale of debentures generated capital. Since no technical expertise was sought, the canal was constructed to resemble nothing more than a small stream.

As serious as these drawbacks were, finances continued to be the most pressing problem. The completion of the C.P.R. had not stimulated the anticipated business expansion. The industries that had been identified as potential consumers of the soon-to-be available electricity failed to materialize. The period of boom began to spiral downward. Once again debentures were sold to meet creditors' demands for payment. This time, however, the town sold an adequate number to enable it to acquire all of the shares in the power company.

Although the town now owned the power company, it was as ill-prepared to assume the financial burden as its predecessors had been. The departure of many of the transient construction workers had caused the tax base to dwindle. As a result, a decreased number of taxpayers was obligated to pay the steadily escalating costs involved in the construction of the hydro facility. Fortunately, the provincial government came to the rescue. An act was passed by the legislature that permitted the town to consolidate its debentures and, more importantly, allowed it to sell the company if a buyer could be found.

The town did not fully comprehend the urgency of finding a buyer until work was completed on the canal in 1894. The first water allowed into the canal caused a corner to collapse and threatened to undo all of the work that had been done. Contractors and construction workers engaged in the second phase of the American ship canal crossed the rapids and made the necessary repairs to the power canal wall. The repairs cost the town all of the money it had saved for completion of the work, and the Ontario and Sault Ste. Marie Water, Light and Power Company was effectively out of business.

Enter Francis Hector Clergue. In March 1894, J.J. Kehoe and H.C. Hamilton, two of the original principals in the Ontario and Sault Ste. Marie Water, Light and Power Company, were travelling to Toronto from Sault Ste. Marie by train. En route, Kehoe fell into

*The core of the industrial empire created by Francis H. Clergue stood on the shores of the St. Mary's River less than a kilometre from the rapids. The various components evolved in a manner resembling an inverted triangle: symmetrical growth continued until the structure became top heavy. The apex as base was unable to support the weight and it collapsed. Courtesy, Sault Ste. Marie Museum*

Francis Clergue built his mansion "Montfermier" atop Moffley Hill, with a view of the hills to the north and west of the town. Built of the finest imported materials, the home reflected Clergue's personal taste for opulence. Courtesy, Sault Ste. Marie Museum

conversation with H.B. Foster of Bangor, Maine. In the course of the conversation, Kehoe described to Foster the difficulties that first the company and then the town had experienced in the development of hydro-electric power. Before they parted company, Foster promised to discuss the project with friends in Maine. The friend with whom he discussed the situation was Clergue.

Shortly after the opportune meeting between Foster and the local industrialists, Francis Clergue arrived surreptitiously at Sault Ste. Marie. He represented a group of Philadelphia financiers eager to invest in a potential hydro-electric plant. The secret arrival and subsequent inspection of the power canal and its environs were carefully orchestrated so as to permit him to impar-

tially study the works.

Clergue, a lawyer by profession, had been involved in a diverse number of economically adventurous exploits before he learned of the investment opportunities at Sault Ste. Marie. Using his vast personal charm and powers of persuasion, he had secured financial backing for his industrial schemes, which ranged from hydro-electric development to street railways to tourist development to the construction of dry docks and banks. Each venture proved to be even more disastrous than the one that preceded it.

In 1888, Clergue became involved in the field of main line railroads when he secured the rights to build a railway across Persia. Unfortunately for his backers, Clergue had little awareness or

*Above: Clergue's industrial network expanded rapidly. The success of the groundwood pulp mill, one of the earliest developments, hinged upon the availability of wood supplies as well as the accessibility of the resources. Courtesy, Sault Ste. Marie Museum*

*Left: Booms of logs for processing in the groundwood pulp mill were moved through the ship canal to a reserve area at the rear of the mill. Daring log rollers equipped with peaveys and pike poles prevented the logs from jamming as the tugboats hauled the booms. Courtesy, Parks Canada, Sault Ste. Marie*

understanding of international politics or of geography. After vast amounts of investment money had been secured and expended, international politics intervened. Russian government officials, concerned with the impact that the construction of such a railway would have on a previously closed frontier, appealed to the Shah of Persia to reconsider his agreement with Clergue. As a result of this intervention, Clergue's contract was unceremoniously terminated. Following this, his most spectacular failure to date, Clergue returned to Maine.

Penurious as a result of his forays into the field of industrial speculation and no longer capable of attracting financial backing because of his dismal record at identifying successful ventures, Clergue went to work for a group of investment financiers. It was in this capacity that he travelled to Sault Ste. Marie. Having learned of the floundering Ontario and Sault Ste. Marie Power Company, and operating under a veil of secrecy, Clergue arrived in Sault Ste. Marie to inspect the power canal.

Before Clergue left the Sault, he had negotiated a contract with the town for the purchase of exclusive rights to the production of hydro-electric power. The town council granted him a conditional title to the power installation in return for the assumption of the debt incurred by the town in the construction of the unfinished and abandoned plant. At this point, it appeared that the power plant, regarded as the economic basis for local industrial development, would finally become operational. As a logical consequence, Clergue came to be regarded as the father of local indus-

try, as the man who would bring wealth and prosperity to a town whose economic outlook appeared dismal.

From the outset, Clergue's development experienced problems. In his own words: "In our simplicity at that time it seemed to us that we had simply to go on, construct the dam, establish the water wheels in place, and that all the manufacturers would come there to seek for power." Unfortunately for Clergue and his backers, manufacturing and industry did not beat a path to Sault Ste. Marie.

It fell to Clergue to determine how the power could most profitably be put to use. To this end, the area's natural resources, most specifically its forests, were studied with an eye to industrial

*The machine shop at the Algoma Iron Works fabricated parts not otherwise available to Francis H. Clergue. It was born of necessity; Clergue began construction of the shop after several Canadian and American plants would not or could not produce the parts he designed to improve the marketability and profitability of the pulp industry. Courtesy, Sault Ste. Marie Museum*

The Lake Superior Paper
Company was incorpo-
rated in 1911, and by
July of 1912 the com-
pany's first two paper machines were producing
newsprint. Later the com-
pany merged with the
Spanish River Pulp and
Paper Company. Cour-
tesy, Sault Ste. Marie
Museum

development. Clergue and his development team discovered the abundance of previously ignored spruce stands. Up until this time only pine and select hardwood had been considered worthy of harvest. Clergue, however, recognized the value of the spruce and obtained the rights to harvest the stands. Close on the heels of this action, he began constructing a pulp mill and began cutting spruce for use in pulp making.

In return for the rights to harvest the spruce, Clergue agreed to invest a minimum of $250,000 in the construction of the pulp mill. A mill of this size, however, did not fit logically into the industrial empire envisioned by Clergue; the scale and proposed output had to be expanded before work on the original works had advanced beyond the initial stage.

Clergue's mill was geared to the production of mechanical or liquid pulp. It was not economically feasible to cultivate foreign markets for the pulp due to freight costs involved in the shipment, since the shipper paid to move not only the pulp resin but also the extraneous water. This particular circumstance led to the decision that if pulp from the Sault Ste. Marie mill was to be sold on the national or international market it would be necessary to devise a method of processing and drying it.

Clergue approached the producers of pulp and paper machinery both in North America and in Europe but found that none was willing to tackle the problem. Invariably, the response was that the scheme was unrealistic and impractical. If Clergue wanted to proceed with his plan to revolutionize the pulp industry, he would have to design

and manufacture his own machinery. Hence the next of the interlocking industries came into being. It was decided that a machine shop, and consequently a foundry, should be built to turn out the equipment necessary to dry the pulp. After a shaky start, the Sault mill was soon the only one in the world turning out sheets of dry pulp. Since chemical processing would improve the quality of the pulp, and therefore increase its value on the open market, the next step was the development of a sulphite pulp mill.

Chemical processing meant that a reliable and cost-efficient supply of sulphur had to be found. After investigating several leads that took him as far afield as Sicily, Clergue discovered the needed sulphite at Sault Ste. Marie's back door—Sudbury.

To obtain the pyrrhotite ore used to produce the sulphite, Clergue was forced to purchase a nickel mine. Clergue's chemists quickly realized that the residue from the sulphur extraction process consisted of nickel and iron, which, when reduced to a metal, produced an alloy of such superior quality that Krupp, the German arms manufacturer, signed a five-year contract with Clergue. Having signed the contract, all that remained for Clergue was the construction of a reduction facility and ferro-nickel plant to enable him to meet his contractual obligations. In other words, the scope of the industrial empire had been extended yet again.

As had been the case in each previous instance of Clergue's insatiable appetite for industrial expansion, there was a qualifying factor. This time it centred on the presence of copper in the

*The discovery of iron ore at Michipicoten was vital to the development of the steel and steel-based industries at Sault Ste. Marie. Initially, the open pit methods of mining were used to extract the ore. Courtesy, Public Archives of Canada*

*Both iron ore and coal arrived at Algoma Steel by boat. Before the advent of self-unloading vessels, ships would dock and be unloaded manually or mechanically. Courtesy, Public Archives of Canada*

nickel ore. Since copper had a potentially disastrous effect on the quality of the nickel-ferro alloy, it had to be removed. The most efficient way of doing this was through the use of an alkali. To obtain the alkali, sodium was brought in from southwestern Ontario. The salt was mixed with water to produce a brine and then an electric current was passed through it. The result was the alkali necessary to the refining process and, in addition, chlorine gas. Holding firm to the adage "waste not, want not", Clergue established a plant to utilize the chlorine gas by-product. Chlorine, since it is a natural bleaching agent,

was adopted as a means of whitening sulphite pulp, which increased its value on the open market.

Clergue's chemists and scientists strove diligently to produce the high-quality nickel-ferro alloy demanded by the Krupp organization, but experiment after experiment ended in failure. When it was discovered that the ore from the Sudbury mine was too rich in nickel to produce armour plate, the solution was at hand. Red hematite (iron ore) could be used to dilute the nickel. Regardless of the fact that geological surveys indicated that the iron ore range on the south shore of Lake Superior did

to have two locomotives, 100 ore cars, and ore dock facilities at the harbour. In August 1899 the first scow loaded with men, horses, and equipment arrived at Michipicoten ready to begin work. They laid 12 miles of track and constructed the dock during the winter of 1899-1900, which enabled the mine to open in the spring of 1900. The first ore cars arrived at the harbour July 12, 1900.

*The Algoma Central Railway had trains running from the Helen Mine to Michipicoten Harbour by 1900. At the Harbour, ore would be transferred from railway cars to lake freighters for transport to Sault Ste. Marie. Courtesy, Sault Ste. Marie Museum*

not extend to the north shore, Clergue was not deterred from searching. As luck would have it, Ben Boyer, a prospector searching for gold at Michipicoten north of Sault Ste. Marie, had instead discovered hematite. He was only too happy to sell the claim to Clergue.

Although the iron ore deposits were located only 12 miles from Lake Superior, a means of transporting the mineral to the factory at Sault Ste. Marie had to be devised. Since the most logical means of moving the ore was by rail, Clergue obtained authorization to build and equip a railway line from the mine to Michipicoten Harbour. The line was

To further facilitate the movement of men and materials between Sault Ste. Marie and Michipicoten, two additional steps were taken: work was begun on the railway line, known as the Algoma Central, northward from Sault Ste. Marie, and Clergue took steps to acquire a fleet of Great Lakes steamers. By 1902 the fleet consisted of eight freight steamers, five barges, three passenger steamers, and a tug.

Until 1900 all of the Bessemer-grade hematite mined at Michipicoten

Above: The trolley line was constructed to provide industrial workers with reliable transportation to and from work. The line travelled to each of the steel-mill gates. Courtesy, Algoma University College

Right: Two million acres of land were opened for settlement as the Algoma Central Railway extended north into virgin territory. Immigration agents such as Duncan Bole, in Sault Ste. Marie, extolled the virtues of Algoma, luring unsuspecting settlers with promises of inexpensive fertile land, plentiful employment, a temperate climate, a long growing season, and absence of illness. Courtesy, Sault Ste. Marie Museum

In 1903, in an expression of anger and frustration, unpaid and unemployed Consolidated Lake Superior Company employees marched on company headquarters where they proceeded to hurl rocks and stones through the windows. The office staff was forced to seek refuge on the upper floors. Although the rioters were turned back by police, they returned later in the day, gained entrance to the building and damaged the interior. Courtesy, Sault Ste. Marie Museum

but not needed at the Sault was shipped to blast furnaces at Midland for use in steel production. But Clergue, in his never-ending search for industrial expansion, recognized the potential for steel development at Sault Ste. Marie. A Bessemer plant and a 28-inch blooming mill were installed in 1901 and were operational the following year. The first rails were rolled in May 1902.

In addition to these major components of his network, Clergue had created a series of smaller but equally integrated industries. The Tagona company, originally empowered to supply the town with power, had its mandate enlarged to provide fresh water as well. For a time it appeared that the company would lose its franchise when the town charged it with providing impure water. Eventually a settlement was reached, but the company's credibility had been called into question. In these early years, Clergue also turned his hand to the construction of electric street railways. Both Sault Ste. Marie, Ontario, and Sault Ste. Marie, Michigan, were beneficiaries of his largesse in this area. On the Canadian side of the border, construction of the street railway began at the corner of Queen and Gore streets in July 1902; the line was completed and operational by the end of that same year.

At about the same time, Clergue instituted his own ferry service between the twin communities. He had attempted to buy out the Sault Ferry Company, owned by two residents of Sault, Michigan, but when they refused to sell their two ferries, Clergue purchased a ferry and offered a competitive service. The ferry war came to an end when the Sault Ferry Company developed financial difficulties and sold out to Clergue.

Other components of Clergue's empire included a veneer mill, car shops, a brick plant, and plants to produce charcoal, acetate of lime, and wood alcohol. There was also a hotel and a boarding house.

The scope of industrial development had a profound impact on the community. The physical size of the community increased, as did the population. Unemployment was virtually nonexistent. On a less obvious level, there was a sizeable influx of settlers and European immigrants, which kept pace with the rate of the industrial growth. The Sault's population quadrupled from 2,000 to 8,000 between 1893 and 1903. Of these 8,000 people, 3,500 worked for the Clergue enterprises.

It was during this 10-year period that large numbers of unskilled workers emigrated to Canada from Europe in response to efforts by the Canadian government to entice immigrants and to encourage settlement. Sault Ste. Marie was fortunate enough to receive a portion of the newcomers. These immigrants settled in the west end of the town near the pulp mill, steel plant, and other industries.

But time was rapidly running out for the industrial empire. It had fallen prey to rapid over-expansion and to unsound financial practices, which created a serious cash-flow problem. The various components of the parent company served as their own customers and suppliers. Clergue, the man responsible for this development, was unable to see the implications of his actions. He was a man of ideas, not a manager or financier. His denial that a problem existed

meant that fresh capital was not infused at a critical time in the company's development. Collapse was imminent.

The danger signs appeared well in advance of the actual 1903 collapse of Clergue's industrial empire. The cracks were evident as early as 1902, ironically the year that marked the company's zenith in terms of both power and prestige. Despite Clergue's protestations to the contrary, the board of directors expressed concern with the steadily dwindling supply of working capital. In dramatic response to the uncertain financial situation, a system of expenditure controls was adopted, all construction was curtailed, track laying was halted, and a loan was secured to ease the immediate cash-flow problem.

The situation continued to deteriorate, and by November 1902 the company was forced to secure another loan both to pay off old debts and to meet current expenses. Speyer and Company of New York, the institution that held the company's notes, was much less lenient with this negotiated loan. In return for the money, they demanded the right to supervise the spending of the loan as well as the right to replace any or all of the company's directors. In addition, the securities of all of the consolidated's subsidiaries were assigned to Speyer.

The Lake Superior company was reorganized in accordance with the terms of the loan agreement in order to meet the stipulations imposed by the Speyer Company. Several directors were forced to resign and their positions were filled by Speyer nominees, and a trustee was appointed to oversee financial operations. Clergue retained

*American-born Francis
H. Clergue (1856-1939)
practiced law in Maine before abandoning his ca-
reer to become a promoter
and entrepreneur. He ar-
rived in Sault Ste. Marie
in 1894 and within a
few years had developed
a family of industries
known as the Consoli-
dated Lake Superior Com-
pany. Clergue's grip on
the industries was loosen-
ed in 1903 and he eventu-
ally lost control of them.
He resigned and moved
to Montreal. Courtesy,
Sault Ste. Marie Museum*

his positions as vice-president and
general manager until April 3, 1903,
when his resignation was requested on
the grounds that his spending practices
were not in keeping with the Speyer
Company guidelines and that he refused to comply with the rules imposed
by the trustees.

Regardless of the changes instituted
by Speyer, the company continued to
lose ground. In an attempt to stem the
downward plunge, Speyer named Cor-
nelius Shields as president to oversee
the day-to-day operations of the company's various components. Further,
the operating and financial departments
were moved from Sault Ste. Marie to
Philadelphia, and all subsidiaries were
brought under two umbrella companies. All Canadian holdings were
merged into the Lake Superior Power
Company while the American holdings
became divisions of Lake Superior Consolidated.

Ultimately, the attempts made to salvage the Clergue empire and to keep it
operating intact ended in failure. It became evident by September 17, 1903,
that the company was financially
embarrassed—there were no funds to
cover the day-to-day operating expenses, but perhaps more importantly
there was no money to meet the payroll.
All subsidiaries except for the Tagona
Power Company, the street railway, and
the weekly Algoma Central Railway Service were shut down. The workers remained unpaid.

The inability of the company to honour its payroll obligations enraged the
unpaid workers. Lumber and railway
workers employed north of town
marched southward where they met a

second group of disgruntled employees who had banded together at the steel plant. The workers, many of whom were armed as the result of a hardware store break-in, moved en masse to company headquarters. The building was surrounded and attacked before the rioters moved on to other company locations. The International Hotel was cordoned off by police and armed citizens in an attempt to protect it from damage or even destruction, and the street railway service was stopped to limit the movement of the rioters. All local bars and taverns were closed, and to prevent the importation of liquor from Sault Ste. Marie, Michigan, the ferry was ordered to return to the American side and remain there indefinitely.

In a last-ditch attempt to restore order, Mayor W.H. Plummer read the Riot Act. When the action proved unsuccessful, the local militia mustered the troops. Word of the industrial unrest had spread by this time, and Lieutenant-Colonel Elliot, commander of the militia, received an enquiry from Toronto regarding the state of affairs. Elliot, like municipal officials, feared further violence on the part of the rioters and requested the support of additional troops. The anger of the rioters had been spent, however, and they took no further action against the company. When the troops arrived from Toronto on the morning of September 28, 1903, they discovered that order had been restored as suddenly as it had been disrupted. Clergue's subsequent arrival on October 2, with funds to meet the overdue payroll, soothed the workers's anger.

The death knell, however, had been sounded for the Clergue industrial network. Speyer proceeded with a foreclosure action, a receiver was appointed, and Speyer gave notice of its intention to dispose of all securities. At a sale of company assets, all securities deposited with Speyer were offered for auction. The only bidder, and consequently the buyer, was Speyer and Company.

The reorganization of the Lake Superior Corporation began with the formation of the reorganization committee. The committee had been formed prior to the crash in an attempt to refinance rather than reorganize the company. The committee designed and submitted a plan for the incorporation of a new holding company that would buy out the Speyer interests and then raise enough money for the continued operation of the company through the sale of bonds. The recommendations of the committee led to the formation of the Canada Improvement Company in 1904; in May the plan became operational and the new company was incorporated in New Jersey. The creation of the Lake Superior Corporation marked the end of the first phase of the reorganization process.

The first task faced by the Lake Superior Corporation was the resumption of operations. Virtually all aspects of the corporation had ceased operating following the crash of September 1903, creating an entirely new set of problems. In addition to the chronic lack of both orders and working capital, the new corporation also had to contend with outmoded and inefficient machinery, and with a lack of workers, since most employees had been forced to seek jobs elsewhere.

## Accident At The Sault Ste. Marie Locks

*Although preventing accidents is difficult, the Sault Ste. Marie canal system has maintained an exceptional safety record. Since the canal opened in 1895 there has been only one major accident. On June 9, 1909, the steamer Perry G. Walker rammed the lower gates while two other ships were preparing to lock down. The force of the released water pushed all three vessels into the shipping channel. Courtesy, Archives of Ontario*

On June 9, 1909, the emergency swing dam built on the north side of the upper entrance to the lock proved its worth.

It was a typical, busy day at the canal; vessels were locking up and down the river, and canal employees steadily went about their duties locking the ships through. Early in the afternoon, the steamer *Assiniboia* was situated in the lock, and the steamer *Crescent City* was slowly maneuvering into position behind it, both vessels preparing to lock downbound. Beyond the closed gates, a dredge was

tied up, waiting to lock upbound once the other two vessels had passed from the lock.

Suddenly, the *Perry Walker*, approaching at a fast rate of speed, rammed the lower south gate, which forced the lower north gate to collapse.

The water already in the lock was released and rushed out. The impact pushed the *Perry Walker* back into the channel and across the river. The *Assiniboia* was borne along by the torrent of water. As it passed the hanging lock gates it smashed into them

before striking the *Perry Walker* and veering into the channel once more. Like the *Assiniboia*, the *Crescent City* was flushed from the lock. As it sped along, it struck the *Assiniboia* before overtaking it.

Fortunately, there were no fatalities or even serious injuries. Some passengers on board the *Assiniboia* thought that the entire incident had been a normal part of locking through and remained on the top deck waving to the horrified by-

standers at the canal. Each of the three ships was towed to Sault Ste. Marie, Michigan, for repairs. The *Assiniboia* resumed its voyage later that day, the *Perry Walker* three days later, and the *Crescent City*, which had sunk while awaiting repairs, was raised and was on its way within a week.

Repair work on the damaged lock gates began immediately; traffic through the canal at Sault Ste. Marie resumed after only nine days.

In spite of the difficulties, progress was made. The steel plant resumed operation in August 1904, when it obtained a large order for rails. Other subsidiaries were also operational by the end of 1904; the railway had resumed operation, and as a result, shipments of ore and lumber were once again moving. None of the subsidiaries achieved their pre-1903 levels, but with the exception of the steel mill, which was forced to close in 1908 due to a lack of orders, all remained nominally operational.

But the lack of orders was not the only problem confronting the rapidly crumbling conglomerate. To its detriment, it had become the centre of a power struggle first between New York and Philadelphia interests and then between American and British parties. The Philadelphia banks emerged as the victors of the first skirmish, but soon disposed of the assets they had acquired. British interests in the persons of James Dunn and financier/industrialist Robert Fleming were wait-

ing in the wings, prepared to step forward and assume control of the conglomerate.

The immediate infusion of new capital revitalized the flagging operations. The steel mill expanded its product line and developed new markets; capital was generated through the sale of iron ore on the open market; and the pulp mill increased its output even though the paper mill component had not yet been completed. Segments of the conglomerate not regarded as vital to its continued operation, such as the railway, were divested. On the other hand, new companies such as Cannelton Coal, Firborn Limestone, and Woodbridge Mining were acquired to provide essential raw materials.

By 1912 the industrial empire initiated by Francis H. Clergue was once again fully operational. The form may have strayed from what he had envisioned, but the intent, the industrial development and diversification of Sault Ste. Marie, was following the pattern.

# Chapter Five

At the turn of the century a tour of the Great Lakes aboard a steamer was the ultimate summer vacation. The ships would frequently tie up at the Government Dock, permitting passengers to disembark and spend time in Sault Ste. Marie. Those who were planning to stay in the Sault would be transported to the hotel of their choice by the waiting station wagons. Courtesy, Public Archives of Canada

# THE EMERGENCE
# OF SOCIETY

Although Sault Ste. Marie remained a small and struggling frontier community throughout the last half of the nineteenth century, local residents and officials never abandoned hope: the community seemed perpetually poised on the brink of growth and prosperity.

Twice in the past, Sault Ste. Marie had found itself in a similar position, only to have the elusive elements of success slip through its fingers. On the first occasion it had appeared, if only briefly, that the reverberations of the development of the surrounding area's resource industries would be felt in Sault Ste. Marie. When the success failed to materialize, the community's residents were down, but not deflated. They simply hitched their wagon to another star, in this case to what they regarded as promising proposals by the government of Upper Canada. Beginning in 1843 with the appointment of the first provincial official, it appeared that the government would take a hand in the development of the area. The survey of park lots in anticipation of the Robinson Treaty, and the creation of the Judicial District of Algoma, underscored the government's intentions. But it all came to naught. These actions, however well intentioned, provided stability to the existing community but did not attract people, money, or commercial ventures to the Sault.

The municipal structure of Sault Ste. Marie experienced a number of changes. Sault Ste. Marie was officially incorporated as a village on July 29, 1871. According to census statistics, the new village had a population of 879 and encompassed approximately 515,000 acres, including the townships of Tarentorous, Korah, Awenge, and St. Mary.

Prior to his death (1870), Judge John Prince had instituted proceedings leading to municipal incorporation. Prince's successor, Judge Walter McCrea, took up where Prince left off, following receipt of a letter and petition from local residents urging the establishment of a formal municipal structure. In accordance with the request, Judge McCrea scheduled a public meeting to be held on June 27, 1871.

The meeting was held at the Court House, and the Sault's first municipal representatives were duly elected. The new councillors—Andrew Hanna, John Carney, Andrew C. McKay, Francis Jones Hughes, and James C. Phipps—held the first meeting of the village of Sault Ste. Marie on July 29, 1871. At that meeting, the councillors appointed Andrew McKay as reeve. Appointments were made to fill a variety of positions, including clerk, treasurer, auditor, and path master. The tedious task of drafting village by-laws also got underway.

Sault Ste. Marie remained a village until April 1887, when it took the next municipal step and was incorporated as a town. William Brown became the first mayor of the newly created town, which by this time stretched from West Street to Church Street and was home to some

1,600 residents.

The 1880s were watershed years in Sault Ste. Marie's history. The Canadian Pacific Railway spurline to Sudbury was completed, and the first train arrived at the Sault on October 20, 1887, connecting Sault Ste. Marie with the rest of Canada by rail. The international railway bridge was constructed across the rapids, affording the community ready access to thousands of miles of rail line throughout the United States. Work was begun on the canal and lock system on the Canadian side of the St. Mary's River, and the idea of using the rapids to produce hydroelectricity was conceived. Each of these colossal projects attracted hundreds of labourers and tradesmen and their families to Sault Ste. Marie. This influx of people taxed available accommodations and forced residential property values to skyrocket. The newcomers added their support to local demands for increased municipal and social services.

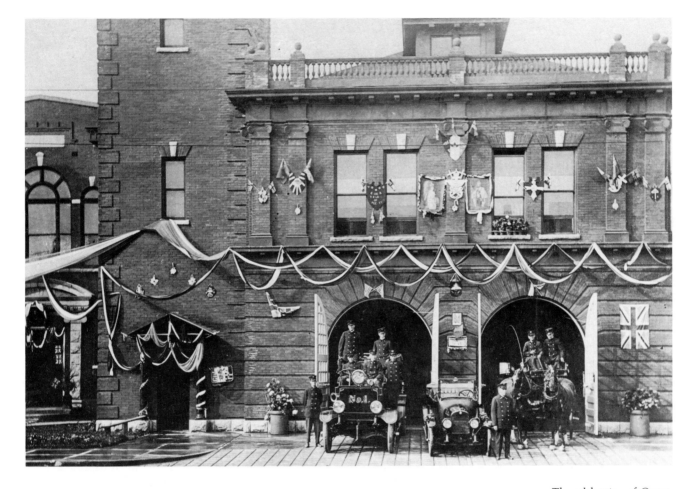

*The celebration of Queen Victoria's Jubilee in 1897 was a major event in Sault Ste. Marie. Buildings were decorated with bunting and pictures of the Queen. There was a grand parade followed by a day of festivities at the Agricultural Grounds. Courtesy, The Sault Star*

# The International Bridge

*The ferries that travelled be-tween the two Saults were retired from service once the International Bridge was opened to traffic. Cour-tesy, The Sault Star*

At its narrowest point below the rap-ids, the St. Mary's River is approxi-mately a kilometre in width. But in the early days of international travel, even this modest distance created in-surmountable difficulties.

The first ferry service between the two sides of the rapids began op-erating in 1873. It handled foot pas-sengers, wagons, and livestock. The ferry operated normally in the summer months, but winter ice con-ditions brought traffic between the two communities to a halt. Only af-ter the ice melted could regular ferry traffic resume. In later years, Coast Guard icebreakers stationed at Sault Ste. Marie controlled ice conditions, permitting year-round transporta-tion between the two cities.

The concept of a bridge linking the two Saults took shape in 1934; a group of local businessmen turned the idea into reality with the forma-tion of the Sault Bridge Authority. The first step toward the eventual construction of the International Bridge had been taken.

The next step was to obtain the necessary legal permissions from the various levels of government in-volved. The State of Michigan in-itially granted approval in 1935; the permission was renewed in 1953. In the following year, 1954, the Michi-gan legislature passed an act authoriz-ing the creation of the International Bridge Authority. The St. Mary's River Bridge Company, the Cana-dian counterpart of the International Bridge Authority, was created in 1955.

The opening of the Mackinac Bridge in 1957 made the construction of an International Bridge even more imperative. The increased flow of traffic into Michigan's upper peninsula would place an even greater strain on the already overburdened ferry system. In addition, the Trans Canada Highway around the north shore of Lake Superior was scheduled to open in 1960, and would bring still more tourists and general traffic to the area. Even before completion of the Mackinac Bridge and the Trans Canada Highway, a four- or five-hour wait for the ferry during peak periods was common. Waiting periods following the completion of both of these construction ventures would have been unimaginably long.

Construction of the International Bridge began on September 16, 1960, and was completed in 1962. The bridge opened to traffic on October 1962, followed by the ribbon-cutting ceremony in May 1963.

*The International Bridge connecting Sault Ste. Marie, Ontario, and Sault Ste. Marie, Michigan, officially opened May 24, 1963. Governor George Romney of Michigan and Premier John Robarts of Ontario made the inaugural trip across the $20 million structure. Courtesy, The Sault Star*

*Born in Ottawa in 1854, James Kehoe practised criminal law in Stratford after being called to the bar at the age of 22. In 1884 he was appointed as Crown Attorney and Clerk of the Peace in Sault Ste. Marie. Courtesy, Sault Ste. Marie Museum*

The population and geographic holdings of Sault Ste. Marie continued to grow at a steady pace. Soon after annexation of the Moffley Hill area in 1912, the town council voted to petition the Ontario legislature to incorporate Sault Ste. Marie as a city. The incorporation bill was introduced in the Private Bills Committee of the legislature in March, and on April 12, 1912, with Mayor W.H. Munro in attendance to witness the bill's passage, Sault Ste. Marie officially became a city.

The amalgamation of Sault Ste. Marie and the adjoining town of Steelton in 1918 resulted in a dramatic jump in population—from 12,200 to 21,500. Steelton had evolved in conjunction with Clergue's industrial complex. It was, in actual fact, a working-class neighbourhood located near Clergue's many industries. The area was

## Sault Ste. Marie During The Depression

The First World War was followed by the fast-paced, free-wheeling decade of the Roaring Twenties. Sault Ste. Marie, like the rest of Ontario, was borne along on the crest of prosperity that engulfed much of North America. When the bubble burst in 1929, the community was plunged into the grim years of the Depression.

Because of the industrial nature of Sault Ste. Marie, it was especially hard hit by the severe downturn in economic fortunes. As businesses and industries were forced to reduce

their work forces, or worse still, to terminate their operations completely, unemployment reached record high levels. Workers fortunate enough to remain on the job were obliged to accept significant reductions in salary.

The economic ramifications of the Depression were evident in all aspects of community life. Many residents were forced to resort to general relief in order to put food on the table. Many more existed at subsistence levels. Housing starts, one of the most accurate economic barometers, were negligible.

In an attempt to at least partially alleviate the poverty and hardship of the Depression, programs were instituted by various levels of government. Citizens were allocated garden plots by the city government to ensure they had sufficient food; on the provincial level, projects such as timbering and road building were initiated to provide employment.

Single, unemployed men were among the most seriously affected during this period. In Sault Ste. Marie this segment of the community sought refuge on Whitefish Island in the St. Mary's River. Camps of these homeless, destitute men were located on the island for the duration of the Depression. The inhabitants existed on handouts of food from area stores and restaurants and on the fish and wildlife they were able to catch.

Ironically, the Depression was brought to an end by a horror of an even greater magnitude—the Second World War.

originally referred to as "The New Settlement", but at that time of its incorporation in 1904 it aquired the name by which it is still commonly known.

If the 1920s was a decade of steady albeit unspectacular growth, then the 1930s was a decade of diametric contradiction. The worldwide economic depression had a devastating impact on the city; while population figures remained steady, the number of available jobs declined as industry after industry experienced production cutbacks. In a letter to Sir James Dunn written in 1934, Mayor James Lyons indicated that 8,000 of the city's 23,000 residents were on relief and that the city had reached the ". . . limit of its financing . . ."

The outbreak of the Second World War in Europe stabilized the Sault's economy. People who were ineligible to enlist in the military arrived in the city to work in the war industries. Bush areas in the hill area and in the Buckley

*William van Abbott arrived in Sault Ste. Marie in 1864 to carry on a wholesale liquor business. He selected the Sault because of its freeport status. Van Abbott returned to his native England in 1865, then made a permanent move to Sault Ste. Marie in 1870. He was appointed village auditor in 1871 and from 1873 he served as Indian agent. Courtesy, Sault Ste. Marie Museum*

section of town were cleared for war-time housing construction to accommodate the growing numbers of war workers and their families.

This growth pattern continued throughout the 1950s and 1960s. In response to an application by the Township of Tarentorous in 1964, the Ontario Municipal Board ordered that the townships of Korah and Tarentorous be amalgamated with the City of Sault Ste. Marie. When the order came into force, on January 1, 1965, the population of the expanded city increased from 44,700 to 70,000.

Education was high on the list of social service priorities mandated by residents of Sault Ste. Marie. The earliest facility for the instruction of local children was established by the Reverend William MacMurray. MacMurray's Anglican Church-funded school provided local and area Ojibway children with a rudimentary scholastic and religious education and at the same time taught them such skills as farming, housekeeping, and basic nutrition.

This type of school had long been the dream of Ojibway Chief Shingwaukonce. In 1832 the chief had snowshoed from Sault Ste. Marie to York to request the services of a teacher. It was partially in response to this request that John Colbourne, governor of Upper Canada, dispatched MacMurray to the Sault.

Classes were conducted in a small one-room building constructed at government expense. The building served as a schoolhouse during the week and as a church on Sundays. It was closed in 1838 with the departure of MacMurray and his wife.

Even though the school was abandoned when MacMurray left, Shingwaukonce never abandoned his dream of a permanent school. After his death in 1854, the task of securing a school for local Indian children fell to his sons, Augustin and Buhgwajene. Almost 40 years after his father had travelled to York on foot, Augustin made a similar trip. This time, the result was the construction of the Shingwauk Residential School and the appointment of the Reverend E.F. Wilson as a missionary and educator. Augustin had hoped the school would provide an academic education that would enable future generations of native children to maintain their cultural identity and their heritage. But, unfortunately for Augustin, Christian doctrine at that time advocated assimilation and integration of native peoples, not the cultivation and protection of their unique identity.

The Shingwauk Residential School was constructed at Garden River in 1873. It opened September 22 with 15 boys and girls enrolled. But, after only six days of use, the building burned to the ground.

Immediately following the fire a reconstruction program was initiated. A much larger site was selected, on the St. Mary's River within the Sault Ste. Marie park lot. The second Shingwauk Residential School opened in August 1875, and accepted only male students. It was not until 1879 that the Wawanosh Home for Girls was opened. Some 20 years later Wawanosh closed and Shingwauk was enlarged to handle the additional female students.

From the time of the closure of MacMurray's school in 1838 until the mid

1860s, little provision was made for the education of non-native children in Sault Ste. Marie. Two maiden ladies, the Misses Hoige, operated the first community facility, a private school. Since attendance was not compulsory, children went to class sporadically as it suited either them or their parents.

A public school was finally built in 1866. A public subscription campaign succeeded in raising adequate funds for the construction of a building near the northeast corner of Pim and Queen streets. As construction neared comple-

tion, a teacher was hired.

According to an 1866 entry in the diary of David Pim, a local businessman, hotelier, and postmaster:

*There were 304 souls in the school district, and of that 79 were between the ages of 5 and 16 years. Heretofore, no provision had been made for the education of the children at Sault Ste. Marie. Mr. William Turner was the first person paid by the town and he gathered 50 out of the 79 scholars available.*

*Properly outfitted barbershops catered to a gentleman's grooming and personal needs. A spittoon accessible to each patron was de rigueur, as was a supply of pipes and tobacco products. Courtesy, Sault Ste. Marie Public Library*

The school, which also served as the Methodist and Anglican churches on alternate Sundays, was appropriated by the Canadian Pacific Railway in 1888 for use as a station house. In 1892, the building was destroyed by fire.

The first permanent public and separate elementary schools were built in 1889. Central School provided a public education to children from the entire town of Sault Ste. Marie. It continued to do so until the Fort School, later King Edward, was built for the convenience of children living in the west end. The Sacred Heart School was the Sault's first separate elementary school. The task of raising funds for its construction fell to Father J.C. Finnett, priest of the Sacred Heart parish. Only two rooms in the school served as classrooms, however. The upstairs was a meeting hall where groups such as the Catholic Order of Foresters gathered for many years.

The city's first high school, the Sault Collegiate Institute, was completed in May 1907. It consisted of four classrooms, a science lab, a commercial room, a basketball court, and an attic with a stage for assemblies. Prior to the construction of the school, post-elementary students attended classes that were held in rooms in three locations in the downtown area, including City Hall. Demand for secondary education was so high that no sooner was the Collegiate Institute opened than an addition was needed.

In 1896 Sault Ste. Marie was struck by a typhoid fever epidemic. Massive numbers of people became infected, and without hospital facilities to stem its tide, the lives of hundreds of local residents were threatened. The town expended $1,600 to acquire an old building for use as hospital quarters and to hire attendants in an attempt to treat the infected and inhibit the spread of the disease. But this solution brought only temporary relief. The fact remained that in the event of another medical emergency, Sault Ste. Marie did not have a hospital and would remain vulnerable.

With this potential threat to the health and welfare of the community foremost in the public mind, efforts to establish a permanent hospital began in earnest in September 1896. Town meetings were held, local organizations offered money and assistance, and the town was granted a free site for the building. Buoyed by the local support, a delegation travelled to Toronto and then to Ottawa to solicit construction funds. To their disappointment, all requests for money were rejected.

Just when it appeared that all hope had been lost, Dr. Chamberlain, Inspector of Public Charities, suggested that the Roman Catholic Sisters of Charity be approached. He spoke to the Sisters in July 1898 on behalf of the town and by September the first two nuns from the Order of the Grey Nuns of the Cross had arrived from Ottawa. They immediately arranged for a temporary hospital in a cottage on Water Street. Once this was completed, the foundation stone for the permanent hospital was laid.

The new 80-bed General Hospital opened its doors in 1899. Equipped with the most up-to-date furnishings and conveniences, the hospital was the area's sole provider of medical services until 1917.

During the first part of the nineteenth century, the town's burgeoning population taxed the facilities of the General Hospital. Uriah McFadden sought and obtained letters of patent authorizing the establishment of the Algoma Benevolent Society, an organization dedicated to the formation of a second non-sectarian hospital. Since provincial law clearly stipulated that the population of an area must exceed 10,000 before a second hospital could be built, the Society was obliged to bide its time. The onset of World War I also caused delay in the establishment of another facility. Finally, in July 1917, the Royal Victoria Hospital opened its doors in a converted house on Albert Street. The hospital was equipped with 20 patient beds as well as living quarters for the staff.

Two years after the establishment of the Royal Victoria Hospital, Captain H.L. Plummer and Mrs. R.A. Lyons, descendants of Mr. and Mrs. W.H. Plummer, offered to donate the Plummer family home, Lynnehurst, for use as a hospital on the condition that the hospital bear the Plummer name.

The Royal Victoria reopened at Lynnehurst as the Plummer Memorial Public Hospital. By 1921, however, three years after the annexation of Steelton, the 35-bed facility was overcrowded. F.J. Davey, president of the Algoma Benevolent Society, acquired adjacent lots for expansion, and in 1928 he launched a successful campaign to raise funds for the construction of a new hospital to replace the renovated Plummer home. Construction of the new facility was completed the following year.

Religion and religious doctrine played a major role in the lives of early residents of Sault Ste. Marie. Religious gatherings were opportunities to meet and exchange news as well as to preach and study scripture. Church services gave settlers and visitors alike a reason and an opportunity to meet on common ground.

The Jesuit missionaries introduced the Christian religion to the Indians of Sault Ste. Marie in the first half of the seventeenth century, and for many years they were the sole purveyors of Christianity in the area. Baptist and Methodist preachers settled on the American side of the river, but worshippers on the British side of the border did not have this variety from which to choose. It was not until 1821 and the North West/Hudson's Bay Company merger that formal Church of England, or Anglican, worship became available. Prior to the arrival of the First Anglican clergymen, Hudson's Bay Company officials were charged with the power of ex-officio deacons. They were authorized to conduct church services and to perform baptisms, marriages, and funerals in the absence of ordained Anglican clergy. The Hudson's Bay Company officials were divested of their religious functions in Sault Ste. Marie in 1830 with the arrival of the Reverend D. Cameron. He was succeeded by William MacMurray in 1832. To fulfill his mandate to establish a mission among the Ojibway people, MacMurray rented the house and property that had been occupied by Charles Oakes Ermatinger until the Ermatinger family's departure to Montreal in 1828. MacMurray also obtained a piece of property on the Great Northern Road

*In 1919 the descendants
of W.H. Plummer do-
nated the family home
for use as a hospital.
The house functioned in
this capacity until the demand for services ex-
ceeded the available
space. The Plummer Memo-
rial Public Hospital was
constructed in 1929.
Courtesy, The Sault Star*

in 1835 for the construction of his school and church. Following the demolition of this building, church services were held at the Old Stone House.

The Right Reverend A.N. Bethune laid the cornerstone for St. Luke's, Sault Ste. Marie's first Anglican church, on July 22, 1870. The ceremony took place in the presence of Colonel Garnet Wolseley and his troops, who were en route to the Red River. The troops provided an honour guard and reputedly contributed generously toward the construction costs of the church. The church was consecrated in October 1870.

A Methodist church was established in 1851 by the Reverend George McDougall. Like the Anglicans, the Methodists conducted their services at the Old Stone House until 1870. The congregation then moved to their new church on the east side of Great Northern Road. The building met the needs of the Methodists until 1900, by which time the congregation had outgrown the available space. The Honourable W.C. Mulock, Postmaster General of Canada, laid the cornerstone for another church at the corner of Spring and Albert streets. A lack of funds brought construction to a halt in 1903, but work resumed in 1905. Central Methodist Church was completed and ready for use in early 1906.

The Presbyterian congregation of Sault St. Marie met in the newly constructed St. Andrew's Presbyterian Church beginning in 1875. For nine years prior to 1875, Presbyterian services had been conducted in the schoolhouse. The church, which accommodated 70 people, was enlarged in 1892 and rebuilt completely in 1908. When the United Church of Canada was formed in 1925, both Central Methodist and St. Andrew's Presbyterian entered the Union and became Central United and St. Andrew's United.

A Roman Catholic church was constructed in 1875 to meet the needs of the diverse religious community. Construction of a new Roman Catholic church began in July 1875, was completed the following year, and was dedicated as the parish Church of the Sacred Heart. The church was selected as the Diocesan Cathedral in 1904 and renamed the Cathedral of the Precious Blood in 1936. The stone structure was intended to replace the wooden building that some accounts indicate may have been constructed as early as 1790. It is more generally accepted, however, that construction of the church was initiated by Father J.M. Menet, a Jesuit missionary, soon after his arrival in 1845.

*In 1904, the volunteer fire department proudly displayed its wagon and team beside the Dominion Building at the corner of Queen and East streets. Courtesy, The Sault Star*

Sault Ste. Marie's Baptist congregation was organized in July 1889. The Reverend Mr. Calder, a pastor from Sault Ste. Marie, Michigan, officiated at the Baptist services, which were held at Dawson's Hall until construction of the church was completed in 1890. According to newspaper reports of 1895, the church was a bright and airy structure, accommodating 350 people, and was blessed with electric lights.

As the population of the community continued to grow, so did the demands for a variety of churches. In response to this demand, other Christian churches were organized, as were the Christian Science Society, Congregation Beth Jacob, the Salvation Army, and the Jehovah's Witnesses.

Residents of Sault Ste. Marie, con-cerned with the protection both of themselves and their property, had established the beginnings of the community's police and fire departments by the end of the 1880s. A volunteer fire department, equipped with hand reels and water buckets, was formed in 1889. In September of that year, the town council formalized its commitment to the development of fire protection when it purchased a horse-drawn hose wagon and authorized the construction of a fire hall on McDougall Street.

A second volunteer brigade was formed in March 1891 following the mass resignation of the original group. William Hearst, later Sir William, was chosen as the first fire chief.

## William H. Hearst—Premier of Ontario

*William Howard Hearst represented Sault Ste. Marie in the Ontario Legislature from 1908 until his defeat in 1919. Hearst was appointed Minister of Lands, Forests and Mines in 1911. Following the death of Premier Whitney in 1914, Hearst became premier of the province of Ontario. Courtesy, Archives of Ontario*

William Howard Hearst moved to Sault Ste. Marie in 1888 and established a law firm with John McKay, a fellow law student from Owen Sound. Hearst quickly became involved in the civic affairs of the community. In 1891 he attended a meeting to form a new volunteer fire brigade following the mass resignation of the original department, and he was elected as chief of the new department. He continued to serve in that capacity until 1892. In addition, Hearst was an active member of the Free Masons Lodge and the Methodist Church.

Hearst entered the field of provin-

*Colonel Sidney L. Penhorwood was one of the key recruiting officers for the Canadian Expeditionary Forces. He went overseas with the 227th Battalion and served as a forester at Windsor Castle, where he came to know King George V and Queen Mary. Courtesy, Public Archives of Canada*

cial politics in 1894. A member of the Conservative party, Hearst made an unsuccessful bid for the seat held by Liberal Charles Farwell. He ran again in 1908 and this time gained the seat. He continued to operate his law practice and to live in Sault Ste. Marie until he was appointed Minister of Lands and Mines in 1911. Following his cabinet appointment, he moved his family from the Sault to Toronto.

Upon the death of Sir James Whitney in 1914, Hearst assumed the premiership of the province of Ontario, the first and only representative from northern Ontario ever to fill the position. He served as premier until 1919, when both he and his party were soundly defeated at the polls.

During Hearst's term as premier, several issues with far-reaching social implications surfaced. His stand on

*W.H. Hearst did legal work for the Lake Superior Corporation before seeking political office. A fervent supporter of the corporation even after his election, Hearst addressed the Canadian Club on the subject in 1912: he indicated that LSC employed ". . . an army of ten thousand men, paying in wages more than $6,000,000 a year . . . What does that mean not only to the Sault and the Province of Ontario? It surely means that the Province at large must be benefitted." Courtesy, Archives of Ontario*

two of these issues, temperance and female suffrage, were partially responsible for his ultimate defeat.

As a war-measure act, the Hearst government advocated the temperate use of alcohol. The open hours of liquor stores were reduced. However, bars, because of their social function, were untouched. The scope of the temperance movement broadened until, in 1916, all bars, clubs, and liquor stores were closed for the duration of the war. The liquor traffic was regarded as a needless waste: it consumed valuable grain, reduced industrial efficiency, and put temptation in the way of the soldiers.

With regard to female suffrage, Hearst impolitically stated in 1917 that the grant of suffrage to women of the province of Ontario was not an issue of compelling interest. He said that although he greatly admired the work performed by women as their contribution to the war effort, he would not and could not insult them by rewarding their contributions with political prizes such as the vote.

Hearst was defeated in his home riding in 1919 by the local Independent Labour party candidate, J.B. Cunningham. His contributions to the province were recognized, however, and he was named a Knight Commander of the Most Distinguished Order of St. Michael and St. George.

Fighting fires was a difficult proposition in those early days. Rocks and posts obstructed the roads, making it difficult for the fire brigade to travel quickly and safely to and from fires. Supplies such as lanterns and rubber coats were chronically in short supply, and by 1894 the hose wagon was in such disrepair that the entire fire brigade threatened to withdraw its services. Evidently their demands were met because the department remained intact.

Beginning in 1893, firemen received nominal payment for their services. They were paid 50 cents for the first hour spent fighting a fire and 40 cents for each subsequent hour. They were also paid 25 cents for each false alarm they attended (a false alarm was defined as a fire where no water was thrown). The firefighters were a highly dedicated group; with few exceptions, they regularly attended not only fires but also scheduled fire drills and practices. Their commitment to service was especially admirable in light of the fact that firemen in other Ontario centres of equivalent size and population earned $5 for each fire they fought and $2 for each practice they attended.

The fire department expanded and updated its equipment in 1912 with the purchase of its first mechanical fire engine. This state-of-the-art pumper truck

*The Ministry of Natural Resources, formerly the Department of Lands and Forests, began using airplanes for fire-patrol purposes beginning in 1921. In that year a survey crew spotted a fire and realized that if a crew and equipment could be flown in, the fire could be extinguished more quickly and the damage done by forest fires reduced. The idea so impressed the Honourable James Lyons M.P.P. that he established the air-service base locally in 1924. Courtesy, Archives of Ontario*

*The growth of the police department kept pace with community expansion. Chief Downey and his staff maintained law and order from police headquarters in the city hall complex. Courtesy, Sault Ste. Marie Museum*

was based at the main fire station on Queen Street. The old hose wagon and team of horses was transferred to the Number 2 station, which had been constructed on Central Park Avenue to service the west area.

By the 1920s, the fire department relied almost exclusively on trucks for transportation. During inclement weather, however, horses followed the

truck in case the vehicle became mired in mud or snow. In more than one instance the equipment was removed from the truck and loaded onto the horse-drawn wagon or sleigh in order to reach the fire.

The police department, like the fire department, kept pace with changes in the community. As the population and physical size of Sault Ste. Marie

*The Post Office on the corner of Queen and East streets was officially completed in 1912 with the installation of a three-day clock in the tower. The clock was ordered from a British manufacturer following completion of the building. Courtesy, The Sault Star*

*Wemyss Simpson was the last factor at the Hudson's Bay Company post in Sault Ste. Marie. From 1867 until 1872 he sat in the Parliament of Canada as the representative for the District of Algoma. Courtesy, Sault Ste. Marie Museum*

expanded, so too did the size of the police force. Sault Ste. Marie hired its first law enforcement officer in 1870 when George Parr was appointed pound keeper. The police force doubled in 1871 with the addition of Andrew McKay as head constable. McKay's duties included such widely diverse activities as weed inspection and tax collection. The most commonly laid charge stemmed from the destruction of gardens by roaming cattle.

Initially, police officers reported to the municipal clerk on a weekly basis. In 1896, however, the first chief of police was appointed and the officers became responsible to him.

The first formal police headquarters was located on East Street just south of Queen, in the same building as

the town council offices. In 1903 the municipal offices were moved out, following the construction of the new civic building, but the police headquarters remained there until 1922. In that year the police moved into space in the city hall that had been vacated by the fire department. In 1945 the police department relocated to the basement of the courthouse, and in 1957 it occupied its own building directly behind the courthouse on Albert Street. It occupied these premises until overcrowding forced the construction of new facilities in 1969.

Because of the isolated location of the Sault, mail service has long been a vital link to the outside world. Canada's Post Office Department was created in 1846, but it was not until 1854 that the first postmaster was appointed at Sault Ste. Marie. According to Post Office Department records, Joseph Wilson was named postmaster in 1854, a role he filled for two years. Wemyss MacKenzie Simpson, the last Hudson's Bay Company factor at Sault Ste. Marie, succeeded Wilson. During his tenure, he moved the post office from the business hub of the community to the Hudson's Bay Company post near the foot of the rapids.

David Pim took over from Simpson in 1858, moving the post office yet again, this time to his own residence, the Old Stone House. Whenever the mail arrived, Pim would hoist a flag to inform the townspeople. Mail was brought to the Sault during navigable months by boat, and by dogsled during the winter. The mail carriers travelled on foot during the in-between seasons.

Growth of the community and

## DEPARTMENT OF THE NAVAL SERVICE.

SEALED TENDERS, addressed to the under-signed, and endorsed "Tender for the Erection of Wireless Telegraph Station," at Sault Ste. Marie, Ontario, will be received at this office until noon, on July Fifteenth, 1911.

Plans, Specification and Form of Contract to be entered into can be seen on and after July First instant, at the office of the Superintendent of Wireless Telegraphs, Department of the Naval Service, Ottawa, the Office of the Agent of the Department of Marine and Fisheries, Parry Sound, Ontario, or the Office of the Superintending Engineer of Sault Ste. Marie Canal, Sault Ste. Marie, Ontario.

Persons tendering are notified that tenders will not be considered unless made on the printed forms supplied, and signed with their actual signatures, stating their occupations and places of residence. In the case of firms, the actual signature, the nature of the occupation, and place of residence of each member of the firm must be given.

Each tender must be accompanied by an accepted cheque on a chartered bank, payable to the order of the Honourable the Minister of the Naval Service, equal to ten per cent (10 p.c.) of the amount of the tender, which will be forfeited if the person tendering decline to enter into a contract when called upon to do so, or fail to complete the work contracted for. If the tender be not accepted the cheque will be returned.

The Department does not bind itself to accept the lowest or any tender.

By order,

G. J. DESBARATS,
Deputy Minister.

Department of the Naval Service,
Ottawa, June 26, 1911.

Newspapers will not be paid for this advertisement if they insert it without authority from the Department.

*Above: Wemyss Simpson began construction of his stone house in 1865 while he was factor at the Hudson's Bay Company post. The house is the second oldest stone house in the Sault and was completed in 1866, the year before Simpson was elected to the Parliament of Canada. Courtesy, Sault Ste. Marie Museum*

*Left: In 1911 the Department of Naval Service placed advertisements in several newspapers calling for tenders for the construction of a wireless telegraph station at Sault Ste. Marie. The station was slated to be constructed at the canal. Courtesy, Parks Canada, Sault Ste. Marie*

In 1911 the first tele-
graph station was con-
structed at the Sault Ste.
Marie Ship Canal. Ser-
vice was instituted at that
time. Several years later
the first telephones were
installed. Courtesy,
Archives of Ontario

resultant increased demands on post office services meant that larger facilities
were required. David and Margaret Pim
moved the postal facilities to the old
schoolhouse on Pim Street. When even
this building proved to be too small, the
search for yet another site began.

In 1902, A.S. Dyment, the federal
member of Parliament for the Sault Ste.
Marie riding, announced plans for the
construction of a federal government
building. The building was intended to
house a variety of government services,
including the post office. Much to the
chagrin of residents of the west end of
the town, the lot on the northwest
corner of Queen and East streets was
chosen for the structure. The location
was ideal from all other points of view,
however, since the winter ice road to
Sault, Michigan (the arrival point of
much mail for Sault, Ontario), was con-

structed annually at the foot of East
Street.

Work on the government building
began in May 1904, two years after the
project had been proposed, and two
years before occupants moved in. The
original plan had called for the building
to open in November 1905, but the delayed installation of a lighting plant disrupted the schedule. The postmaster at
the time of the move was Dr. W.A.
Adams; he supervised an expanded staff
of seven.

A three-day clock was installed in
the Federal Building's tower in 1912. In
the same year, eight letter carriers were
hired, and free door-to-door mail delivery was instituted. Although the service
proved convenient for the community,
the lack of roads and sidewalks and the
distances between houses created hard-
ships for the carriers.

# The Trans Canada Highway

During the early years of development, Sault Ste. Marie relied heavily upon water transportation. As a result of this dependence, the community was isolated for several months of the year. This situation gave rise to a growing awareness that land transportation was essential if further settlement was to take place.

Albert P. Salter surveyed the area for a road in 1859. The result of his survey, the Great Northern Road, was to extend from the Spanish River to the mouth of the Goulais River in a northwesterly direction. Work began on the road in 1860. Although the original plan called for the construction of a road approximately 150 miles in length, only half of the work was completed.

*The Government of Canada passed the Trans-Canada Act in 1949, authorizing the construction of a highway linking all of the provinces. The stretch of road from Montreal to Sault Ste. Marie was completed in 1960. Work on the road westward continued, linking with towns such as Wawa that previously were accessible only by rail. Courtesy, The Sault Star*

The McKay Road, the portion of the roadway extending from Sylvan Valley to Echo Bay, along the north shore of the St. Mary's River to Sault Ste. Marie, and then along what are today the Black and Old Garden River roads, was the first road link between Sault Ste. Marie and other communities. Large tracts of land were finally opened for farming and

*This arch, formed of cedar logs, was erected on the highway east of Sault Ste. Marie. It served to remind visitors to the Sault how sorry the residents were to see them leave. Courtesy, Lillian M. Quinn*

settlement. In a move common to the time, people living along the road were assigned responsibility for its maintenance. Unfortunately, most of them were too busy with their day-to-day chores to devote much time or energy to road work, and the road quickly deteriorated into an unusable state.

It was not until 1911 that efforts to build an access road to Sault Ste. Marie were renewed. Construction

of the roadbed between Sault Ste. Marie and Sudbury took 14 years. Residents of both communities, as well as points in between, were so pleased to finally have a road that they paid little heed to the spring mud and summer dust conditions. By 1935, however, the novelty of the road had worn off and motorists were less prepared to accept the poor road conditions. A delegation led by Sault Ste. Marie lawyer Harry Hamilton, representing some 150 communities, travelled to Toronto to demand that improvements be made.

Construction of a new road westward to the lakehead began during the Depression. Road work had progressed only as far as Batchewana when Mitchell Hepburn, Premier of Ontario, halted the project due to lack of funds and dismissed the 1,800 men engaged in the construction work. Although work was scheduled to resume once funds were available, construction was further delayed by the outbreak of World War II.

In 1949 the Government of Canada passed the Trans Canada Act, authorizing construction of a highway linking each of the provinces. The federal and provincial governments agreed to share the cost of constructing 5,000 miles of highway. The stretch of the road from Montreal to Sault Ste. Marie, which roughly follows the old fur-trade route, was completed in 1960.

*Below: In 1924 the Soo Greyhounds won the Allen Cup for the first and only time in the team's history. The day the team arrived back in town following the momentous victory was an unofficial holiday. Thousands of local residents turned out to welcome the hometown heroes. Courtesy, Sault Star*

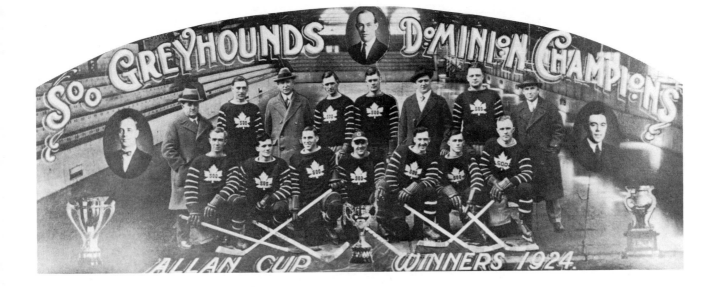

an additional ice surface exclusively for curling.

Hockey and Sault Ste. Marie have long been synonymous. In the days before organized hockey leagues, pick-up teams were the norm. Gradually, schools, clubs, and businesses became involved and competitive leagues were born. The Sault Ste. Marie Greyhounds were formed in 1919, just in time to take part in the 1919-1920 hockey season. The highlight of the team's history was their spectacular 1924 season, when they captured the Allen Cup for the first and only time. Thousands of local residents gathered at the train sta-

tion to welcome home the hockey heroes. The team was presented with an Algoma Steel slagpot decorated to resemble a huge trophy. As a result of the victory, the team's manager, George MacNamara, was inducted into the Hockey Hall of Fame.

While the Greyhounds continued to participate and to excel in their loop, other leagues were formed in the city. One of these was based at an outdoor rink on Ferris Street. A group of men and boys from the Pim Street Hill area had gotten together and built a rink where people could skate and play hockey. Their concept was well timed; they began their efforts at the beginning of the Great Depression when people had plenty of spare time, little to do, and no spending money. As the reputation of the rink spread, its popularity grew and so too did its size. Soon music and lights were added. Skaters would have exclusive use of the ice until 10 P.M. Then the hockey players would take over and play until 2 A.M. In 1934, a men's team, the Pim Hill Bullies, was formed to compete against teams from Echo Bay, Bar River, Bruce Mines, Thessalon, and Richard's Landing. A women's counterpart, the Bullets, was organized to play in 1939 in an expanding women's league. The Pim Hill rink remained an important social and recreational centre until 1948.

Beginning in the early twentieth century the YMCA provided facilities for year-round recreational activities. Construction of the Sault Ste. Marie YMCA began in 1912, the year Sault Ste. Marie was incorporated as a city following its annexation of the Moffley Hill area with the resulting increase in

*Construction of the YMCA began in 1912. When it opened the following year, the March Street facility was designed to serve a community with a population of 10,000. The facilities, including a swimming pool, gymnasium, meeting rooms and later an outdoor tennis court, were large enough to accommodate 500 men and boys. Courtesy, The Sault Star*

When the Orpheum The-
atre opened its doors on
April 15, 1912, there
were already four other the-
atres in the downtown
area. The theatre had to devise an innovative means
of attracting patrons. The
solution was the Or-
pheum Komedy Concert
Band. The group would
entertain passers-by on
Queen Street, encourag-
ing them to buy a ticket
and see the show. Cour-
tesy, Sault Ste. Marie
Museum

*Henry Wadsworth Longfel-low's poem* Hiawatha *was based on the lore and legend of the local Ojibway. The poem was turned into a play by L.O. Armstrong and was first staged by the Garden River band in 1900. Between 1901 and 1904 the production toured the United States and Europe. In subsequent years it was presented at Garden River, often in the Ojibway language. Courtesy, Sault Ste. Marie Museum*

population. By the following year local men and boys were using the pool, gymnasium, and meeting rooms. Since the YMCA was designed to accommodate a city with a population of 10,000, demands for services soon exceeded the available space. It was not until 1965, however, that a new, larger building was constructed.

Not all recreational activities were of a sporting nature. When the Orpheum Theatre opened in 1912, there were already four other amusement houses in the downtown area. Animal acts, comedy troupes, and vaudeville

acts such as the "Dumbelles" performed for the city's entertainment. During the era of the silent movie, an orchestra provided music to accompany the on-screen action. The same orchestra entertained during intermission and in case of technical difficulties. Local theatre productions such as the enactment of Henry Wadsworth Long-fellow's *Hiawatha*, a poem based on Ojibway lore, attracted large audiences. In later years a variety of musical and theatrical organizations evolved to meet the entertainment needs of the community.

## Visits By Royalty

On September 4, 1919, thousands of people lined the streets of Sault Ste. Marie to catch a glimpse of His Royal Highness, the Prince of Wales. The dashing Prince had succeeded in charming the entire country on his cross-Canada tour, and Sault Ste. Marie crowds were no exception. A holiday had been declared, houses and businesses were decorated, and special welcome arches were erected, all in honour of his visit.

The Prince arrived at the Sault aboard a special Royal Train and was met by local dignitaries, including Sir William Hearst, the premier of

*Above: The Prince of Wales visited Sault Ste. Marie in 1919. Accompanied by local dignitaries, the Prince crossed the lock gates to the Islands to get a better view of the famed St. Mary's Rapids. Courtesy, Parks Canada, Sault Ste. Marie*

*Left: Before touring the community the Prince met with local residents including Mayor George Boyd and his family. Courtesy, Dawna Macgregor*

Ontario, and George Boyd, the mayor of Sault Ste. Marie, as well as by a crowd of cheering residents. The Prince's entourage left the Canadian Pacific Railway station and proceeded to the Sault Collegiate Institute, where Mayor Boyd officially welcomed the Prince on behalf of the citizens of Sault Ste. Marie. A band was there to perform, a children's choir sang, and a group of war veterans, including William Merrifield, a Victoria Cross recipient, was introduced.

Following the program at the high school, the royal motorcade made its way down the freshly paved Queen Street en route to the Spanish River Pulp and Paper Mill for a scheduled tour. After viewing the operation, and then proceeding to the bascule bridge for a closer look at the St. Mary's rapids and the islands in the river, the Prince requested a tour of the steel mill. His trip to the Sault was capped by a journey northward aboard an Algoma Central Railway train.

Residents of Sault Ste. Marie, like the rest of the world, were shocked in 1936 by the abdication of their beloved Prince of Wales shortly before his formal coronation as King Edward VIII. He had become the King upon the death of his father, King George V, but renounced his

claim of the throne in order to marry the woman he loved, the twice-divorced American, Wallis Warfield Simpson.

Sault Ste. Marie was not included in the 1939 Canadian tour made by King George VI and Queen Elizabeth II. When Queen Elizabeth and Prince Philip toured Canada in 1959, however, following the opening of the St. Lawrence Seaway, Sault Ste. Marie was included on the list of stops.

The royal yacht *Britannia* anchored in the St. Mary's River on July 5, 1959, and the Queen and Prince were transported to shore. They spent the day in Sault Ste. Marie attending civic functions, touring Algoma Steel, and meeting with young people. Residents and visitors alike lined the streets to catch a glimpse of the royal couple.

*The Rotary Community Night was held during Wolf Week in 1932. Harry Gagnon's Choir, winners of the Sweet Adeline singing contest, rode on a float bearing a miniature of the Windsor Hotel. Courtesy, Lillian M. Quinn*

*Right: Mrs. Alice Ross Brown, a Sault Star employee, was a participant in the five-mile swim race in the St. Mary's River as part of the Wolf Week program. Courtesy, Lillian M. Quinn*

*Below: Plans for the first Bon Soo Winter Carnival were presented to local residents in 1963. A myriad of activities including the construction of an ice palace, outdoor activities and indoor events such as dances and fiddle contests were designed to entertain people of all ages during the mid-winter period. Courtesy, The Sault Star*

As Sault Ste. Marie continued to grow, so too did its reputation as a tourist centre. Cruise ships that sailed the Great Lakes regularly stopped at the Sault. Frequently, passengers would disembark and spend time exploring the city before continuing on their way. Hotels and businesses in the downtown core grew and prospered.

Annual events celebrated by the residents of the community drew visitors from near and far. The Rotary Club's Community Night has attracted summer tourists since 1922; more recently, the Bon Soo Winter Carnival has invited people to participate in and to enjoy Sault Ste. Marie's winter.

The Sault Ste. Marie Rotary Club staged the first Community Night on September 13, 1922. The evening's festivities included a parade with floats and bands. This is a tradition that continues today. Courtesy, The Sault Star

# Chapter Six

The first annual Lockfest celebrations were held in 1984 to commemorate Ontario's Bicentennial. The Tug Boat Races, held on the historic St. Mary's River, are an important component of the festivities. Photo by Sault Star Photography Department. Courtesy, The Sault Star

# SAULT STE.
# MARIE TODAY

I mmigration and colonization agents, intent on luring settlers to Sault Ste. Marie during the latter years of the nineteenth century, predicted a rosy and prosperous future for the community and its residents. In the manner of true carnival pitchmen, they prepared and presented stories about the town and its environs that were a curious amalgam of fact and fiction. Duncan Bole, the pre-eminent government immigration agent, boasted to David Spence, Secretary of Immigration, that he had ". . . succeeded in locating quite a number of thrifty farmers in Algoma," no mean feat considering "the depression of trade in almost every portion of the Dominion." In his usual confident manner, Bole reported to Spence that land enquiries had increased and that he anticipated ". . . a large influx of settlers during the coming season [1897]." The substance of the reports submitted by Bole to Spence was basically the same as the presentations he made to prospective settlers.

Like the optimist viewing a partially filled glass of water and declaring it to be half full rather than half empty, Bole looked at the obvious advantages of life in Sault Ste. Marie without giving any thought to the disadvantages. According to Bole, Sault Ste. Marie offered "to the industrious immigrant . . . advantages surpassed by no other part of the Dominion . . ." Among the benefits of living in the community Bole identified were the ability to settle without a large amount of capital; an abundance of well-paid industrial jobs to supplement farm earnings; fertile soils whose yields exceeded even the most fertile of the American states; availability of cheap fuel and building materials; proximity to markets via water and rail transport; a "temperate" climate; and an "absence of fever and ague," inferring that there was "no healthier country under the sun." In conclusion, Bole prophesied that the area was "capable of maintaining hundreds of thousands of people in agriculture, mining, manufacturing and general industries."

*The Hudson's Bay Troupadors entertained the crowds at the ox roast before the ox was carved and served. Courtesy, Lillian M. Quinn*

There can be little doubt but that Duncan Bole's prophesies were overly optimistic for the time. The Sault Ste. Marie he envisioned is only now emerging.

Implicit in Bole's comments were promises for an improved quality of life. Unquestionably this promise served to entice people to relocate to Sault Ste. Marie. They came not only from the rapidly filling southern and eastern portions of Ontario and Quebec but also from the United States, Great Britain, and continental Europe.

The newcomers were doubtlessly disillusioned upon their arrival. True, settlers could establish themselves with very little capital. But the reason for their disappointment quickly became apparent: no societal, economic, or transportation infrastructures existed— they had to be constructed from the ground up. Fuel and building materials were cheap and abundant because they came from the land; if a settler wanted to farm his land he first had to clear it of trees and brush. Hence, he provided himself with the materials with which to construct his home and fuel to heat it. Once the land was cleared the prospective farmer may or may not have found fertile soil capable of supporting a variety of crops. Rich pockets of loam appear in bands interspersed with bands of sand or clay or with rocky soil incapable of supporting anything but meagre, stunted vegetation. It was possible to transport goods to markets both in Canada and the United States by rail and seasonally by water, but the distance from viable markets made it impractical to ship anything but durable or industrial products. Industry was developing at this point in the community's history, but it was still in the neophyte stage. It provided only temporary, sporadic, and in some cases, seasonal employment.

For many years Sault Ste. Marie had been like a diver poised on the edge of a springboard trying to decide whether to stay on the board where it was relatively safe or whether to take the plunge, a move that could ultimately result in failure. At several junctures it seemed that the community was going to throw caution to the wind and jump. It wasn't until the decision was made to harness the hydro potential of the rapids that the Sault took up its final po-

Left: The early twentieth century was a time of rapid growth for YMCAs in Northern Ontario, and Sault Ste. Marie was no exception. By the early 1960s, however, demand for services far outstripped the space available at the old "Y." Following an intensive fundraising campaign a new facility was constructed on McNabb Street. Photo by Sault Star Photography Department. Courtesy, The Sault Star

sition on the end of the board. With the collapse of the original hydro development plans and the subsequent arrival of the charismatic and persuasive Francis H. Clergue, the community took a deep breath and jumped. It had taken the first step towards changing its frontier-town image.

Sault Ste. Marie, like Rome before it, wasn't built in a day. As you survey the city as it exists today, it reflects the successful attainment of many of the more realistic of Duncan Bole's predictions.

Sault Ste. Marie is a modern, bustling community of 84,000 people. The economic base of the city continues to be the industrial foundation designed and created by Francis Clergue. The success, growth, and economic well-being of Sault Ste. Marie can be tied directly to the progress of local industry. Although the city experienced a serious economic downturn in recent years as a result of a decline in industrial activity, economic stability and prosperity has returned.

Algoma Steel's leadership position in steelmaking is being enhanced by the purchase of Algoma by Dofasco Ltd. of Hamilton in 1988. The acquisition, which makes the Dofasco-Algoma combination Canada's largest steelmaker, has been welcomed by both companies' boards of directors as well as by organized labor and the business community at large. The alliance promises an even brighter future for the Sault's operation.

The Sault's traditional industrial

Above: The Art Gallery of Algoma, designed to be compatable with its water front surroundings, has been open to the public since 1980. The prime objectives of the gallery are to exhibit, promote, collect and preserve visual art. Photo by Sault Star Photography Department. Courtesy, The Sault Star

*Sacred Heart Separate School is the oldest continuously operating school in Sault Ste. Marie. Built in 1889, it continues to provide educational facilities for children from the central portion of the city. Photo by Sault Star Photography Department. Courtesy, The Sault Star*

base has begun to expand and diversify. Tourism, once an interesting albeit seasonal adjunct, has grown to become one of the largest and most lucrative of local industries. Whereas tourists had previously only visited during the summer months and sportsmen had come only during specific hunting and fishing seasons, they now come on a year-round basis. Winter recreation enthusiasts, convention attendees, and tourists attracted by specific events such as the Ontario Winter Carnival Bon Soo, have swelled the number of tourists travelling to the area.

The decision of the Ontario government to decentralize certain of its ministries and to relocate their operations to centres outside of Toronto has had beneficial effects for Sault Ste. Marie. As a result of this Ontario initiative, the Sault will be the new home of the Ontario Lottery Corporation as well as a forensic science laboratory and a natural resources research unit.

Duncan Bole would marvel at the

strides that have been taken to ensure that a high quality of life is available to all citizens of Sault Ste. Marie. From a rugged frontier community without benefit of social amenities such as schools, hospitals, municipal agencies (including fire and police departments), or a print medium, the Sault has evolved into a socially progressive community.

During Bole's tenure in Sault Ste. Marie there were very few schools in town. As a matter of fact, the first full-time, permanent schools had not been constructed until 1889. These two schools (which, incidentally, are still intact—Central Public School as the offices for the Sault Ste. Marie and District Public School Board, and Sacred Heart as an operational school in the Separate School system) served as the only educational facilities for all of the children in Sault Ste. Marie for many years. As the community expanded, first westward and then northward and eastward from the core area, elementary schools developed in the newly emerging neighbourhoods.

The secondary school system evolved much more slowly than the elementary system. Until the Sault Collegiate Institute was constructed in 1907, only a limited number of high school classes were offered in vacant spaces above and behind several downtown businesses. The Collegiate Institute remained the only secondary school until the Sault Technical School began offering classes in 1922. This enabled post-elementary students to choose between a technical or commercial high school education and an academic course of study. Subsequently, both the public and separate boards have added several

high schools to their systems, enabling them to serve students in all areas of the city as well as the outlying areas.

Post-secondary education was introduced to Sault Ste. Marie in 1964 with the opening of the Ontario Vocational Centre. When the Ontario community college system was created in 1967, the Centre became a satellite campus of the Sudbury-based Cambrian College of Applied Arts and Technology. The Sault campus gained its independence from the Sudbury college in 1972; it was renamed Sault College of Arts and Technology.

Although Sault College began accepting students sooner than Algoma University College, Algoma has the longer history of the two. Local citizens, concerned with the lack of facilities for an academic post-secondary education, launched a movement as early as 1950 to establish a liberal arts college in Sault

Ste. Marie. It wasn't until 1964 that the Algoma College Association was incorporated, but once the incorporation was complete, plans for the realization of a university in Sault Ste. Marie moved quickly. Algoma College, in affiliation with Laurentian University in Sudbury, began offering classes in 1965. Because facilities had not been secured, instruction took place in public school classrooms and in empty office space. When first-year full-time studies were offered beginning in 1967, portable buildings were acquired on the campus of the community college. Algoma remained in these portables until 1971 when it leased and renovated the former Shingwauk Residential School; the move was significant in more ways than one—it signalled the beginning of a full-time Bachelor of Arts programme and also a change in the institution's name. It became known as Algoma University

*The Korah Collegiate and Vocational High School, which opened in 1968, is one of the Sault's newer high schools. The school, which is located in the city's west end, won several awards for its innovative design. Photo by Sault Star Photography Department. Courtesy, The Sault Star*

*Sault College of Applied Arts and Technology offers a wide variety of course options. Many of the courses deal with natural resources and the environment. Forestry is an especially popular course; students learn not only how to manage forestry resources but also how to protect them from destruction from disasters such as forest fires. Photo by Sault Star Photography Department. Courtesy, The Sault Star*

College rather than Algoma College. Over the years numerous significant changes have taken place: Algoma purchased the land and buildings it had leased from the Anglican Church of Canada, and the Arthur A. Wishart Library was added. Recently, Algoma was granted permission and funding to renovate and expand its facilities. Ultimately, Algoma will achieve its goal of independence from Laurentian University. While this severing of the apron strings is not imminent, there can be little doubt but that Algoma University College will be awarded independent degree-granting status by the turn of the century.

Health care is another field where great strides forward have occurred. Duncan Bole would have been in Sault Ste. Marie in 1896 to experience firsthand the devastating outbreak of typhoid fever that threatened to destroy

the community. He would have witnessed the attempts made by local citizens to secure a hospital. Perhaps, although his name is not mentioned, he even lent his support to the cause.

The first positive step was the establishment of a small hospital in 1898. The Grey Sisters moved their hospital from a cottage on Bay Street to a specially constructed building on Queen Street in 1899. The General Hospital remained the only one serving Sault Ste. Marie and the outlying areas until the Algoma Benevolent Society established the non-sectarian Royal Victoria Hospital in 1917. Following the death of W.H. Plummer and his wife, the Royal Victoria moved from its rented premises to the Plummer home, Lynnehurst, and assumed the name Plummer Memorial Hospital. As demand for hospital services increased, the hospital outgrew the available space. A new hospital was

*The Plummer Hospital, like the General, backs on the St. Mary's River. With the rationalization of hospital services, the Plummer will offer unique services such as oncology, nuclear medicine and psychiatry. Photo by Sault Star Photography Department. Courtesy, The Sault Star*

constructed on the Lynnehurst site in 1929.

Throughout the years, the hospitals have undergone numerous renovations to make efficient use of available space and to allow for the introduction of the most up-to-date medical services. Ongoing rationalization of hospital facilities is eliminating the duplication of services and enabling the hospitals to offer specialized treatment such as oncology, intensive care, and neonatal intensive care. The General Hospital acquired a C.A.T. scanner in 1988.

An innovative approach to health care was introduced to Sault Ste. Marie in 1963 when the Group Health Centre opened in September of that year. The project was initiated by six locals of the United Steelworkers of America. Initially, membership was limited to union members, but in 1969 membership was opened to the general public. The Clinic, as it is known to local residents, provides a variety of services, such as

x-ray, laboratory, physiotherapy, and dentistry, in addition to regular medical treatment. It has served as a model for similar types of broad-spectrum clinics throughout Canada and the United States.

The introduction of a fire protection service meant that many buildings of wooden construction were spared an untimely end. Winter was an especially disastrous time; sparks from fireplaces

*The Group Health Centre, spearheaded by the steelworkers union as a community service, became operational in 1963. It has become a model for community health centres across North America. Courtesy, United Steel Workers of America Local 2251*

and wood- and coal-burning furnaces often started chimney fires. The lack of water due to the freeze-up meant that homes—and sometimes lives—were lost.

During Duncan Bole's years as immigration agent, the Sault acquired not only its first volunteer fire department, equipped with hand reels and water buckets, but also its first fire hall, on Queen Street near East Street. Volunteer firefighters received nominal payment for the time they spent training and fighting fires. The first chief of the volunteer brigade was none other than William Howard Hearst, a local lawyer who went on to become Premier of the Province of Ontario during the First World War.

As the community grew and diversified, the need for expanded fire protec-

tion became evident. Horse-drawn hose wagons were replaced by mechanical vehicles, and new stations were constructed—in the centre of the city on Bruce Street, and in the west end on Central Park Avenue.

Today there are stations situated throughout the city. A new fire station on Bay Street recently replaced the old Bruce Street station, which was torn down.

The first law enforcement officer was hired in the Sault in 1870; a policeman was hired to collect taxes and mediate the problems stemming from marauding cattle and roaming dogs. The community's growth meant that not only were additional officers needed but they were also required to be trained to deal with the issues inherent in an industrial community.

*Right: Sault Ste. Marie's newest fire hall opened in late 1983. It replaced the station on Bruce Street at Albert which was demolished in the summer of 1987. The new station houses some of the most modern and up-to-date equipment available. It also has a tower to facilitate training programs for firefighters. Photo by Sault Star Photography Department. Courtesy, The Sault Star*

*Facing page: As twilight envelopes the Sault Ste. Marie harbour, fireworks begin. Photo by Colin Shaw. Courtesy, Westfile Inc.*

*Actors in native costume participate in the visitors' reception at St. Joseph Island National Historic Park. Photo by Howe Photography. Courtesy, Westfile Inc.*

*The hilly north shore of Lake Superior in Ontario is the site for a superbly detailed group of Indian pictographs found on the Agawa Rock. Photo by Wayne Lankinen. Courtesy, Valan Photos*

Above: The oldest stone house in Western Ontario was built in 1814 by the Swiss fur trader Charles Oakes Ermatinger for his Ojibway wife Charlotte. Photo by Howe Photography. Courtesy, Westfile Inc.

Right: The construction of the Lockhouse Administration building was coordinated with the construction and completion of the entire Canadian lock system. The official opening was in 1895. Photo by L.A. Morse. Courtesy, The Stock Market Inc.

*Above: Algoma University was established in 1967 as a Liberal Arts and Science college. The facility maintains an enrollment of approximately 1,000 full and part-time students. Photo by Bill Howe. Courtesy, Westfile Inc.*

*Left: These women soccer players practice their technique faithfully, every day during the season. Photo by Howe Photography. Courtesy, Westfile Inc.*

*The Algoma Central Railway begins its continent-famous Agawa Canyon Train Tour at the Soo. This vivid, colorful trip twists around hills and river gorges, rattles over 130-foot high trestle bridges, and then plunges into the Agawa Canyon. Left: Photo by Colin Shaw. Above: Photo by Howe Photography. Courtesy, Westfile Inc.*

Above: This tranquil reflection of foliage was found along the Goulais River near Searchmont. Photo by Howe Photography. Courtesy, Westfile Inc.

Facing page: The natural splendor of the Aubrey Falls may be viewed from Highway 129. Photo by Howe Photography. Courtesy, Westfile Inc.

The decision to build the
Soo locks on the Cana-
dian side of the St.
Mary's River was made
in 1870, following the
Chicora Incident. Photo
by Howe Photography.
Courtesy, Westfile Inc.

*Above: The International Bridge linking Sault Ste. Marie, Ontario, with its sister city Sault Ste. Marie, Michigan, was completed and officially opened on October 31, 1962. Photo by Howe Photography. Courtesy, Westfile Inc.*

*Left: These sailboats are "locking through" the Canadian locks in preparation for the Trans Superior Boat Race. Photo by Howe Photography. Courtesy, Westfile Inc.*

*Above: Built in 1920, this hunting and fishing camp is located just off of Highway 556 (Ranger Lake Road). Photo by Howe Photography. Courtesy, Westfile Inc.*

*Right: This idyllic farmhouse is tucked away in the Sylvan Valley. Photo by Howe Photography. Courtesy, Westfile Inc.*

*The Sault Ste. Marie City Hall Civic Centre is a 90,000 square-foot structure which has as its most significant features gold-tinted glass and brown porcelain steel panels. Construction and the furnishing of the building was completed in December 1974 at a total cost of $4.3 million. Photo by Gera Dillon. Courtesy, The Stock Market Inc.*

*Above: The 1988 Bon
Soo Winter Carnival will
celebrate the twenty-fifth
anniversary of festivities.
Opening ceremonies in-
clude a torchlight parade
and the infamous polar
bear swim. Photo by
Howe Photography. Cour-
tesy, Westfile Inc.*

*Right: Pairs of cross-
country skiers frequent
the plentiful, well-
groomed trails surround-
ing Sault Ste. Marie
proper. Photo by Howe Photography. Courtesy, West-
file Inc.*

*Dancing, snow-sculpting and Bingo actively engage all members of the local community during the Bon Soo Winter Carnival. Photo by Howe Photography. Courtesy, Westfile Inc.*

The annual Bridge Trot Race is held during Lockfest activities in early July. Photo by Howe Photography. Courtesy, Westfile Inc.

The expansion of the police department kept pace with the growth of the Sault. As the number of police officers increased—to say nothing of the number of crimes they were obliged to investigate—the department secured larger premises. The shared space in City Hall was replaced by a new building on Albert Street and subsequently by a large and ultramodern structure on the Second Line.

During the 1920s the Ontario Provincial Police and the Royal Canadian Mounted Police established detachments in the Sault, which enabled them to better serve their particular jurisdictions.

Sault Ste. Marie has a very rich military history, and Duncan Bole would have been a keen observer if not an actual participant. In its early years the militia's purpose was to preserve and protect the quality of life in the community. Joseph Wilson was the driving force behind the Sault's first rifle company. Although Wilson's initial attempt to form the company in 1849 ended in failure due to a lack of both weapons and ammunition, subsequent attempts were more successful, and when the threat of a Fenian Raid frightened the community in 1866, the Sault had a strong and sturdy military force ready and willing to offer a defense.

*When the Sault Ste. Marie Armoury was officially opened in January 1952, the Honourable Louis St. Laurent, then Prime Minister of Canada, predicted it would be the last of its kind to be built. In addition to a drill hall, the Armoury houses a gun shed, garage, theatre, offices and bowling alley. The Armoury is the site of numerous local events and activities. Photo by Sault Star Photography Department. Courtesy, The Sault Star*

# Sault Ste. Marie in the World Wars

*In addition to manning the three guard posts that served as canal security, the officers of the 51st Soo Rifles trained units in preparation for military service overseas. Courtesy, Parks Canada, Sault Ste. Marie*

Troops from Sault Ste. Marie played a vital role during World War I both in Europe and on the homefront. The home unit of the 51st Soo Rifles, which had been organized in November 1913, was ordered to guard the Sault Ste. Marie canal as well as the local wireless installation and station. The soldiers assumed their duties the day that war was formally declared; it was feared that new Canadians of enemy nationality and/or sympathy living in Sault Ste.

Marie might attempt to sabotage these key links in the chain of the Canadian defense network.

The 51st Rifles also acted as the Northern Ontario Recruiting Depot for the Canadian Expeditionary Force. Recruiting for the 119th Battalion began in November 1915. Once fully recruited, the battalion was sent to England and then to France where the troops were used to reinforce the battle-weary Canadian contingent. Although the battalion

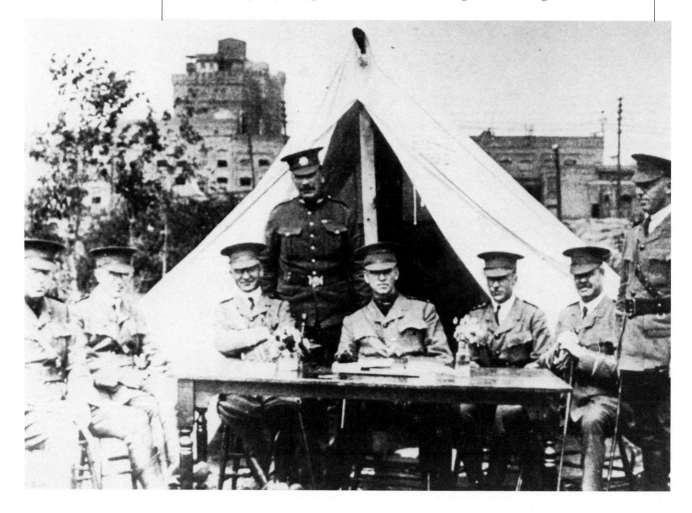

had been recruited and shipped overseas on the understanding that it would go into battle intact, the heavy casualties suffered by the Canadians made this impossible.

Before the 119th left for Europe, recruitment for the 227th Land Battalion had begun. This battalion, which set sail for England in April 1917, met the same fate as the 119th—it was absorbed into other units. Both battalions were disbanded in 1923.

In 1923, the newly formed Sault Ste. Marie Regiment, which replaced both the 119th and 227th, was awarded battle honours in recognition of the role played by the members of the battalions in Europe during World War I.

When it appeared that a second world war was imminent in the late 1930s, the government of Canada took steps to increase the security measures taken at previously identified strategic defense locations. Locally, the Sault Ste. Marie and Sudbury Regiment was charged with the responsibility of guarding the Sault shipping canal. They assumed their duties on August 26, 1939—less

*Once basic training had been completed at the Sault Canal, the soldiers were marched up Queen Street to the CPR train station for the first leg of their trip overseas. Courtesy, Public Archives of Canada*

than 48 hours after the formal declaration of war was made. A tent camp was established on the canal grounds and a lower room in the canal administration building was designated as headquarters for the canal guard. All matters relating directly to the protection of the canal were relegated to this office.

The headquarters of the regiment remained at the Armoury on Brock Street. Since the building was not equipped to serve as a barracks, the arena and the curling rink were taken over for use by the regimental soldiers. Once the additional sleeping quarters, dining room, and kitchen facilities were built, the temporary barracks reverted to their original status and the tent camp was dismantled.

The Sault Ste. Marie and Sudbury Regiment reverted to its prewar, non-active status in November 1939. The task of guarding the canal was reassigned to the Royal Canadian Mounted Police. Demobilization of the Sault Ste. Marie and Sudbury Regiment was completed by the end of the month, and members were given the option of taking a discharge or being absorbed into the regular

forces. This did not mean, however, that Sault Ste. Marie was without any form of military organization for the remainder of the war. The 23rd Reserve Company, Reserve Guard, was formed in May 1940 to assist with regional defense. As a result, military training continued throughout 1940 and 1941, escalating both with the collapse of the French Army and with the spread of the war to the Pacific theatre.

The United States' entry into the war in December 1941 meant yet another change in the canal defense program: American anti-aircraft batteries were transferred to both sides of the St. Mary's rapids. The Reserve Guard remained under the direction of the United States Army until all danger of possible foreign raids had passed.

On the industrial scene, Algoma Steel fulfilled its national obligations toward the war effort by supplying Canadian armament manufacturers with steel. Contracts with the federal Department of Munitions and Supply enabled Algoma to embark on an extensive construction program and to expand product lines through the addition of new facilities.

*Facing page: During World War II the United States Army floated barrage balloons over the American and Canadian canal systems to disguise them from enemy attack. Courtesy, Gordon Daun Collection, Judge Stere Room, Bayliss Public Library*

Since the inception of the first military unit, Sault Ste. Marie has enjoyed a continuous relationship with the military. Although the units have tended to maintain a low profile in the community, in times critical to the military history of Canada they have come to the fore prepared to protect and defend. During World War I, the Soo Rifles provided local protection by guarding the Sault Locks, and in addition became the recruiting unit for the Canadian Expeditionary Force. The regiment supplied three overseas detachments and two overseas battalions to bolster the battle-weary Allied troops in France. During World War II the Sault Ste. Marie and

*In 1932, at the Agricultural Grounds the U.S. soldiers presented a British flag to civic officials. The flag represented the one seized by American troops during the War of 1812. Courtesy, Lillian M. Quinn*

Sudbury Regiment, followed by the 23rd Reserve Company, performed a similar function.

A succession of changes in military organization took place following World War II. Currently, the 49th Field Regiment and the 26th Service Battalion, as well as the Northern Ontario Militia District, serve the community, with headquarters in the Sault Ste. Marie Armoury.

The most common form of communication in Sault Ste. Marie during Duncan Bole's years was by word of mouth. However, there were other mediums. The *Sault Courier*, the forerunner of today's *Sault Star*, would have been the newspaper of the day. The *Algoma Pioneer* and the *Express* were other early day newspapers.

In 1901 James Curran purchased the *Courier* and renamed it the *Sault Star*. The first edition under Curran's editorship hit the newstands on August 31, 1901. The paper joined the daily "world news service" of the Canadian Press and went into production as a daily on March 16, 1912.

A second newspaper began publishing in Sault Ste. Marie in June 1963. *Shopper's News* began as a weekly advertiser, and since that time has expanded to include several pages of news and sports stories. To reflect this added dimension, the paper changed its name to *Sault This Week* in the summer of 1975.

Telephone communication began to replace chatting over the back fence in 1889 with the installation of the Sault's first pair of phones. Three years later a Bell Telephone exchange was installed and the community entered the world of telecommunications.

## The Federal Airport

The construction of the Sault Ste. Marie Federal Airport in 1961 linked Sault Ste. Marie with the national and international air passenger network. Trans-Canada Airline had inaugurated service to Sault Ste. Marie in 1948. Since there were no airport facilities on the Canadian side of the St. Mary's River, all flights were serviced from the air strip at Kinross, Michigan, just south of Sault Ste. Marie.

A committee was organized in 1952 to select a suitable site for the Sault airport. Negotiations for the purchase of land at Pointe des Chenes began in 1956, and plans for runway construction were drawn up at the same time. Actual construction of the runway and terminal facility began in 1957 and was completed four years later.

*The General Hospital, which backs on the St. Mary's River, is still administered by the Grey Sisters of the Immaculate Conception. In addition to other facilities, the hospital boasts a helicopter pad to facilitate the transport of patients by Air Ambulance. Photo by Sault Star Photography Department. Courtesy, The Sault Star*

Duncan Bole would approve of the Sault Ste. Marie that has grown out of his dreams. He would be pleased with the educational facilities, the hospitals, and the health care facilities. The police and fire departments are unsurpassed in protecting the lives and property of local citizens. But there are facets of the community that add to the quality of life that Bole could never have imagined. Parklands dot the community, including along the waterfront, which allow residents and visitors alike an opportunity to enjoy the strength and beauty of the St. Mary's River. The Art Gallery of Algoma introduces to the community culture and forms of art that otherwise could be experienced and appreciated only by travelling to major centres. The Sault Ste. Marie Mu-

seum collects and preserves the heritage of the city so that future generations may fully appreciate the strides she has made towards her future.

Sault Ste. Marie's contemporary community services and technical innovations are light years beyond Duncan Bole's time. Sault Ste. Marie has caught up with the optimistic and beneficent projections that Bole envisioned at the end of the last century. Perhaps a Duncan Bole of today would not be accused of such overt optimism for predicting the Sault's continued climb to prominence. Sault Ste. Marie will never have a temperate climate. Nor will it ever be free of current-day "fever and ague," but neither of these factors detract from the positive qualities of the community. The good far outweighs the bad.

*The Sault Ste. Marie Museum opened in its new location at the corner of Queen and East streets in December 1983. Museum exhibits interpret the history of the community for visitors and residents alike. Photo by Sault Star Photography Department. Courtesy, The Sault Star*

In an effort to revitalize and rejuvenate the downtown shopping district, the section of Queen Street East from East Street to Dennis Street was converted into a semimall. By widening the sidewalks in strategic areas and interspersing green spaces it was hoped that the downtown would revert to its original status as a people area. Photo by Sault Star Photography Department. Courtesy, The Sault Star

# Chapter Seven

*In the days before self-service grocery stores, sales clerks would fill a customer's order from supplies stored behind the counters. Liquor and beer were sold in grocery stores before specialty stores were created to market them. Courtesy, Sault Ste. Marie Public Library*

# PARTNERS IN PROGRESS

F ounded on furs and built on steel, Sault Ste. Marie has grown from an Indian trading settlement to a major industrial centre. Nestled on the banks of the busy St. Mary's River, its location has been attracting commerce for almost 5,000 years. The native people settled on Whitefish Island as early as 3,000 B.C. to fish and trade.

The economic and military potential of the site first attracted the French. Later, when Great Britain conquered Canada, British troops took over the fort, and by the late eighteenth century the North West Company had a thriving post on the north side of the river.

Through the mid-1800s the community's development lagged. But in 1887 the Canadian Pacific Railway completed a line to the newly incorporated town, and an international rail bridge provided a link to the United States. The Sault began to boom, and within two years 27 new stores were under construction.

A lock to aid shipping was built on the Canadian side of the river. This mammoth project changed the town's economic and social structure with an influx of Slavic, Irish, Finnish, and Italian workers.

In 1894 American entrepreneur Francis H. Clergue used the area's rich natural resources to build his empire. From his mining and shipping interests, utilities, foundries, pulp and sawmills, railway, and steel company came the lifeblood of present-day Sault Ste. Marie.

The waterfront, important in the town's beginnings, continues to be the focus of development. Tourism, government, and health and education services are targeted for growth as Sault Ste. Marie diversifies.

The organizations whose stories are related in this chapter have chosen to support this important literary and civic project. They illustrate the ways in which individuals and their businesses have contributed to the Sault's growth.

# SAULT STE. MARIE CHAMBER OF COMMERCE

Two years after the first Canadian Pacific Railway train reached Sault Ste. Marie, a group of businessmen formed an organization dedicated to community welfare and development.

The rail connection, completed in 1887, also included a bridge linking the town with American railway systems, and has spurred an economic boom that doubled the population to 4,000. Business prospered, 27 new stores were constructed, and on June 25, 1889, forty businessmen organized the Board of Trade.

The 100-year-old Sault Ste. Marie Chamber of Commerce originated with this group of businessmen. John Collins, a town councillor, is listed as the first president of the Board of Trade, although no formal records were kept for the organization's first 40 years. It is known, however, that one of the first acts of the fledgling group was to write the federal government commending Ottawa's plans to build a shipping canal on the Canadian side of the St. Mary's River.

In December 1937 the *Sault Star* reported that a committee had been established to set up the first international chamber of commerce in the world following a meeting of Canadian Sault and Michigan Sault residents. Co-operation between the sister cities, particularly in tourism promotion, was the goal of the group, which had R.H. Elgie, president of the Canadian Sault Board of Trade, as an executive member.

While the international chamber apparently existed for only a short period, the Board of Trade continued to operate and by 1936 had its own building, a log cabin it shared with the Algoma Travel Bureau. Located on the corner of Brock and Bay streets, near the ferry dock where vehicles and passengers were transported back and forth across

*During the chamber's centennial year, the position of president is shared by Paul Dalseg, president 1988-1989 (above, left) and Larry Whalen, president-elect, 1989-1990 (above).*

the river, it was the chamber's summer headquarters. Each fall the chamber moved its offices to the second story of the Virene building on Queen Street East until 1948, when the cabin was winterized and it became a year-round operation.

During the 1940s—probably after World War II—the Board of Trade was renamed the Sault Ste. Marie Chamber of Commerce, and then, in 1960, became the Sault and District Chamber of Commerce.

Jack Hambleton was the first paid secretary, a position he received in 1938. He was followed by John McLeod, and during the war years Dave Cohen was honorary secretary. David Bews was secretary/manager from 1946 to 1948, when Wilf Hussey was appointed to the job. Hussey served in the manager's job until he retired due to ill health in 1967.

The ferries that brought thousands of tourists and visitors to the Brock Street area stopped running in 1962, when the new $20-million International Bridge connecting the two Saults opened. The chamber office remained at its downtown location for another nine years until it was forced by an urban-renewal project to relo-

cate. It moved to a temporary site on Great Northern Road until it opened a new office in a hotel-tourism complex at 360 Great Northern Road.

At the same time as the chamber acquired new premises it also named its first female manager; Nancy Fitzpatrick held the job for three years. In 1965 Hazel Chitty became the first woman to serve on the chamber's board of directors and then, four years later, became the first female president in the chamber's 80-year history.

Since the 1930s the Sault Ste. Marie Chamber of Commerce ("District" has been deleted from the name) has promoted tourism enhancement and marketing. It also promotes civic, commercial, and industrial development in the community, and works for sound legislation and efficient administration of the municipal, provincial, and federal levels of government. Economic growth and encouraging policies to ensure improved business opportunities in Sault Ste. Marie also are among the 950-member chamber's concerns.

The chamber initiated, and for a number of years ran, the annual Bon Soo Winter Carnival, which grew to become one of the largest winter carnivals in North America. It also assisted with the establishment of the Algoma Fall Festival, a yearly cultural event offering theatre, music and art shows, workshops, and performances. It has been involved with Lockfest, an international festival of joint celebrations for the July 1 Canada Day and U.S. July 4 Independence Day holidays. And in 1987 it helped organize a first-ever bridge walk to mark the 25th anniversary of the International Bridge, the 75th anniversary of the incorporation of the city of Sault Ste. Marie, Ontario, and the 150th anniversary of Michigan's statehood. The walk attracted 7,000 people and became an annual event.

A lobbying group, the chamber strongly advocated an Economic Development Corporation, established in 1986 to promote industrial, commercial, and tourism development and to try to switch the community's reliance away from a single employer. It also operates three tourism information centres and a consumer relations department, provides nonfinancial assistance to prospective and existing businesses, and organizes various trade shows annually.

Active with both the Ontario Chamber of Commerce and Canadian Chamber of Commerce, the Sault organization has built a reputation as one of the most dynamic chambers in the country with its pro-active role.

*In 1936 the log cabin at the corner of Brock and Bay streets became the summer offices of the Sault Chamber. The cabin was winterized in 1948 and became the year-round headquarters until the chamber relocated during an early 1970s urban renewal period.*

# ALGOMA STEEL CORP. LTD.

A sparkling curtain of fire that lit up the sky on a winter afternoon in 1902 signalled a historic moment for Sault Ste. Marie.

The sparks were created on February 13 at 3:15 p.m., when the first steel produced in Ontario was "blown" in the Bessemer converter of a small steel plant. The steelworks were part of a burgeoning industrial empire that American entrepreneur Francis H. Clergue was building on the banks of the St. Mary's River. And while the company faltered in its early years, it grew to be an industrial giant that pumps the lifeblood of the community.

The power potential of the river's turbulent rapids had piqued Clergue's

*Algoma Steel is one of the leaders in Canada in the production of continuously cast steel.*

interest in the area during a visit in 1894. Impressed with the industrial possibilities, the leader of a group of Philadelphia investors purchased the town's partially completed power project.

He then began to establish his own industries to use the hydro-electricity. By 1902, when the steel plant started production, Clergue had a pulp and paper mill, railway, steamship company, and numerous nickel, iron, and gold mines.

Algoma Steel Co. Ltd. was incorporated in 1901, and by the end of the year the Bessemer and a 28-inch

*A 1986 aerial photo of Algoma Steel Corp. Ltd., located on the St. Mary's River.*

blooming mill had been constructed. Early in 1902 a rail mill with a capacity of 1,000 tons per day began producing the first railway rails in Canada. Although company directors believed there was a sure market in Canada for rails, Algoma had problems securing orders. The lack of orders forced the plant to close in late 1902, and no rails were produced the following year.

As the steel plant was struggling to get established, Clergue's Consolidated Lake Superior Company, which controlled his other interests, faced a financial crisis. The crash came in September 1903. Lake Superior went into receivership. With no money to meet payrolls or operating expenses, the industries shut down.

Angry construction and bush workers, who had not been paid, headed toward the Sault. Days passed with no sign of the promised payment, and on September 27 the men gathered in front of the steel plant. The mob headed to the company's general office on Huron Street, where the crowd found the building locked and guarded by police. The workers tried to force open the doors but could not get inside. Windows were smashed with bricks, gunshots were exchanged, and

*The legendary Sir James Dunn, the self-made millionaire and main shareholder who revived the Lake Superior Corporation and took over Algoma Steel in 1935.*

the rioting soon spread to other Consolidated enterprises.

Mayor W.H. Plummer read the Riot Act and the local militia was called out. The following day troops arrived from Toronto to quell the disturbance. The riot marked the end for Clergue. His financially unsound business was bailed out by the provincial government; but when he and his associates tried to reorganize it, he was forced out.

A new company, Lake Superior Corp., was formed in 1904, and within four years control had passed from American hands to a British group, headed by well-known financier Robert Fleming.

Over the next few years demand for rail was extremely high and the first hearth furnaces were installed. These additions were followed by more expansion—additional coke ovens, blast furnaces, and merchant mills were constructed.

The outbreak of World War I brought another serious setback to the steel plant. Demand for rails dried up and the company was forced to change production to steel shells. By 1917 Algoma was engaged entirely in manufacturing war materials, and used this as a lever to have one of its executives returned from overseas to the Sault, "where he could best serve his country as general manager of the plant."

David Kyle had been assistant general manager until the war. When he returned he was made general manager, and in 1918 was named a director and vice-president. On February 7, 1920, the popular executive died at the age of 35 after a bout of influenza developed into pneumonia.

A Military Cross winner, Captain Kyle was buried with full military honors on February 20. He was paid the highest tribute when the steel plant's machinery and men stopped work for 10 minutes during his funeral. Kyle was held in such high esteem by the workers that 2,000 of them donated money to erect a bronze monument to his memory nine years later.

By 1920 Algoma was making fairly substantial profits, but the following year deficits were growing as production was curtailed. The next decade was a roller coaster ride from boom to bust that ended with the collapse of the company during the dark days of the Depression.

When the Lake Superior Corp. collapsed in 1932, one of the principal bondholders was an eccentric, strong-willed financial wizard—Sir James Dunn. The bankrupt firm became the property of its bondholders, and in 1935 the self-made millionaire, who held the majority of shares, became chairman and president.

Dunn, a New Brunswick-born financier awarded a baronetcy in 1921 for hazardous undercover missions

*The 12-inch bar mill in the 1930s at Algoma Steel, a mill no longer in existence.*

during the war, first saw Algoma Steel in 1907. The man who eventually would salvage the company from bankruptcy and breathe new life into the city's economy had been brought to the Sault by an American investment syndicate to help restore Clergue's faltering enterprises. Dunn and Clergue toured all the operations, and Sir James, intrigued by the area's rich resources, began purchasing Algoma bonds.

When Dunn took over in 1935, he embarked on a long-term program to modernize and diversify the steel company's products. His aim was to obtain a larger share of the nation's steel markets for Algoma. He revitalized the plant with new methods and equipment, and expanded facilities. Employment grew, wages improved, and the Sault was back on the road to prosperity.

World War II brought new contracts for steel and government subsidies for expansion. Constant programs of modernization fol-

*Algoma Steel's operations shut down for the dedication of the David Kyle Memorial in 1929.*

lowed in all parts of the plant.

With his quick temper and autocratic control of Algoma, Dunn was the subject of numerous legends. In 1947 Algoma Steel purchased the nine-storey Windsor Hotel in downtown Sault Ste. Marie. Sir James, so the story goes, was dissatisfied with food served him in the dining room. He complained to the chef and was told if he did not like the food he could go elsewhere. Dunn bought the hotel so he could fire the man. Sir James Dunn was still in charge of the company when he died on January 1, 1956, at the age of 81.

After the 1950s, with the addition of the most up-to-date equipment and latest technological advances in the industry, Algoma Steel Corporation, Limited, grew to be Canada's third-largest integrated steel producer. Nearly $196 million was spent modernizing the firm between 1952 and 1962. The country's first wide-flange beam mill was constructed at a cost of $20 million in 1961, and 10 years later Algoma took over Mannesman Tube, establishing its tube division.

Algoma prospered and grew until it hit record earnings of $165 million in 1981 and a total work force of 13,500. But a worldwide slump in steel markets and low oil prices soon took their toll on the company, and Algoma's fortunes plummeted for the next five years. It was not until 1987 that the steelmaker rebounded and again turned a profit.

A fully integrated steel producer, Algoma has five major product lines—sheet and strip, plate, seamless tubulars, structural shapes, and rails—and employs 9,000 workers in Canada and its U.S. subsidiaries.

In August 1988 Hamilton-based Dofasco Inc. took over Algoma Steel, and together the two companies became Canada's largest steel company and the fourth largest in North America.

# SAULT COLLEGE

The first students enrolled at Sault Ste. Marie's Ontario Vocational Centre in 1965 were participating in an ambitious new educational concept—the creation of a provincewide system that would become the colleges of applied arts and technology.

It was an idea that blossomed, and today Sault College, as it was named in 1972, is one of 22 community colleges across Ontario. The college grew rapidly from a fledgling vocational centre with 313 students to a respected institute of higher learning with 1,400 full-time postsecondary students and 6,500 people participating in continuing education programs.

It has an annual operating budget of $30 million, three campuses in the Algoma District, and 400 full-time employees, including academic, support staff, and administration personnel. More than 8,000 students have graduated from Sault College's postsecondary programs since the Northern

*A robotics course is offered as a component of the several engineering and technology programs at Sault College.*

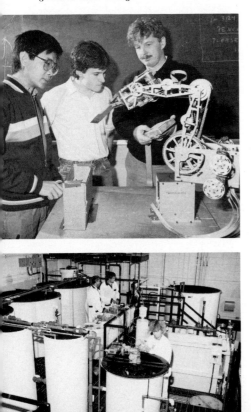

*A program in advertising art and graphic design was added to the curriculum in 1987.*

Avenue campus was established. They have earned certificates and diplomas in aviation technology, nursing, chef training, early childhood education, computer engineering technology, and dozens of other programs.

Located in an area rich in natural resources, Sault College has specialized programs such as forestry, geology, pulp and paper engineering technology, and water resources engineering technology that tie into this environment.

In addition to postsecondary programs, the college provides retraining and upgrading for unemployed or under-employed adults, and apprenticeship programs.

From one small building nestled in the north end of the city, the college has developed into a sprawling campus with additions that include a 16,490-square-foot visual arts wing (1976), a three-level Learning Resources Centre (1980), and a $2-million Technical Training Centre (1984).

The first satellite campus was opened in Wawa, 140 miles north of the Sault, in 1973. The North Algoma campus, which since 1985 has also operated a campus in Chapleau, serves numerous communities in the Wawa area with upgrading, extension, and retraining programs.

The Elliot Lake campus, established in 1976, offers a range of postsecondary, career-oriented, and vocational studies. It now has a subcampus (the North Shore campus) in

*Located in an area that is rich in natural resources, Sault College offers several ecology and environment-related programs in such areas as water resources engineering technology, for which the college has recently built a new waste-treatment plant.*

*Sault College began as Ontario Vocational Centre in 1965 in a small building tucked away in the north end of the city. Today the sprawling North Avenue campus is part of a network of 22 community colleges across Ontario, with more than 1,400 students enrolled in dozens of programs ranging from computer engineering technology, aviation, and applied arts to nursing, forestry, and chef training.*

Blind River, 83 miles east of the Sault, enabling the college to service an area that stretches to the eastern boundary of Algoma District and includes several Indian reserves.

In 1987 Sault College signed a reciprocal agreement with Lake Superior State University in the Michigan Sault, which will allow students who have earned a diploma at Sault College to gain advanced standing in LSSU degree studies. The university's students can obtain credits for specialized courses taken at Sault College.

# ALGOMA CENTRAL RAILWAY

When Algoma Central Railway was incorporated in 1899, American entrepreneur Francis H. Clergue conceived it as feeder service for the industries he was developing in Sault Ste. Marie. It would haul pulpwood, logs, and iron ore from the dense forests and rugged hills of northern Ontario to his paper mill and steel plant on the banks of the St. Mary's River.

Today what began as a wilderness railroad is a diversified transportation company moving cargo by water and rail, and carrying thousands of passengers on its Agawa Canyon excursion tours.

The ACR operates a fleet of 18 ships on the Great Lakes and St. Lawrence Seaway, owns 850,000 acres of land (including mineral and timber rights) in the Algoma region, and has developed commercial real estate complexes in the Sault and Elliot Lake. Its main rail line, running 295 miles north from the Sault to the lumbering town of Hearst, serves the natural re-

*Building a rail line through the rugged terrain of northern Ontario required the construction of numerous trestles, such as this arcing one near the Montreal River.*

*One of Algoma Central's old steam units being serviced in the shop in 1952—the year the railway converted to diesel.*

*In 1899 Algoma Central Railway began carving a rail line through the northern wilderness from the Sault to Hearst. Here workers prepare rock cut for blasting.*

source, manufacturing, and tourism industries of the Algoma region.

Each summer, winter, and fall more than 100,000 Canadian and American visitors follow the "tracks of the black bear" on a one-day excursion to Mile 114 to view the scenic beauty of Agawa Canyon.

Algoma Central Railway was incorporated under a dominion charter on August 11, 1899, and construction began that year. Two years later it became the Algoma Central and Hudson Bay Railway Company, with plans to extend the line north to the Moosonee area on James Bay, a dream that never materialized.

By 1903, when Clergue's empire crashed in financial ruin, track had been laid 56 miles north from the Sault. Twenty-one miles of branch line had been built from Michipicoten Harbour on Lake Superior, near Wawa, to the Helen and Josephine mines, the site of iron ore deposits so important to the steel industry. The line to Hearst, the northern terminal, was eventually completed in 1914, af-

ter Clergue's industries had been taken over by a London, England, financial group.

The firm's marine division is the oldest bulk freight carrier with continuous service on the Great Lakes. It was also started to handle coal and iron ore for Algoma Steel Corp. and to ship the Sault-based steel mill's finished products.

It began in 1900, when Algoma Central acquired four bulk freight carriers—the steamers *Paliki*, *Theano*, *Munkshaven*, and *Leafield*—and three passenger boats—*Ossifrange*, *King Edward*, and *Minnie M.* The fleet was augmented with many vessels over the

*Algoma Central Railway president L.N. Savoie (left), and H.R. Jackman, chairman of the board.*

years, until 1964, when the ACR undertook a major rebuilding program.

One ship, the *E.B. Barber*, was converted to a self-unloading vessel, and a new bulk carrier, the *Sir Denys Lowson*, was constructed. Realizing the increasing demand for self-unloading-type ships, the company commissioned a new, larger class of vessel. The *Roy A. Jodrey* was launched in 1965, followed by construction of the *Algorail* in 1968, the *Agawa Canyon* in 1970, the *Algoway* in 1972, and the *Algosoo* in 1974, the *Algosea* in 1976, the *Algolake* in 1977, the *Algobay* in 1978, the *Algoport* in 1979, the *Algowood* in 1981, the *Algowest* in 1982, and the *John B. Aird* in 1983.

The marine division continued to expand, and in 1986 the firm purchased Nipigon Transport Ltd. and Carryore Ltd., obtaining four seaway-size, bulk ships and bringing the ACR fleet to 18 vessels.

Algoma Central further diversified its transportation interests by pur-

*The* John B. Aird, *a self-unloading ship commissioned by Algoma Central Railway in 1983 and shown here at Algoma Steel's coal docks, is one of the fleet of 18 vessels comprising ACR's marine division—the oldest bulk freight carrier with continuous service on the Great Lakes.*

chasing a southern Ontario trucking company in 1972: Algocen Transport Holdings Ltd. grew to employ 800 people in communities including Windsor, London, and Chatham; controlled about 1,100 units of equipment; and had revenues of more than $65 million. The trucking division was sold in October 1987 to the GTL Transport Group.

In 1973 Algocen Realty Holdings Ltd., a wholly owned company of ACR, was incorporated, and it embarked on a development program in downtown Sault Ste. Marie that changed the city's waterfront. On land reclaimed from the St. Mary's River near its Bay Street office building and freight operations, the firm built a shopping mall and a major hotel, leased to Commonwealth Holiday Inns, which opened in 1974. Near the same location it constructed a new passenger terminal to handle its train service and moved the freight operation.

The Station Tower, a six-storey office building, had its first tenant in 1975, and senior citizens occupied the 101 units in Algocen's waterfront apartment building by May 1978. The Station Mall, with 40 stores, officially opened October 30, 1973. Since that time the complex has been expanded, more than doubling the number of stores. A major $18-million, 82,000-square-foot expansion is planned that will add another 40 stores and services to the 93 already located there.

Algocen branched out its real estate development to the uranium town of Elliot Lake in 1980, when it opened the Algo Centre shopping/office complex and a hotel, the Algo Inn.

Algoma Central Railway also has investments in U.S. real estate and in 1985 became sole owner of a luxury Florida condominium project it had embarked on as a joint venture with a partner. By 1986 all of the 108 units in the first building had been sold. Two additional buildings of 134 units each are now under construction.

*As part of its downtown redevelopment program, Algocen Realty Holdings Ltd., a wholly owned company of ACR, constructed Station Mall in the early 1970s on reclaimed land along the Sault Ste. Marie waterfront.*

# HOLIDAY INN

The Holiday Inn has played a major role in the redevelopment of Sault Ste. Marie's waterfront and will have an integral part in future development along the banks of the St. Mary's River.

The nine-floor hotel opened in July 1974 as part of a riverfront project that included a giant shopping mall developed by Algocen Realty Holdings, the real estate division of Algoma Central Railway. Owned by Algocen, it is leased to Commonwealth Hospitality Ltd., which operates Holiday Inn, Radisson, and Best Western hotels across Canada. Commonwealth is a division of Scott's Hospitality, which purchased the company in 1979. With the ownership change, Commonwealth spent $255 million retrofitting and refurnishing its 44 hotels nationwide.

The Holiday Inn in downtown Sault Ste. Marie has a new look since its doors first opened for business. The change reflects a change in the needs of the market. The switch has been away from an emphasis as a

family-type hotel to a business hotel with the addition of facilities and amenities catering to business and corporate customers.

In 1987 a convention centre and a fitness club were added in a $2.5-million expansion. The hotel has

a total of 15 meeting rooms with the smallest boardroom capable of holding 10 people and the largest 400. Bridgewater Fitness Centre is a fully equipped and staffed health club that has a swimming pool, whirlpool, sauna, fitness classes and testing, workout equipment, change facilities, and lockers. The fitness club is open to hotel guests and offers memberships to the public as well.

The Holiday Inn has 194 rooms, six suites—two hospitality and four residential—a piano bar and restaurant, and a staff of 100 full-time and 35 to 50 part-time employees.

A fishing charter boat operation is based at the hotel, and horse-and-buggy tours of the city are available, along with a view of the most stunning sunsets on the river.

Community involvement is an important part of the Holiday Inn's operations. Hotel staff sit on the chamber of commerce, Sault College advisory boards, and various tourism-related organizations, thus supporting the growth of the tourism industry and ensuring future growth in Sault Ste. Marie.

# CANADIAN TIRE ASSOCIATE STORE

Paul Dalseg recalls the days when his employees came to work in the morning and he never saw them again until 6 p.m., quitting time, because they were so busy scurrying like ants from one warehouse to another searching for merchandise.

But this all changed in 1974, when the proprietor of the Canadian Tire Associate Store relocated his business from Queen Street to the corner of Great Northern Road and McNabb Street. The new site enabled him to expand under one roof a growing business that had been housed in one store and five outside warehouses.

Ten years later the store expanded again, when it became the south anchor of the newly con-

structed Cambrian Mall, a major shopping complex in the city's north end. A half-century after it was established in Sault Ste. Marie, the Canadian Tire franchise has grown from a store with a staff of six to one with more than 160 employees and an annual payroll exceeding $2 million. Retail floor

*Vic and Wib Muncaster opened the first Canadian Tire franchise at 368 Queen Street East in 1938, moving to this location at 344 Queen Street (where the business was run until 1974) two years later. Previously stocking mainly automotive parts and accessories, farm goods, and hardware, Canadian Tire was once viewed as an exclusively "man's store"; today, with the addition of sporting and seasonal items, Canadian Tire Corporation has become known as a "family store with something for everyone."*

*Once a small franchise with six employees, Canadian Tire Corporation is today an anchor store on the south end of Cambrian Mall, an extensive shopping complex on McNabb Street. The company currently occupies 28,500 square feet of retail floor space and 16 service bays, and employs a staff of more than 160 on an annual payroll exceeding $2 million. Courtesy, The Sault Star*

space has increased from 1,900 square feet to 28,500 square feet, and the building has 50,000 square feet of warehouse space plus 16 service bays.

The first Canadian Tire store opened its doors in the fall of 1938. Brothers Vic and Wib Muncaster founded the outlet at 368 Queen Street East, and then, two years later, moved into larger quarters at 344 Queen Street. It was established as a franchise store (No. 095) and made purchases from CTC Toronto, which was started in 1922 by the Billes Brothers. Vic Muncaster operated the business for some 26 years, with the franchise passing to two others before Dalseg took over in January 1971.

Born and raised in northern Ontario, Dalseg established the first Canadian Tire store in Dryden in 1961 and four years later moved east to Port Credit, where he remained until he obtained the Sault franchise.

Inventory is controlled by a computer system, introduced, along with an on-line cash register for credit approval, when the new store opened. Electronic systems maintain constant contact, and the future will bring a satellite hookup to improve inventory control and provide an improved service level to customers, with information channels and delivery systems.

# PLUMMER MEMORIAL PUBLIC HOSPITAL

It was 11 years after the drive first began that a man who became known as Sault Ste. Marie's "Good Samaritan" succeeded in establishing the city's second hospital.

In 1917 Frank J. Davey was elected president of the Algoma Benevolent Society, an organization that had been trying since 1906 to set up a nonsectarian hospital. Thanks to his untiring efforts, the Royal Victoria, a 20-bed hospital located in an Albert Street East house, opened its doors in July 1917.

Two years later heirs of W.H. Plummer (a former mayor) offered to donate Lynnhurst, the family estate located on Queen Street East, to be used as a hospital. There was one condition—the name had to be changed to the Plummer Memorial Public Hospital. The association accepted, and in 1920 the new 35-bed facility opened.

Within a year the Plummer Memorial School of Nursing was established and four women enrolled. By the time the school closed its doors 50 years later, 475 nurses had graduated from the program.

*With 971 employees and 139 doctors, Plummer Memorial Public Hospital serves the community of Sault Ste. Marie. Because of the growing need for increased services, Plummer will be cooperating with General Hospital to improve and divide services.*

*Frank Joseph Davey. It was 11 years after the drive first began that a man who became known as Sault Ste. Marie's "Good Samaritan" succeeded in establishing the city's second hospital. Courtesy, The Sault Star*

In 1921 Davey purchased two adjoining properties, and seven years later, in 1928, he launched a campaign to raise money for a new $207,000 building. At that time a patent was signed officially naming the hospital Plummer Memorial Public Hospital. When it was completed in 1929, the Plummer Hospital had 48 beds. A plan to increase the size to 108 beds had to be abandoned, but a smaller, 20-bed addition was constructed in 1951. This still was not enough. Demand for beds far exceeded the supply, and three

years later the building was again enlarged to accommodate 150 beds and 32 bassinets.

Expansion continued over the years with the addition of two more wings in 1962 and in the 1970s and 1980s. Two satellite hospitals were included, as well as numerous units, such as detoxification, psychiatric, and oncology, and an ambulance base.

The hospital staff grew in 70 years from three nurses, nine student nurses, one orderly, a cook, a maid, and a laundress to a modern facility with 971 employees and 139 doctors. It has an annual budget of $35 million, with 89 percent of the funding from government and the rest from other sources.

A 180-member hospital auxiliary provides numerous services to patients, operates a gift shop, and raises money through special events such as teas and fashion shows.

In 1986 Plummer signed a rationalization agreement with General Hospital, the Sault's other hospital, to improve and divide services. Implementation of the plan will take at least 10 years, and Plummer Memorial Public Hospital will be responsible for all critical and acute medical and surgical care, as well as psychiatric and alcohol treatment for adults in the Sault and Algoma district.

# R.M. ELLIOTT CONSTRUCTION LTD.

Ronald Elliott can claim two connections to one of Sault Ste. Marie's prominent buildings. The forerunner of his construction firm helped build the courthouse, and some of the brick inside the historic Queen Street building came from his family's brickyard.

The history of R.M. Elliott Construction Ltd. is intertwined with several local families and business enterprises. The Elliott family—five brothers—came to the Sault in 1901 from Wingham, Ontario, where they had operated a brickyard. They acquired 45 acres of land on Rossmore Road and began producing 800,000 bricks per year in a brickyard that was the first established business in Korah Township. Hardwood fired the kilns, and a steam engine powered the machinery.

By the early 1920s the plant was converted to electrical power and James Elliott, Jr., had bought out his brothers. During this time most of the houses and many public buildings in the Sault were built with the red-colored bricks from the Elliott yard.

In 1947 the business was purchased by James' sons, Thomas and Stanley, who operated it until Stanley's death in 1968. The property was

*Elliott's Brickyard at Rossmore and Elliott roads (now the site of James Elliott Park), provided the brick for many of the Sault's homes and public buildings in the early 1900s.*

then sold to the municipality and became James Elliott Park.

Meanwhile Stanley's son Ronald had left the family business in 1946 to work as a carpenter for E.D. Jannison, General Contractor. Its predecessor, D. Jannison & Son, had been in the area from approximately 1900, and built parts of the Abitibi Paper Mill, the courthouse, and many city streets and sidewalks. When John Scott joined the firm in 1947, it became Jannison and Scott.

An office and warehouse, constructed at 35 Cedar Street (still the site of Elliott Construction) in 1952, was destroyed in a September 1963

*These villas at the Searchmont Ski Resort north of the Sault comprise one of Elliott Construction's recently completed projects.*

fire and replaced by three buildings.

After Jannison retired in 1955 and Scott died unexpectedly the following year, longtime employees Norman Caughill and Ronald Elliott purchased the firm. It continued to operate as Jannison and Scott until Caughill's retirement in 1971, when the name became R.M. Elliott Construction Ltd.

Since 1974 the company has been a franchised dealer for Butler Pre-Engineered steel buildings, and has expanded into the design-build field. Over the years Elliott built many local structures, including the Steelworkers Union Hall, Parkland School, and Riverview Centre. Recent projects include Searchmont Ski Lodge and Villas and Pathfinder Beverage Warehouse.

The firm has branch offices in Wawa, managed by Brian Elliott, and in Elliot Lake, which operates as an equipment rental centre.

R.M. Elliott Construction Ltd. became involved in equipment rental in 1956 and includes stores in the Sault, Wawa, and Elliot Lake, as well as an affiliated company, Repeat Rentals Ltd., in the Sault. The largest equipment rental centre in the district, it is managed by Stanley Elliott.

*E.D. Jannison and Sons, General Contractors (which later became Elliott Construction), operated in the Sault since about 1900 and was involved in the construction of the Abitibi Paper Mill, several of the city's streets, and the courthouse. This photo, taken in 1920, includes James Elliott (third row, fifth from left).*

# TRADERS METAL CO. LTD.

In 1901 Benjamin Cohen brought his new bride, Esther, to Sault Ste. Marie for their honeymoon. The young couple obviously liked what they saw, because by February 1902 they had moved from Sherbrooke, Quebec, and had established a scrap-iron business on the banks of the St. Mary's River.

Today, 85 years later, a third-generation Cohen, grandson Robert, still operates the family business, Traders Metal Co. Ltd., along with Benjamin's son Wilfred.

Originally called The Superior Iron and Metal Co. Ltd., the firm was initially located near the Government Dock at the foot of Pim Street. Now the site of the Ministry of Natural Resources Air Base, Cohen's iron, steel, coal, and wood operations remained there until 1913, when the company moved to its present five-acre waterfront site on Queen Street West.

What began as a scrap-iron business had expanded by 1905 as Benjamin Cohen brought the first domestic coal by boat to the Sault. "Cohen's Clean Coal" and firewood, another

*Scene from Sault Ste. Marie scrapyard in 1948.*

fuel the business sold, were used to heat the community's homes. Large barges transported the wood from extensive timber-cutting operations on nearby St. Joseph Island, and during the winter months, when the river froze, firewood was transported by sleigh to the town's American neighbor, Sault Ste. Marie, Michigan.

Teams of horses also were used to move scrap iron across the ice to Michigan Sault for shipment to U.S. consumers, in the days when goods flowed freely across the international border. The wood and coal branch of the business was later discontinued, but the scrap operations expanded until the firm became one of the best known in Canada, with branches in Lachine, Quebec, Toronto, and Dollar Bay, Michigan.

When the Depression hit in the 1930s and the city's major industry, Algoma Steel Corp., was in dire straits, it was devastating to Traders, Wilf Cohen says. Business began to pick up in 1937, and during World War II, when the men were overseas, women kept the scrapyard operating.

Today Traders Metal Co. Ltd. has operations in the Sault and North Bay. It continues to buy and sell **scrap—an essential business recycling**

*Benjamin Cohen in a 1915 photograph.*

metals that Robert Cohen is pleased to note is ecologically beneficial. Obsolescent items ranging from demolished buildings and ships to household objects and vehicles are collected from a 600-kilometre radius of the Sault. They are stockpiled, graded, cut, or crushed into portable size, and then transported out of the city, mainly to steel mills and foundries in the United States and Canada.

# CLIFFE PRINTING 1979 LIMITED

Charlie Cliffe is a third-generation printer, working at a trade that has undergone a technological revolution since his grandfather opened up shop in 1902.

The old mode of printing with hot metal has been replaced by a lithograph process that utilizes computers, enabling Cliffe Printing 1979 Limited to do all types of commercial printing, including full color. The process has changed dramatically, says Cliffe, who entered the family business in 1953.

His grandfather, Charles Cliffe, came to Sault Ste. Marie from British Columbia in 1902. He purchased a weekly newspaper, the *Algoma Pioneer*, which he converted to a daily paper. The paper closed down six years later, after a fire destroyed the plant located on the west side of Pim Street. After the fire he moved to March Street and then, in 1926, to larger quarters and the firm's present location at 118 Spring Street.

Charles Cliffe also edited the

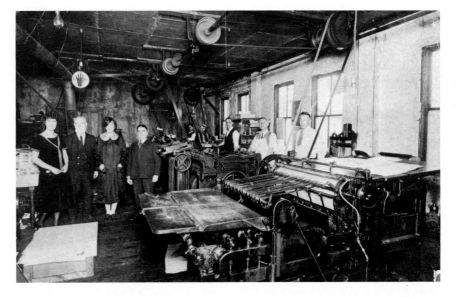

*Charles Cliffe (with beard) and his son Herbert (fourth from left), at the March Street printing plant with employees and the old hot metal printing presses. This photograph was taken in 1922, roughly eight years before Herbert and his brother, Osborne, converted this one-time newspaper operation—which Cliffe had run since 1902—into a commercial printing plant.*

*Using today's modern, computerized printing process, Charlie Cliffe (left) carries on the business started by his grandfather more than 85 years ago. He and a staff of 12 use up to 50 tons of paper annually to produce brochures, folders, books, and all types of commercial print work for a market that extends to Wawa in the north and to Chapleau in the east. Enduring many changes over the years, Cliffe Printing 1979 Limited has been doing business at its present location at 118 Spring Street since 1926. Courtesy, The Sault Star*

*Steelton News*, and had a china shop and bookstore at 506 Queen Street East. He operated a newspaper until approximately 1930, when his two sons, Herbert and Osborne Cliffe, joined the business and started a commercial printing plant.

After Charles' death in 1931, the two brothers continued their partnership until 1938, when Osborne moved to Chicago to set up his own printing shop. Herb remained with the business until his death in 1974, then his son Charlie took over. In 1979 Charlie Cliffe sold the company to four employees, with himself remaining principal shareholder.

A total of 12 employees are currently employed at the print shop that serves a market covering not only Sault Ste. Marie but Wawa to the north and Chapleau to the east. The business, which 35 years ago used roughly 10 tons of paper annually, now goes through 50 tons, producing folders, brochures, books, and all types of commercial printing.

Charlie Cliffe continues to carry on not only his family's trade, but their record of community involvement. His father headed a group of local businessmen who in 1919 organized the Soo Greyhounds, a senior amateur hockey team that in 1924 won the Allan Cup, a national championship, and was active with the Northern Ontario Hockey Association.

Charlie has been heavily involved with the Sault branch of the Canadian Cancer Society and served as campaign chairman for the province of Ontario. A member of the Rotary Club, he will serve as district governor in 1988-1989, encompassing an area from Wawa to Grand Rapids, Michigan.

# SAULT STE. MARIE ROTARY CLUB

Thirteen years after the establishment of Rotary International, a group of Sault Ste. Marie business and professional men formed the Sault Ste. Marie Rotary Club. The club's charter was presented at a banquet at the March Street YMCA on July 20, 1918. Harry Hollinrake was the first president of the service club, which had 53 members.

Rotary soon became involved with a project that is synonymous with its work in the Sault. The club's first Community Night parade, an idea originated by *Sault Star* founder Jim Curran, was staged on September 23, 1922. Proceeds from the event were used to purchase a car for the city nurse. The parade became an annual event that has since raised thousands of dollars for the group's work with crippled children. Rotary began working with crippled children in 1923 and over the years organized numerous events, such as the sports celebrities dinner, to support its projects.

The club also has been involved with other youth projects, including a boys' camp and international student exchanges, and during World

*In 1922 Rotarian Jim Curran helped establish Community Night, a fund raiser for Rotary's work with disabled youth. The celebration takes place every third Saturday in July. Courtesy, The Sault Star*

War II it sent parcels to soldiers overseas. It has donated equipment to hospitals, provided scholarships, and worked with the Duke of Edinburgh Awards program.

In 1949 the club began participating in the Ontario Society for Crippled Children Easter Seal campaign, another major project, along with the Snowarama snowmobile marathon it continues to sponsor to raise money for crippled children and its other youth work. The club's contribution of funds to a rehabilitation unit for children led to its being renamed the Rotary Children's Rehabilitation Unit in 1964. In 1981 Rotary collaborated with the Easter Seal Society to establish the Rotary Easter Seal Superthon on Sault Ste. Marie's CHBX-TV and CJIC-TV. This major fund-raising project accounts for thousands of dollars raised on behalf of handicapped children. The 1989 Superthon will be held in March.

Over its 70-year history the Sault Ste. Marie Rotary Club has made significant contributions to Sault Ste. Marie's recreational facilities by constructing tennis courts throughout the city. Rotary's tennis program has provided facilities such as RYTAC (Rotary-YMCA Tennis and Aquatic Club). Rotary is one of the first organizations in Ontario to establish the program known as Partners in Educa-

tion with Bawating Collegiate & Vocational High School. It is also a community leader in its support of the Sault's hospitals, with major contributions to the CAT Scanner Campaign ($25,000) and the Plummer Hospital Campaign.

Until 1961 the Rotary Club of Sault Ste. Marie was the only Canadian club in its district, which encompassed the Upper Peninsula of Michigan. The decision to attach the club to this district was made in 1923, resulting from the vast distances separating it from other clubs in Ontario. A club sponsored by the Sault club was chartered in Wawa in 1961, and a second Rotary Club was formed locally a decade later and named Sault North Rotary.

Over the years eight members have served as district governor: James Shaw (1938-1939), Fred Wilson (1957-1958), Alan Broughton (1960-1961), Russell Ramsay, Jr. (1968-1969), Skipper Manzzutti (1972-1973), Norman Candelori (1976-1977), H.S. "Mac" McLellan (1981-1982), and C.O. "Charlie" Cliffe (1988-1989).

*Until the International Bridge was built, this sign, at the Brock Street ferry dock, greeted American visitors. Sault Rotarians organized the project in the late 1930s; local firms provided free labor and materials. Courtesy, The Sault Star*

# SOO MILL BUILDALL

Soo Mill Buildall has been a family business for nearly three-quarters of a century—since 1915, when F.E. "Lynn" Hollingsworth purchased a half-interest in a local lumber company.

By 1923 he had bought out his partner in the Corrigan Lumber Co. and renamed it Soo Lumber Co. (later changed to Soo Mill and Lumber Co.). The firm used the Corrigan mill on North Street until 1922, then built a new plant in four stages during the next 16 years.

Hollingsworth, who came to the Sault Ste. Marie area from Montreal as a child, was active with the firm until he left in 1952 to become president of Great Lakes Power Ltd. After his retirement his three sons, Simpson, Lynn, and Ian, took over operation of the company, and in 1988 five third-generation members of the family were working at the business.

Soo Mill's first retail outlet was opened on North Street in 1915; a de-

cade later a store was added in Wawa. The Sault's second store was opened on Second Line in 1973, and another branch was added in Elliot Lake the following year. In 1986 Soo Mill sold the Second Line store, bought Dubreuil Lumber Co.'s outlet on Great Northern Road, and reopened it as a Soo Mill Buildall.

Lumber, plywood, home and builders' materials, electrical and plumbing supplies, hardware, floor coverings, and paint, along with prefab homes and cottages are handled. During the Depression the firm began manufacturing butcher blocks and hardwood table tops, and later added laboratory tops, altars, and church furniture, now shipping these custom wood products across Canada and to markets outside the country.

In 1955 Soo Mill began constructing houses; it built more than 1,000 in the Sault, and developed 1,500 to 2,000 lots. Sue Maid cupboards, produced by the firm, have been installed

in many local homes.

The organization has grown from 28 employees in the early days to more than 200, including those in Wawa and Elliot Lake. Another Sault company, Downey Building Materials Ltd., is a wholly owned subsidiary of Soo Mill, which also has a major investment in Huron Broadcasting Ltd.

Soo Mill Buildall president Simpson Hollingsworth and his brothers Lynn and Ian have been active on the boards of the Sault's two hospitals and with many other organizations. Four Hollingsworths—now into the third generation—have been chairman of the United Way campaign, and F.E. Hollingsworth was the first president of the Welfare Federation, which initiated the United Appeal in 1957.

*Soo Mill's Great Northern Road store in Sault Ste. Marie is one of two Soo Mill stores in the city that service retail and commercial customers.*

# UNITED STEELWORKERS OF AMERICA

*John Barker, "the grand old man of the Sault's labor movement," served as Local 2251 president from 1946 to 1948 and was the driving force behind establishing a community health centre. At left the longtime labor leader receives an honorary Doctor of Laws degree from Laurentian University.*

The first steelworkers union meeting took place in Sault Ste. Marie on a June night in 1935. The men gathered in the Sons of Italy Hall had been talking union for a while, meeting secretly in small groups in out-of-the-way places.

The Algoma Steel Corp. workers were tired of the low wages and long hours—working 11- and 13-hour shifts, toiling in the mills seven days a week for less than 30 cents an hour. Wages were poor, but the workers were even more worried about job security, and this played the biggest factor in the formation of the Algoma Steelworkers Union.

A few years later the independent union affiliated with the Steel Workers Organizing Committee (SWOC), which became the United Steelworkers of America in 1942. And the union, organized seven years earlier in a Queen Street West hall, was chartered as USWA Local 2251 and grew to be the third-largest steelworker local in Canada. It also earned the label as one of the most progressive union

locals in the North American labor movement, and has produced an impressive list of members who have made an outstanding contribution to the United Steelworkers of America.

In 1940 a Welsh-born electrician's helper who had gone to work in Algoma's mills at the age of 17 was elected the local union's secretary/treasurer. The election marked the beginning of William Mahoney's long union career—a career that spanned 37 years and included 20 years in the top Canadian steelworker job. Mahoney was named a staff representative with SWOC in 1941 and continued in that post with the United Steelworkers. After spending two years on the West Coast assisting the Canadian Congress of Labor, he became assistant to C.H. Millard, the USWA's first Canadian national director, in 1949.

When Millard left in 1956 to become director of the International Confederation of Free Trade Unions, Mahoney became acting Canadian director. The following year he was

unopposed in his bid to keep the director's job, and held the position until he decided to step down in 1977. Mahoney was one of many USWA officials and staff people to come up through the ranks of the giant Sault Ste. Marie steelworker local.

John Barker, who attended the first steelworkers meeting in 1935, has been called the grand old man of the Sault's labor movement. A USWA staff representative for 24 years before retiring in 1971 as area supervisor, he had started at Algoma Steel as a pipefitter's helper in 1926. He rose from the rank and file to serve as local president and vice-president then full-time staff with the steelworkers in 1947. Barker was the driving force behind what's been called the Sault steelworkers' finest hour—a community health centre that has become a model for health care in Canada and the United States. He was assigned the task of organizing the establishment of the centre in 1958, and after a five-year struggle, marked by a display of solidarity and strength by the steelworkers, the Sault Ste. Marie and District Group Health Centre opened.

When Barker retired in 1971, he was replaced as northwestern Ontario supervisor by Paul Krmpotich, another Sault steelworker who had become a staff representative, in 1954. He started at the plant in 1937, and after his fellow workers in the scarfing department elected him a delegate, he became involved with the union.

He served on the strike committee during the lengthy, controversial nationwide steel strike in 1946, when 14,000 men simultaneously struck three of Canada's steel producers. When the two-month dispute ended, the Algoma workers had won a 13-cent-an-hour wage increase and improved benefits. But one of the major gains, Krmpotich said in his book, *A Tribute to the Members of Local 2251*, was the "feeling of establishing the kind of respect workers need in the workplace." The pay raise was secondary to the solidarity and strength the union members showed, he said.

Thirty-six years after he went to

work in Algoma Steel Corporation's open-hearth plants, Bern Schultz took over the senior staff job when Krmpotich retired in 1978. Schultz had taken on an assignment as one of three union representatives on Algoma's co-operative wage study committee in 1954 and never returned to the shop floor. Local 2251 was the first USWA local to negotiate such a job evaluation program, which rated every job according to skill and labor needed to perform it.

Once the new system of standardized pay rates had been established, eliminating arbitrary differences between departments, the union's national office hired Schultz to work

with other locals to establish similar pay systems. He was later transferred to the regional office in the Sault as a staff representative. He retired in 1981 after 25 years as a USWA staff representative.

Les Woodcock, a structural ironworker who started with the company in 1942 and returned after service in World War II, held various positions, including president with Local 2251, before being appointed a staff representative in 1972. He worked with Barker on the committee that raised

*John Ferris served as president of Local 2251 for 13 years, became a city alderman, and was acclaimed for his community involvement.*

*Les Woodcock, Local 2251 president (1962-1964), later became a staff representative and was active in the community.*

$800,000 to build the group health centre by a $135-per-family subscription of steelworkers. Woodcock, who retired in 1987, was a trustee and vice-chairman of the Sault Board of Education for many years, served on the board of the health centre, and was one of the directors of the Algoma Steelworkers Credit Union.

The steelworkers have always had a high profile in the Sault, and play an important role in community services and organizations. They are active supporters of the United Way and serve on city council, the boards of local institutions such as Sault College, the Group Health Centre, and credit unions and many other local agencies and bodies.

John Ferris, a union activist for 40 years, served 13 years as Local 2251 president and as a city alderman for four years. He earned a city Medal of Merit in 1974 for his community work.

Sault Ste. Marie has 9,000 steelworkers, including members of Local 2251, the giant production local of Algoma Steel; Local 4509 (formed in 1952), which represents ASC office workers; and Local 5595 in the steel plant's tube division. The USWA district office in the Sault, located in the steelworkers' hall on Dennis Street, covers an area that stretches northwest to the Manitoba border and services 12,000 union members. It is part of District 6 (the province of Ontario), the largest district in the union, which has 400 locals and a membership of 80,000 men and women. While the majority of its members work in mining and basic steel industries, the USWA also represents workers in the chemicals, electronics, and furniture industries as well as office, professional, and technical workers.

Canada's largest industrial union, the USWA has been in the forefront of the labor movement, taking many innovative and precedent-setting steps. The steelworkers led the fight

for improved safety in the workplace and workers' compensation. In 1985 the union set up a humanity fund to help those suffering in third world countries, and District 6 locals agreed to donate a penny an hour to the fund. Sault steelworkers were the first to negotiate a wholly company-paid, non-contributor pension plan and an almost completely paid medical, surgical, and hospitalization plan.

USWA locals in the Sault and Hamilton negotiated a reduction in work hours in their 1949 contracts

*Paul Krmpotich served on the strike committee in 1946, when steelworkers established "respect" in the workplace. He later served as a staff representative.*

with the steel companies that dropped the week to 44 hours from 48. In 1950 the 40-hour week became standard at Algoma Steel.

As the largest union in Sault Ste. Marie, the United Steelworkers of America sets the pace for a prosperous community with a good standard of living.

# MAJOR CONTRACTING (ALGOMA) LTD.

*Tony Ruscio overlooks the Sault, with the City International Bridge in the background, from the balcony of his seventh-storey office.*

When Tony Ruscio arrived in Canada from his native Italy in 1955, he had a suitcase full of clothes and only a couple of dollars in his pocket. The young stonemason took a job in London, Ontario, at a poultry business, where he earned $17 per week, and made a deal with a parish priest to repair his church's steps in return for English lessons.

In 1957, with $300 in savings from his work with a local contractor, he moved to Sault Ste. Marie, intent on establishing his own construction company. Major Contracting (Algoma) Ltd. was in business the following year, doing small jobs and repairs and building fireplaces, and it was not long before Ruscio's firm was building homes.

After a few years of doing masonry work and building homes, Major Contracting branched out to apartment construction and development. Then, in 1966, during a Sunday afternoon drive, Ruscio spied a vacant Allard Street lot, cluttered with rubble and debris from a nearby construction site. The potential of what to most eyes was a pile of dirt was not lost on Ruscio, who immediately secured an option on the land. Construction of a 12-unit apartment building

began in 1967 as a centennial project. Another 12 units, followed by 45 units were added to the complex, named Ruscio Villa. That project was followed by Ruscio Court, with two 11-unit buildings and a 38-unit complex on Boehmer Boulevard.

Major Contracting diversified further a couple of years later when it ventured into office buildings. Walrus I, an office complex on Albert Street East, was erected in 1969, followed two years later by Walrus II. During 1974 and 1975 apartment buildings with 32

units and 41 units were being constructed on Trunk Road, and the fun of building swimming pools began.

The developer and businessman then turned to the hospitality industry. A convention-hotel-sports complex was his next project, and on April 27, 1978, the two-storey, 110-room Ramada Inn and Convention Centre, with a ballroom to accommodate 1,000 people, located at 229 Great Northern Road, officially opened its doors. As owner and operator of the hotel, Ruscio continued to expand the facility, constructing a million-dollar sports complex, including squash and racquetball courts, and 22 additional rooms.

In 1987 the entrepreneur's hotel complex had grown to 220 rooms with an eight-floor tower, convention rooms, swimming pool, whirlpool, sauna, bars, and 200-seat restaurant. The 24-lane automatic scoring Cambrian Bowling Centre, linked by tunnel to the hotel tower, has a 120-seat lounge, snack bar, and underground parking. Golfers can tee off at the nine-hole indoor Wilderness Golf Course and Driving Range. A clubhouse, pro shop, and nineteenth hole have replaced part of the racquet club facilities—and this is only the beginning.

*Ruscio reviews promotion in the boardroom of Major Contracting.*

# GREAT LAKES POWER LIMITED

Sault Ste. Marie's industrial growth was generated by an American dreamer who recognized the immense power potential of the St. Mary's River rapids when he first visited the community in 1894. Francis H. Clergue harnessed the "untold millions of horsepower energy" that rushed over the rapids, and created an industrial boom in the early 1900s that gave the Sault a steel company, railway, pulp and paper mill, electric utility, and a foundry.

Today Great Lakes Power Limited's modern, $118-million generating station, completed in 1983, bears the name of the man who developed the first hydroelectric generating power plant on the river. Great Lakes traces its ancestry back to Clergue and the day in 1894 when he assumed the $260,000 debt on the town's white elephant and acquired the partially completed power project. He named the new organization the Lake Superior Power Company. Two days after he purchased the power company, Clergue obtained a franchise from the town council to supply the community's electric lighting and water, and formed the Tagona Water and Light Company.

The power facility changed hands in 1912, when its assets were transferred to Algoma Steel Corp., another of Clergue's businesses. When the outbreak of World War I brought a sudden end to the demand for rails, the steel company's principal product, it sold off the power rights to provide

*Great Lakes Power's $118-million Clergue Generating Station on the St. Mary's River was named for Francis H. Clergue, one of Sault Ste. Marie's industrial pioneers. The new station was officially opened in 1983.*

capital to increase production of shells. Tagona Water and Light was taken over by the city in 1915 and, as the Public Utilities Commission, continues to distribute power to the Sault.

Another new venture—The Great Lakes Power Company—was formed and incorporated in 1916. It took over the power plant, power rights on the river, land and power lines owned by the steel company, and the International Transit Co. The transit company operated streetcars within the city of Sault Ste. Marie and a ferry service between the Sault and its twin city, Sault Ste. Marie, Michigan, on the U.S. side of the river.

The challenge of providing the power needs of a growing industrial centre attracted men of high calibre, imagination, and drive to head a utility from its formative years to the present. Founder John A. McPhail, company president until 1952, was a lawyer, alderman, and mayor of the city from 1914 to 1915. He served as an officer and director of other companies, and was instrumental in bringing millions of dollars of capital into the district.

In 1952 Fremlin E. Hollingsworth left an active and progressive lumber and hardware business in the hands of his family to assume the presidency of Great Lakes Power. Seven years later the reins passed to William M. Hogg, one of the Sault's most civic-minded citizens. He was named to the Order of Canada, received a city Medal of Merit, and was involved with numerous organizations—an involvement that continued after his retirement in 1976.

Hugh L. Harris, who currently holds the office of company president, continues the tradition of combining responsible corporate leadership with many varied and demanding civic positions.

*Construction of the Clergue Generating Station, which replaced the deteriorating 70-year-old plant, was begun in the spring of 1979. It was completed nearly four years later and ceremoniously activated with the push of a button by Ontario Premier William Davis.*

Two years after Great Lakes Power was formed, a new generating station with a capacity of 15,600 kilowatts was completed on the St. Mary's River. A further expansion of that plant added another 5,400 kilowatts in 1922. Four years later another company, the Algoma District Power Company Limited, was formed to generate power for the growing and important mining development at Michipicoten (110 miles north of the Sault) and Goudreau.

A new generating station was built at High Falls on the Michipicoten River in 1929-1930, and a transmission line using aluminum as a power line conductor was built to transmit power to the Sault. Building power lines through the North's rough and mountainous terrain was difficult. Poles and line material had to be hauled along logging roads by teams of horses, and workers had to fight sub-zero temperatures in the winter and black flies in the summer.

In 1931 Great Lakes Power and Algoma District Power merged to become Great Lakes Power Company Limited.

During the early 1930s more lines were built north of the city and

*The International Transit Company Limited, at one time owned by Great Lakes Power, operated streetcars within the city of Sault Ste. Marie and a ferry service between the Sault and its twin city, Sault Ste. Marie, Michigan, on the U.S. side of the river.*

*MacKay Generating Station, constructed in 1937, is 90 miles north of the Sault and one of four hydroelectric plants on the Montreal River.*

east to Bruce Mines and St. Joseph Island. In 1937, to further assist the district's mineral and industrial growth, a new power station was constructed on the Montreal River, 90 miles north of the Sault. In the same year that this station at Montreal River Upper Falls was completed, work began on a hydro power plant 11 miles downstream at the river's Lower Falls.

In the following decades Great Lakes Power continued to expand until its generating system consisted of nine hydroelectric generating stations—four on the Michipicoten River, four on the Montreal River, and one on the St. Mary's River. Power requirements for the needs of the district beyond Great Lakes Power's generating capability are supplied through power purchased from Ontario Hydro.

In 1949 Great Lakes Power was incorporated to become the owner of all the generating stations, while Great Lakes Power Company Limited acted as operating agent for the corporation. The company's corporate structure changed in 1973 when Brascan Ltd. acquired more than 99 percent of the shares and its operations were continued by the corporation's utilities division. In December 1980 ownership of the company was transferred from Brascan to Great Lakes

Group Inc. In May 1987 Great Lakes Group Inc. became a public company.

Great Lakes' biggest project, and perhaps the largest in the Sault's history outside Algoma Steel, was construction of the Clergue Station to replace the aged and deteriorating plant built nearly 70 years earlier. Construction began in May 1979, and on February 21, 1983, Ontario Premier William Davis activated the first of the station's three generating units. The horizontal, bulb-type units of the Clergue Generating Station are notable, as they are among a limited number of such units in North America.

In 1987 Great Lakes Power Limited began a $100-million power development on the Magpie River, near Wawa. The project, scheduled for completion in 1989, will harness three falls—Steephill, Magpie, and Mission—to develop power-generation sites on the river. This development will be a step toward limiting the company's dependence on purchased power as well as assisting it in serving the domestic and industrial needs of the Sault and Algoma District.

# LYONS BUILDING CENTRE LTD.

James Lyons was lured to Sault Ste. Marie from a small Lake Simcoe farming settlement by reports that laborers in the Sault were earning $1.50 a day. The 22 year old arrived at the turn of the century with his young family, little money, and no formal education. He soon began laying the foundations for successful business and political careers.

Lyons worked as a stonemason, butcher, grocer, and laborer before getting involved in construction and real estate. Then, in 1912, he established Lyons Fuel, Hardware, and Supplies Ltd., a business that 75 years later still bears this pioneer's name (as Lyons Building Centre Ltd.).

Lyons' political life began in Steelton in 1908 as a councillor and later mayor (1911 to 1913). After Steelton's amalgamation with the Sault, he served on the city council as alderman in 1922 and 1923, when he was elected to the provincial legislature. He was appointed Minister of Lands and Forest in the Conservative government, a portfolio he held until 1926. Lyons was reelected as the Sault's Member of the Provincial Parliament

*Lyons has undergone many changes over the years. In its early days (below right)—photo circa 1920—it sold coal and lumber and included a sawmill. Today Lyons Building Centre Ltd. is still located at the same Wellington Street site (below). The two-storey brick building at the right of the old photograph is still in use and can be seen in the recent photograph at far right, beyond the lumber piles in the foreground.*

in 1926 and 1929 but lost in the two following elections. During the darkest years of the Depression he served as the Sault's mayor.

His son Harry C. Lyons later followed in his father's footsteps and was elected Member of the Provincial Parliament in 1951. He held the seat until his death in 1962. Harry and his brothers, Earl and Bill, were actively engaged in management of the business after their father died in 1947.

Earl recalls his father had 10 teams of horses to deliver coal and coke, and one team would make seven deliveries per day. The teamsters could unload one ton of coal in five minutes. The shovels held 50 pounds, and 40 shovelfuls equalled a ton. A disastrous fire swept Lyons' stable in 1922, killing 19 horses. It was replaced with a fireproof brick barn.

Coal was the first material handled by the firm, but the enterprise grew to include a sawmill and lumber business, a hardware store, a concrete plant that supplied pipe to Algoma Central Railway and the city, and a ready-mix cement plant.

Lyons Building Centre Ltd. is still located at the same Wellington Street West site, but it has expanded from a wholesale and contractor-oriented firm to include a retail outlet offering ready-mix concrete, concrete products, building materials, lumber, paint, and plumbing supplies.

President Richard Beaumont was part of a group of local businessmen who purchased the company from the

*Before founding Lyons Fuel & Supply Company, of which he was also president and general manager, in 1912, James Lyons had worked as a stonemason, butcher, grocer, and laborer. Active in city politics shortly after his turn-of-the century arrival in Sault Ste. Marie from a small Lake Simcoe farming community, he became a Steelton councillor in 1908, served as Steelton mayor from 1911 to 1913, was appointed Minister of Lands and Forest in Conservative government, and was elected Member of the Provincial Parliament in 1926 and 1929.*

Lyons estate in 1958. A few years later he became sole owner, and continues to operate the firm with his son, David.

Beaumont has been president of the Kiwanis Club, the United Way of Sault Ste. Marie, and the Construction Association. He has also served as northern Ontario representative on the United Way national board and as chairman of the board of the Algoma District Homes for the Aged.

# DAWSON AND KEENAN INSURANCE LTD.

For nearly a century the name of one of Sault Ste. Marie's pioneer families has been associated with insurance and real estate. English-born John Dawson emigrated to Canada in 1869, and although the date of his arrival in the Sault is unknown, he is listed in the 1881 census, and by 1892 had established Dawson Real Estate and Fire Insurance.

The first agent for London Life in the Sault, his business was located on the corner of Queen and Elgin streets, but later moved to 112 East Street. Influential and respected, he was considered one of the town's prominent men. He was an alderman and was active with many local organizations, including the Children's Aid Society, which he was instrumental in founding. Also a partner in a grocery business, Dawson preferred to stay in the background, channeling his energy into real estate and insurance.

In 1898 he built a three-storey sandstone building at the busy intersection of Queen and East streets. The Dawson Block (708-714 Queen Street East) housed the grocery operated by his two sons, James and George. Four years later he sold the block to his sons.

James Dawson joined his father's insurance business in 1915—the same year its founder died. For three years James and George attempted to carry on both businesses, but by 1918 they had split the operations. James was running the insurance firm, and George had a new partner in the Dawson and Gibson Grocery.

James continued his father's community involvement. An alderman for two years, he was mayor of the city from 1922 to 1925. Born in the Sault in 1879, he gained the distinction of being the city's first native-born mayor.

A third generation of the family became part of the business in 1932, when James' son Fred joined the firm,

which became Dawson and Dawson Real Estate and Insurance. After his father's death in 1941, Fred became owner-manager of Fred J. Dawson Real Estate and Insurance.

In September 1959 the firm moved to a new building at 121 Brock Street, and three years later Dawson merged with competitor Clifford Keenan.

In 1978 the firm became associated with the Century 21 real estate network and continues to market real estate very successfully using the Century 21 referral system.

A new era came to Dawson and Keenan Insurance Ltd. when Arthur Day joined the firm as a junior partner

*The Dawson Block, built in 1898, housed both the family grocery operation and the real estate and insurance business. Standing in the doorway (in black suit and bowler hat) is John Dawson.*

in 1962. By 1973 he had purchased the business from the now-retired partners. He continues to operate Dawson and Keenan, but a second generation of his family, daughter Elaine Foster and son Laurence Day, are company shareholders.

Thirty-two people are employed by Dawson and Keenan Insurance Ltd., which offers a complete insurance and real estate service, at its offices in the Sault, Wawa, and Toronto.

# ST. MARYS PAPER INC.

*This building, which houses the headquarters of St. Marys Paper Inc., once included the offices for the Clergue empire. In 1896 a mill was completed on the site.*

St. Marys Paper Inc. can credit its existence to two entrepreneurs—Francis H. Clergue, who built the mill in the 1890s, and Dan Alexander, who gave it a new lease on life 90 years later.

Attracted to Sault Ste. Marie by the hydroelectric potential of the St. Mary's River rapids, Clergue found, after harnessing the turbulent waters, that the town lacked the industrial development to purchase the power. The most obvious answer to his dilemma was to establish his own industries. His Lake Superior Corp. constructed a pulp mill, a steel plant, a railway, and foundries. The Sault Ste. Marie Pulp and Sulphite Company groundwood paper mill was completed in 1896 on land that in the late 1700s had been the site of a trading post. The sulphite mill went into operation between 1901 and 1902.

In September 1903 Clergue's empire crashed. With no money to meet payrolls or operating expenses, the industries were shut down. Unpaid bush, mine, and construction workers rioted, smashing windows in the firm's Huron Street office. Local militia and troops from Toronto were dispatched to quell the disturbance.

Operations at the groundwood mill continued until 1910, when it was shut down for reconstruction, and the first newsprint paper mill was built in the Sault by a new organization known as the Lake Superior Paper Co. Four new paper machines were installed before 1913, and between 1915 and 1917 the sulphite pulp mill doubled its capacity. In 1917 Lake Superior amalgamated with the Spanish River Pulp and Paper Mills.

The groundwood mill was expanded further in 1918 and 1926. Abitibi Power and Paper Co. bought the Sault operation in 1928. Major alterations to the four paper machines followed during the next two years, and they operated almost continuously until World War II. After the war more changes and modernizations took place, and in the 1970s the mill moved to groundwood specialties, paper used in catalogues, paperbacks, telephone directories, and advertising supplements.

Then, in May 1983, Abitibi-Price Inc. permanently shut down the No. 2 paper machine in an attempt to increase the ageing mill's efficiency. The mill, however, continued to incur substantial losses; with the threat of closure looming, its sagging fortunes and those of its 460 workers got a reprieve.

Chicago businessman Dan Alexander, heading a three-company con-

*The stores department in the Sault mill of the Spanish River Pulp & Paper Mills, three years after Lake Superior Paper Co. amalgamated with Spanish River.*

sortium, purchased the failing Sault mill and set about turning it into a profitable operation. The consortium included D.C. Northam Inc., a firm created by Alexander to fulfill his dream of acquiring his own paper mill.

St. Marys Paper Inc., taking its name from the river adjacent to which it stands (minus the apostrophe lost in the bureaucratic shuffle of registering the company's name with the federal government), began business on June 1, 1984.

The fledgling company immediately undertook a $20-million project to convert the mill to produce supercalendered paper, a glossy paper stock used in full-color advertising

A new building (above) is being constructed to house the PM No. 5 paper machine (left), a new addition to St. Marys Paper Inc.

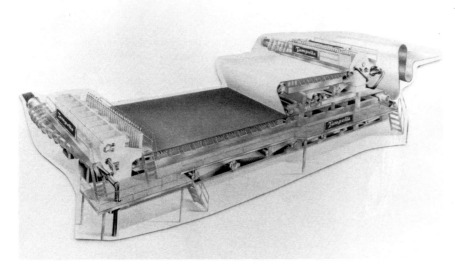

such as newspaper inserts.

After St. Marys took over, the once-struggling mill began turning a profit, and in 1985 president and chief executive officer Alexander announced the firm, along with a major Finnish pulp and paper manufacturer, would look for expansion possibilities in Canada and the United States. Rauma Repola OY of Helsinki became the fourth shareholder in St. Marys when it acquired an interest in the company in April 1985.

Weak markets for supercalendered paper in 1985 forced St. Marys

to delay plans to expand the mill. Two years later, however, work began on a $135-million expansion that will create roughly 30 jobs and double the mill's output. Another 150 independent loggers will be employed in neighboring woodlands, cutting and transporting logs to the mill. When completed in November 1988, annual production capacity will have increased 88 percent, to 220,000 tons from 125,000 tons, and its modern technology will enable the mill to compete with any other producer in the world.

Alexander, sitting in his office in the historic Huron Street sandstone building that once housed Clergue's operations, describes the expansion as "the most significant thing to happen to the mill in 75 years." Installation of the new equipment at the mill, which employs 405 workers, will give St. Marys the first machine in Canada "specifically designed to manufacture supercalendered paper."

Ninety-seven percent of St. Marys Paper's $100 million in annual business is in the American market. Following the expansion it will become the second-largest producer of supercalendered paper in North America.

Alexander says he and his fellow shareholders in St. Marys Paper Inc. are extremely proud of the accomplishments of senior management and all of the employees in making the company a success. It is their hard work, dedication, and drive to succeed that has enabled the mill to return to profitability and to receive its first new paper machine in 75 years.

# WOOD GUNDY INC.

While Wood Gundy Inc. may be new to Sault Ste. Marie, the investment firm has been a Canadian institution for more than 80 years.

Officially opened on October 15, 1987, at 659-661 Queen Street East, the Sault branch is the third brokerage office in the city. It also is part of a network of financial services organizations that began in Toronto 83 years earlier and now includes 50 offices operating in eight countries and staffed by 1,950 people.

The network traces its roots to George Herbert Wood and James Henry Gundy, who formed a partnership in 1905 and entered the investment business under the name of Wood, Gundy and Co. The business was confined primarily to underwriting and distributing government and municipal bonds, but this began to change after World War I.

As Canada developed industrially, investor interest extended to the bonds and shares that resulted from the growth of the country's railways and transportation systems, production of hydroelectric power, and the development and expansion of many basic industries, including newsprint and forest products, cement, steel, chemicals, agricultural machinery, and the operation of retail stores.

Wood Gundy entered the international financial markets arena in 1910, when it opened an office in London, England, to assist in raising capital to meet Canada's growing financial requirements. At that time London was the principal source of capital funds available to Canada, but during World War I the London market gave way to the U.S. capital market, and Wood Gundy established an office in New York in 1916. That same year the firm opened its first Canadian branch office in Montreal, followed by Winnipeg in 1920 and Vancouver in 1928.

The firm was incorporated as a private company, Wood, Gundy and Company Ltd., in 1925, with G.H. Wood as chairman and J.H. Gundy as president. Wood remained with the firm until he retired in 1932, and Gundy, who was succeeded as president by his son C.L. Gundy in 1948, continued as chairman until his death in 1951. C.L. Gundy remained as chairman until his death in 1978.

Wood Gundy Inc. employees are encouraged to become involved in community projects, and over the years a number of its directors have headed major charitable and public interest fund-raising campaigns. During the two world wars members of the firm took a prominent and active part in the Victory Loan committees and National War Finance committees that organized the distribution of War Loan and Victory Loan Bonds.

*G.H. Wood (left) and J.H. Gundy formed a partnership in 1905, entering the investment business under the name Wood, Gundy and Company. Originally limited to underwriting and distributing government and municipal bonds, the firm expanded into international markets in 1910, when it established an office in London, England.*

# FLEMING AND SMITH LTD.

E. Bruce Fleming's name is synonymous with real estate in Sault Ste. Marie. He first started in the real estate and insurance business in 1927 and, except for five years during World War II, worked in the profession until his retirement in 1977. The Sault Ste. Marie native remains chairman of the board of Fleming and Smith Ltd., a company he formed in 1966 with Ray Smith.

Fleming started in the business with Tom Chitty Insurance, and by the time he went overseas in 1940 he was a junior partner. Discharged in 1945 with the rank of major, he returned to the Sault, where he purchased the Hesson Insurance Agency and formed Fleming Insurance Services.

In 1950 he purchased 354-356 Queen Street East and formed E. Bruce Fleming Ltd. Eleven years later he sold the insurance business to his nephew and godson, David Sawer, and relocated his real estate office, then called North Channel Realty, upstairs.

Fleming and Smith Ltd. was founded on December 5, 1966. Rod McLeod joined the firm a year later as a partner, and when Fleming retired, he and Smith bought the com-

*Rod McLeod and Ray Smith purchased Fleming and Smith Ltd. in 1977.*

pany. In the late 1960s Fleming purchased a building at 378 Queen Street East, and in 1970 the firm moved to this location, which it still occupies.

Fleming and Smith has the oldest and largest property management department in the Sault, managing more than 800 residential, commercial, and industrial units. It has had a separate appraisal department since 1966, and was the listing agent for all Canada Mortgage and Housing Corp. properties in the area for more than five years.

The firm assembled land for the first phase of the municipality's Industrial Park, and negotiated all easements and land purchases for the new west end sewage disposal and treatment plants.

Fleming was the first president of the Ontario Association of Real Estate Boards (1962) from outside the major southern Ontario centres. In 1984 he received a life membership from the Ontario Real Estate Association, as it was later renamed. In addition, he served as president of the Sault Real Estate Board, as president of Plummer Memorial Hospital, and

was a member of the Downtown Kiwanis Club.

Toronto born and educated, Smith moved to the Sault in 1962, and received his real estate licence two years later. A two-time president of the local real estate board, he has also been president of the Lakeshore Kiwanis Club and the Sault Ste. Marie Mental Health Association. Smith sat on the Sault Planning Board for two years and is a former member of the Court of Revision and the Sault Ste. Marie Economic Development Advisory Board. Currently he is a member of the Ontario Assessment Review Board and has been since its inception in 1971.

McLeod, the only chartered accountant practicing real estate in the Sault, is treasurer of the real estate board and a member of the Waterfront Steering Committee. He is a past president of Lakeshore Kiwanis and a former treasurer of the Sault Ste. Marie Chamber of Commerce.

*E. Bruce Fleming rose to the rank of major during World War II, and when the conflict ended he returned to the Sault and the insurance business.*

# J.P. PIERMAN CONSTRUCTION LTD.

In 10 years J.P. Pierman Construction Ltd. has grown from a one-man operation in John Pierman's Goulais River home to the largest general contractor in Sault Ste. Marie. With headquarters in a 4,000-square-foot building on Drive-In Road in the Sault and a business volume of $22 million in the 1987 fiscal year, the company has come a long way from the days when it was renovating cottages and building decks.

Headed by 33-year-old John Pierman, the firm does commercial, institutional, and industrial construction work throughout northern Ontario, and has been involved in projects as far away as Nova Scotia, where it helped Rio Algoma open up the first tin mine in North America. The East Coast project took 18 months, and Pierman compares it to building a "little city" in the bush. The company did all the clearing, grading, sewer, and water work, as well as constructing an administration building and carpenter shop for the mine.

In the years when the recession slowed down the construction industry in the Sault and most of northern Ontario, Pierman's firm

*J.P. Pierman's many construction projects have included Chapleau Co-generation Station (left) and Sault Ste. Marie Federal Airport (above).*

managed to keep busy. "When there wasn't much going on in the whole north it made us get versatile, working out of town," says Pierman, the company's owner and only shareholder. He estimates the corporation still does 50 percent of its work outside the Sault.

His volume of business has ballooned from $1.5 million in 1982 to $7.9 million in 1985 and $15.3 million in 1986. Pierman's interest in construction dates back to his childhood, when he helped his dad

build cottages and houses in the Goulais River area, where his family lived and operated a sawmill. During his high school years he worked with his brother's excavation business.

A graduate of Sault College's construction engineering and technology program, Pierman was employed with R.M. Elliott Construction Ltd. for two years before venturing out on his own. He set up his own business in 1976, incorporated it in June 1977, and for the next four years did small residential projects.

The first major contract came in 1981, when the young firm built Ferroclad Fishery Ltd.'s processing plant at Mamainse Harbour north of the

Sault. The following year it constructed the city's new $1.2-million central firehall, and "it mushroomed from there."

Pierman was soon putting up buildings in the Sudbury area, Manitoulin Island, Marathon, New Liskeard, Kapuskasing, Elliot Lake, and Owen Sound. The enterprise renovated and built a $3.2-million addition to Sault Ste. Marie's federal airport, and in 1986 it was involved with an unusual project—constructing the first waste wood-burning hydroelectric plant in Ontario. The plant produces electricity for the town of Chapleau and three local lumber mills.

The Tarentorus Fish Hatchery, a welfare building for employees at

Algoma Steel Corp.'s No. 2 tube mill, and an extension to the F.J. Davey Home for the Aged are among the long list of buildings that attest to Pierman's construction abilities. A $6.4-million addition to a hospital in Espanola is the company's largest single project, but Pierman anticipates he will be involved with larger projects in the years to come. Construction of a $4.6-million hospital project began in the spring of 1988 in Hornepayne.

After operating out of his garage in the early years, Pierman set up a little office in a 10- by 12-foot room above the H.R. Lash clothing store on John Street in 1980. He later moved to the industrial mall, before erecting his own building in 1985.

In February 1988 the company expanded its operations, opening an office in Sudbury, 185 miles east of the Sault, where Pierman does a lot of work. Among the projects his operation has worked on in the Nickel City is Crothers Ltd.'s headquarters.

Depending on the season and the work, Pierman's work force varies from 30 to well in excess of 100 employees—a substantial jump from the early days, when it numbered the founder and three or four others. Pierman's wife, Vicki, is the company's vice-president and runs the office.

J.P. Pierman Construction Ltd. is a dealer for Robertson Building Systems (pre-engineered metal building structures), and in 1984-1985 was third in sales in Canada.

John Pierman serves on the board of directors of the Sault Ste. Marie Construction Association and the Canadian Construction Association. He also is first vice-president of the Economic Development Corporation, a body established by the city council to switch Sault Ste. Marie's emphasis from a single major employer (Algoma Steel), and to create and promote commercial, industrial, and tourism development.

# CHITTY INSURANCE BROKERS LTD.

Thomas Chitty first came to Sault Ste. Marie at the turn of the century as a secretary to financier Francis H. Clergue. A graduate of Pitman's Shorthand College in London, England, he was employed by the American-born founder of the city's steel, paper, and rail industries for five years, before moving to Espanola to work in the sales department of the Spanish River Pulp and Paper Co.

After following the lure of the gold rush to Porcupine, Ontario, where he was involved in mining properties and real estate, he returned to the Sault in 1910 and established a business that still bears his name. Mr. Chitty founded his real estate and insurance agency in partnership with John W. Moffly and Charles Chipley. Located at 518 Queen Street East, it also had an office in the Michigan Sault, listed the choicest business properties in town, and wrote all forms of insurance.

When Moffly died in 1914, the partnership was dissolved, and Chitty joined James W. Blair to form the Chitty-Blair Agency at 496 Queen Street East. In 1933 Blair retired, and the agency became Chitty Insurance Agency Ltd. It was then located at 485 Queen Street East, next to its present office.

When World War II ended in 1945, son William R. Chitty, a distinguished veteran who had served with the Royal Canadian Artillery, joined

*The Chitty Insurance Agency at 485 Queen Street. Photo circa 1935*

the firm. A new building was erected at 495 Queen Street East. Thomas Chitty retired four years later, and the firm became William R. Chitty Insurance and Real Estate Ltd. William Chitty ran the business for 10 years, until he died of a heart attack in 1959. His wife took over the family business after his death, and in 1960 her brother-in-law, E.L. "Ed" Klym, became associated with the agency.

The first female broker in north-

*Chitty Insurance Brokers Ltd., located at 495 Queen Street, adjacent to its previous location, is owned and managed by Ed Klym, a relative of the Chitty family.*

ern Ontario, Hazel Chitty was also the first female to serve as president of the Sault Ste. Marie Real Estate Board (1965) and the first female president of the Sault and District Chamber of Commerce (1969-1970).

In 1978 Mr. Klym became owner/manager and incorporated the name Chitty Insurance Agency Ltd. When he purchased the firm, it was still a real estate and insurance company, but he decided to concentrate on just one area—insurance. With the advent of the Registered Insurance Brokers of Ontario Act, the name was changed in 1981 to Chitty Insurance Brokers Ltd.

Today the firm, an independent insurance brokerage representing such well-known corporations as Zurich Insurance Co., Economical Mutual, and Halifax Insurance Co., specializes in personal lines of insurance. Many of the customers who have life, automobile, and homeowners' coverage with Chitty Insurance Brokers Ltd. are the third and fourth generations of their families to be insured by the firm.

# THE PROCTOR & REDFERN GROUP

The Proctor & Redfern Group has been involved with all major sewer and water projects in Sault Ste. Marie since the firm of consulting engineers and planners was founded in 1912. But the Toronto firm's association with the Sault goes even deeper. One of its early principals, W.B. Redfern, was town engineer for Steelton, an adjoining community that amalgamated with the Sault in 1918.

The Sault office, opened in 1959, also is among the oldest existing branches of Proctor & Redfern, which is one of the oldest consulting engineering firms in Ontario.

E.A. James, the first engineer for the Toronto and York Roads Commission, founded the organization in 1912 when he set up his private practice. The rapidly growing number of cars in the province had created a demand for roadway engineering, and many centres had requested his assistance. In 1916 engineer E.M. Proctor joined the firm to head up the bridge design section, and three years later Redfern, a classmate of Proctor's, entered the business.

They became owners of the practice with James in 1922, and it was incorporated as James, Proctor & Redfern Ltd. James died five years later, but his name was carried through to

*Sault Ste. Marie Public Utilities Commission Water Filtration Plant.*

*Proctor & Redfern has been involved with many municipal engineering projects, including the Sault Ste. Marie Water Filtration Plant. W.B. Redfern (at right center, standing on pipe) was the consulting engineer. Photo circa 1934*

1945, when the firm became the partnership of Proctor & Redfern. Later both Proctor & Redfern's sons joined the firm, taking the association into the second generation.

When the firm marked its 75th anniversary in 1987, it had grown to one of the largest consulting firms in the province.

In Sault Ste. Marie, Proctor & Redfern has done municipal engineering projects—sewer, water, roadwork, and bridges. The water-filtration plant, sewage-treatment plant, water tower, and most of the

watermains were all done by the firm. It was the engineer for the Queenstown development in the city's downtown, and all major flood-control channels throughout the city. It also has been involved with subdivision developments, site plans for small shopping centres and mini-malls, and projects for the two local school boards and Algoma Steel Corp.

The Proctor & Redfern Group has broadened its base, augmenting its municipal services to provide a full range of engineering services, including mechanical, electrical, and structural to institutional, commercial, and industrial projects. With a staff of 25, including nine engineers, the Sault office services a vast area, reaching from Sudbury in the east to Marathon in the west.

# BOSTON MOTORS LTD.

The Boston name has been a driving force in Sault Ste. Marie for more than 55 years.

After trying his hand at many businesses and trades, A.F. "Fergie" Boston began selling cars at Lynch Auto Sales in 1928. Five years later, heading a group of shareholders, he took over the Ford dealership and formed the company that bears his name. Gradually he bought out the other stockholders, and by the mid-1950s he gained full control of the firm, then located at 66 Spring Street. Under his leadership Boston Motors Ltd.'s sales moved from 75 units in the early days to more than 200 by 1940.

In 1952 Boston switched from a Ford to a General Motors dealership, and sales of new units soon reached the 450 mark. The Spring Street garage, with its service department, offices, and showroom, was expanded over the years, but by 1957 the firm needed more room. Construction of a modern building began at 775 Queen Street East, and the structure was opened in February 1958. The new building contained a combination showroom, sales office, and maintenance centre to tie in with Boston's body shop on nearby Thomas Street.

Fergie Boston's sons, Robert and Pat, began operating the business in 1960, renaming it Boston Bros. Seven years later Pat left to open his own firm and Bob became sole owner. In 1977, following Bob's death, his son, Fergie Jr., who had been working with the company since 1975, took over. Brothers Robert and William also work in the business.

The firm, which originally started with 18 employees, boasted 60 in 1988, working in the sales, service, leasing, and parts departments. On May 1, 1988, Boston's added a new operation, selling and servicing cars at 826 Queen Street East.

Fergie Boston, the third generation of his family to sell cars, has noted a vast change in the industry in the past years. "In the past we sold cars; now I run an organization with more than $20 million in business a year," he says.

A past director of the Ontario Automobile Dealers Association, Boston is a director of the Northern General Motors Dealers Association and the General Motors Dealer Council for Ontario. He is active with a number of community organizations, serving as a director with the Economic Development Corporation, the Industrial Accident Prevention Association, and the Kidney Foundation. In addition, he is chairman of the Heritage Committee, which is working to revitalize the Pim to East Street blocks of Queen Street.

*A.F. "Fergie" Boston (below), who founded Boston Motors Ltd. in the early 1930s, started with 18 employees. He was succeeded by his son, Robert S. Boston (below right), who owned the company until his death in 1977. Today Boston Motors Ltd., still owned and operated by the Boston family, boasts 60 employees and more than $20 million in business per year.*

# NORTHERN CREDIT UNION LIMITED

Northern Credit Union Limited, a financial cooperative, got its start when 28 people employed in various city departments and Great Lakes Power signed the original charter. Each kicked in two dollars, and this initial deposit of $56 started the ball rolling. From this humble beginning the credit union's membership has swelled in its 30 years to reach 29,000 members across northeastern Ontario (18,000 in Sault Ste. Marie), and its assets have increased to more than $99 million. Northern Credit Union is now a community bond credit union serving members of all ages, occupations, and income levels in five major areas of northeastern Ontario.

Credit unions were organized to fill a critical need, says Len Strom, now Northern Credit Union's general manager. "At that time banks were not really taking care of the needs of working persons," he recalls. "Their personal loan and mortgage policies were very restrictive."

The first Northern Credit Union loan was made in February 1958 at the kitchen table in treasurer Len Strom's home. The Sault Civic Employees Credit Union, as it was incorporated November 17, 1957, had its office in Strom's basement for six years. During that time it was operated by Len; his wife, Geri; and Roy Bernardi. A permanent home was not

found until September 1964, when the office was relocated to a frame farmhouse at 264 McNabb Street.

Construction of a new building began in 1969 at the same site, and by the following year the Sault of Ontario Credit Union, as it had been renamed, officially opened its doors.

The credit union underwent a name change in 1977, when it became the Soo & District of Algoma Credit Union, to reflect the area and people it served after opening a branch in Wawa. Over the years the Sault-based financial institution purchased the assets of numerous other credit unions organized by groups of employees and labor unions. In 1985, after merging with two smaller credit unions located in North Bay and Timmins, it became Northern Credit Union Limited.

A total of 80 full-time and part-time workers are employed at the credit union's branches in Wawa, Elliot Lake, North Bay, Timmins, Thessalon, and the Sault. A full-service financial institution, it offers loans, mortgages, chequing and savings ac-

*Arthur A. Wishart, provincial attorney general, and John Rhodes, mayor, participated in the steel-ribbon-cutting ceremony celebrating the completion of the new offices in 1970.*

counts, Term Deposits, Registered Retirement Savings Plans, Registered Retirement Income Funds, MasterCard II, Northernline, Gold MasterCard, Club 55, the Business 1, the Investment 1, and automated teller machines, which are connected with the INTERAC and PLUS Systems, at six branches.

Northern Credit Union was one of the first Sault Ste. Marie financial institutions to computerize and the second to install automated teller machines. It began offering daily interest savings accounts in 1968, more than a decade before banks introduced the service, and was the first credit union in northern Ontario to go into weekly and biweekly payment plans for mortgages. In April 1988 it became the first credit union in the nation to offer a Gold MasterCard. Over the years Northern Credit Union has helped thousands of members finance homes, cottages, boats, vacations, and educations for their children.

With its quality service and competitive rates, Northern Credit Union Limited can be expected to continue to grow in the coming years.

*Northern Credit Union Limited got its start in 1957, but it wasn't until 1964 that it relocated to 264 McNabb Street. Shown in front of that first office are charter members Chester Edwards, Harry Wiley, Doug Gemmel, Ray Stares, and Len Strom.*

# DOWNTOWN INSURANCE AND REALTY LTD.

While the "Dial" name has been associated with insurance and real estate in Sault Ste. Marie for 20 years, the company has roots that go back to 1945. That is the year World War II ended and E. Bruce Fleming returned from duty overseas, where he had earned the rank of major and was company commander in the first battalion of the Hampshire Regiment, 50th Division.

Fleming had entered the insurance business in 1927 and became interested in real estate four years later. When he returned to civilian life in Sault Ste. Marie, he established an insurance and real estate business.

He opened the offices of Fleming Insurance Services on Queen Street East, in a building that had housed Sault Business College. John A. Furse, who also was in the insurance and real estate business for many years, operated the business college there from 1911 until his death in 1943. The land-

mark building, later a Barnes Wines store, was destroyed by fire in 1980.

Four years after Fleming set up

shop, Charles H. Lefave started with the company as the first salesman.

In 1954 Fleming purchased another downtown building at 356 Queen Street East and relocated his business. Along with the new facility came a new name—E. Bruce Fleming Ltd. The same year that he moved to the new office, David B. Sawer joined the company, and then, in 1957, Donald McBain started working with them.

Sawer and McBain purchased the business from Fleming in 1961, and eight years later they also purchased the building. The two men changed the name to Downtown Independent Associates Ltd. and began using the trade name Dial.

In January 1977 Vincent Tagliabracci, Peter Orlando, Charles Lefave, and John M. Campbell pur-

*Above: The staff of E. Bruce Fleming Ltd. when the office was located at 356 Queen Street East.*

*Left: E. Bruce Fleming (at door) opened an insurance and real estate business after World War II.*

chased the business from Sawer. Tagliabracci had joined the firm in July 1973, and Orlando three years later in March 1976. After the sale in 1977, the name was changed to Downtown Independent Associates Insurance and Realty Ltd. Campbell sold his shares to the remaining shareholders in 1979.

In 1982 Dial Insurance and Realty Ltd. moved across the street into 2,500 square feet of sales space on the ground floor of the McCarda office building (former Sault Star building) at 369 Queen Street East. Efficiency was improved with the move. The company was able to "go on line" with its computer centre, and the new location also enabled the owners to introduce the latest in telephone and filing systems. With the relocation the corporate name was short-

*Charles Lefave (third from right in the back row), Donald McBain (second from right), and David Sawer (first on right), with the staff in the late 1960s.*

*The Dial staff in the early 1970s.*

ened to Downtown Insurance and Realty Ltd. Lefave retired in January 1986, and in October of that same year the business moved to its present location at 384 Queen Street East.

Downtown Insurance and Realty Ltd., owned by Tagliabracci and Orlando, employs 25 people and offers a range of general insurance and real estate services. All types of insurance, including home, auto, commercial, industrial, business, boats, motorcycles, and life insurance, are handled by the company.

Residential, commercial, business, and industrial real estate, along with mortgages and property management, are among the realty services available at Downtown Insurance and Realty Ltd.

# THE SAULT STAR

The first edition of the *Sault Daily Star* rolled off the press on March 16, 1912, with the news that Sault Ste. Marie would soon be incorporated as a city. The newspaper's debut as a daily sold for 2 cents and came 11 years after veteran newsman James W. Curran launched *The Sault Weekly Star*.

Curran and his brother John had purchased the paper from two other brothers, Uriah and Moses McFadden. The McFaddens had been publishing the weekly, believed to have been founded in 1895, under the name of the *Sault Courier*.

Located in a 16- by 40-foot frame building on East Street, the newspaper's equipment had seen better days when Curran took it over. The paper, with a total circulation of fewer than 2,000, was printed on an ancient, hand-operated flat-bed press that had printed Winnipeg's first paper years earlier. The *Star*'s tiny office could not serve a growing community, so in 1905 Curran relocated to a two-storey building at 374 Queen Street East. These quarters were home to the paper until 1951, when it moved across the street to a newly constructed building at 369 Queen Street. This facility was expanded seven years later to accommodate the growing newspaper operation.

*The present home of* The Sault Star *is at 145 Old Garden River Road.*

Curran believed a newspaper had a duty to promote its community and used the *Star* to boost the Sault and Algoma district. He gained the most publicity for the area by "crying wolf" in his articles, and his challenge that "any man that says he's been et by a wolf is a liar" became legend. He offered $100 to anyone who could prove he was "et by a wolf." No one ever collected, and his book, *Wolves Don't Bite*, made the *Sault Star* wolf world famous. The newspaper, which in 1988 boasted a circulation of roughly 27,000, continues to have a wolf on its front page masthead, a symbol that has been part of the daily paper for more than 60 years.

Ill health forced Curran to resign in 1941. The paper remained family owned, with his son Robert L. Curran as publisher until 1975, when it was sold to Southam Press Ltd. (now Southam Inc.).

After the sale William Dane, who had been publisher of another Southam paper in Owen Sound, was named publisher. When he retired in 1987, Sault native Clifford Sharp, publisher of the *North Bay Nugget*, re-placed him.

*The Sault Star* ("Daily" was dropped from the name in 1975) moved to a new, $1.4-million building at 145 Old Garden River Road in 1979. Along with the move, part of a major $2.35-million expansion program, came a new offset press and technological changes that have computerized production of the newspaper.

*From 1905 to 1951 this building at 374 Queen Street East was home to* The Sault Star.

# YMCA

The Young Men's Christian Association of Sault Ste. Marie was organized at a December 17, 1900, meeting in St. Andrew's Presbyterian Church. Its goal, like other YMCAs of the day, was the spiritual improvement of young men.

In the early years the Y was located in the Express Building on Queen Street, but following a 1912 fund-raising campaign, it was able to construct its own building. Official opening of the $70,000, three-storey brick building at 123 March Street took place in the spring of 1913.

Financing the institution was a problem, and in 1920, struggling under a burden of debt and declining interest, the Y was forced to cease activities and lease the building. For the next four years it was operated as an Algoma Steel Corp. athletic club with accommodations for bachelors employed at the plant.

In 1925 a group of citizens determined to revive the YMCA were able to reopen the March Street facility. This was accomplished with financial assistance from 10 local men who promised to contribute $5,000 annually for three years and a group who guaranteed $2,500 toward retiring the mortgage. The Y rented rooms on the third floor of its building and, although women and girls were allowed membership privileges in 1915, the accommodations were for men only.

By the late 1950s the YMCA was the "busiest place in town." The ever-increasing membership was taxing the facilities, and the board of directors began looking at expanding or constructing a new, larger building. It

*In the late 1950s the YMCA was "the busiest place in town." Shown here is the swimming pool at the former March Street facility, built and opened in 1913.*

*The YMCA relocated to its present McNabb Street facility in 1965 because of increasing membership. It was expanded in 1972 and 1982.*

took time, but a site was finally obtained in 1963, and a campaign to raise one million dollars was initiated.

The new family YMCA on McNabb Street officially opened in 1965. It underwent a major expansion in 1972 and another one a decade later as memberships soared to 5,300, more than double the number than when it moved to the new site. With the advent of health spas, membership dropped and settled at 3,800 in the mid-1980s.

Funded 86 percent through membership and program fees, with the remainder coming from the United Way and government sources, the Y's facilities include men's and women's health clubs, indoor track and fitness area, gymnasium, weight rooms, saunas, whirlpools, racquet courts, and two swimming pools. It operates a 64-place day nursery, a Youth Employment Services centre, and many recreational and leisure programs.

For many years the Y had a residential camping program at Camp Pauwating at Upper Island Lake north of the Sault. In 1963 it began using the site as a day camp, and as a youth hostel from 1967 to 1972. The waterfront portion of the camp was sold in 1977, but the YMCA still retains the rest of the property for hiking and other outdoor activities.

# CITY OF SAULT STE. MARIE

"Ojibwa Kitche Gumeeng Odena—Ojibway town next to big body of water" reads the inscription on the City of Sault Ste. Marie's crest. The words are as symbolic as are the other parts of the crest, created in 1912 when Sault Ste. Marie was incorporated as a city. A British crown, a Canadian beaver, maple leaves, a steelworker, an Indian, steel rails, the ship canal, a steamer, and pine and hemlock trees represent the heritage and history of a community that traces its origins back thousands of years to when the Indians gathered at the rapids to trade and fish.

When the Sault was incorporated as a city on April 16, 1912—25 years after incorporation as a town and 41 after gaining status as a village—it had a population of 13,502. Seventy-five years later it had swelled to more than 80,000, a major northern Ontario urban centre at the hub of the Great Lakes.

In 1918 the Sault and Steelton, a nearby town that grew up around Algoma Steel Corp., were amalgamated, boosting the population to 21,500. The union of the city with the townships of Tarentorus and Korah in 1965 increased the population to 70,052.

In 1912 the City Hall, Carnegie Public Library, and Fire Hall were located on Queen Street East in a complex that had been reconstructed after fire had ravaged it five years earlier. The blaze destroyed three buildings that had cost $39,000 and were only insured for $19,000. The library, constructed with a $10,000 grant from American steel magnate and philanthropist Andrew Carnegie, had only been insured for $4,500. The fire department was next door, and, as town clerk Charles Pim put it, "both were considered as absolutely safe from destruction by fire." Carnegie accused the Sault of being "penny wise and pound foolish" but eventually was persuaded to provide an additional

*W.H. Munro was mayor when Sault Ste. Marie officially became a city in 1912.*

$5,000 to rebuild the library.

The Queen Street buildings housed the city fathers and municipal offices until a new $4.3-million Civic Centre, overlooking the St. Mary's

*Sault Ste. Marie's new waterfront Civic Centre opened in 1975.*

River, was opened in 1975. The new building, with its distinctive porcelain steel panels and gold tint glass, is the focal point of the city's waterfront development.

The fire department had been relocated to a new central fire hall at the corner of Bruce and Wellington streets in 1922. In 1983 a $1.7-million facility at Bay and Tancred streets replaced the 60-year-old fire hall.

A new library opened in 1967 on East Street, and by 1987 circulation of books stood at 660,048 at the main library and its three branches. In 1912 circulation was 27,901.

W.H. Munro was mayor when the Sault officially became a city; when the municipality celebrated its 75th anniversary in 1987, Joe Fratesi was the 23rd mayor since incorporation.

*Mayor Joe Fratesi, Sault Ste. Marie's 23rd mayor.*

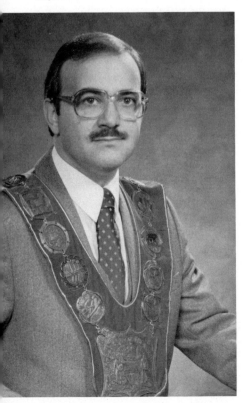

The city embarked on a new form of municipal government in 1962, when a city administrator was appointed to co-ordinate all activities of civic administration and implement the city council's policies. W.J. McMeeken, who had served 13 years as alderman, 9 years as mayor, and 17 years as city treasurer was named to the position, which he held until his death in 1967. Allan Jackson, who became administrator in 1981, says the city has been functioning as a true council/administrator form of local government since 1967. Issues are dealt with by the council—the mayor and 12 aldermen—through the co-ordination and direction of the administrator with 10 civic departments.

A modern, bustling border city on the banks of the St. Mary's River, the Sault has been linked to its Michigan twin by the International Bridge since 1962.

The municipality provides numerous services, ranging from transit to cemeteries, day care centres to marinas, sports complexes to garbage collection and snow removal.

Bellevue Park on Queen Street East has picnic areas, a wild animal zoo, greenhouse displays, summer concerts, and winter skating and cross-country skiing. Pointe des Chenes Park, 10 miles west of downtown Sault Ste. Marie, offers camping, picnic, and swimming areas on Lake Superior. The city also operates playgrounds and neighborhood parks throughout the community, two indoor pools and two outdoor pools, three arenas, a drop-in centre for senior citizens, and a fish hatchery.

For most of the century Sault Ste. Marie has been largely dependent on the fortunes and jobs at its major employer, Algoma Steel Corp. However, when the steel industry underwent a worldwide slump in markets in the early 1980s, Algoma cut back its operations and the number of jobs. The

*Allan Jackson has served as city administrator since 1981.*

city then began a concentrated effort to diversify the economy so there would be less dependence on the steelmaker in the future. An Economic Development Corporation to promote industrial and commercial development, Hospitality and Travel Sault Ste. Marie (HATS), an umbrella organization to promote and co-ordinate the tourism industry, and other special initiatives were undertaken.

A major waterfront facelift has been initiated that is dramatically changing the city. Industries such as A.B. McLean Ltd.'s gravel operation, which was situated next door to the Civic Centre, was relocated from the downtown and projects such as condominiums, apartments for senior citizens, and marinas are being developed.

# ARTHUR FUNERAL HOME

While the building and owners have changed in the 50 years since the Arthur Funeral Home was established, its location has remained the same. It has been at 492 Wellington Street East since Jim Arthur came from St. Marys, Ontario, and went into business with his uncle, John Furse, owner of Soo Business College.

Furse and Arthur Funeral Home opened in 1937, and from that time until 1951, as often was the practice, it also operated an ambulance service. Arthur owned the funeral home for 37 years until he sold the business to Chuck MacLeod in 1974.

The original building, which was remodelled and an addition constructed in the early 1950s, was gutted and underwent extensive renovation in 1959. Over the years more expansions took place, with another major one in 1977 increasing storage area for caskets and adding space to the east side of the structure to serve the families of Sault Ste. Marie.

In 1983 Bob Linklater and Bill Kiteley formed a new company and purchased the Arthur Funeral Home and Barton and Kiteley Funeral Home on Brock Street. Including the two owners, 11 full-time and 10 part-time employees work at the two funeral homes, providing service 24 hours a day, 365 days a year, to families of all

faiths.

Among the staff are two female funeral directors, a growing trend in a once male-dominated profession. Educational requirements include one year in a funeral service education program at a community college and a one-year apprenticeship followed by board examinations through the provincial Ministry of Health. Every five years a funeral director must attend a postgraduate refresher course.

Funerals are a celebration that a death has occurred and a life was

*Arthur Funeral Home, opened in 1937, has remained at its original location at 492 Wellington Street East for 50 years. The home, which employs 21 staff to serve the needs of families of all faiths 24 hours a day, 365 days a year, is unique in that it is one of the first to hire women as funeral directors.*

lived, Linklater says. They are both social and spiritual events, where the funeral home will do anything to assist a family during this emotional time. This can include directing them to various agencies, assistance with life insurance and settling estates, and after-funeral counselling where the funeral home staff works closely with the clergy and pastoral care workers at the city's two hospitals.

Education plays an important role in the services offered by the funeral homes. Presentations are made to organizations, schools, service clubs, and churches.

Both Linklater and Kiteley are active in the community. A member of Central United Church, Kiteley is involved with the Rotary Club, Algoma University College Building Development, and the Ontario Commemorations Committee of the Canadian Cancer Society. Linklater, a member of Gospel Hall, is involved with Light Haven Christian Home in Bruce Mines and the Interschool Christian Fellowship. He also plays hockey, is an avid boater, and is a member of the Canadian Power and Sail Squadron.

*In 1983 Bill Kiteley (left) and Bob Linklater (above) formed a new company by purchasing the Arthur Funeral Home and the Barton and Kiteley Funeral Home on Brock Street. In addition to operating the two homes, both men are active in area civic and religious groups.*

# TOSSELL AND CAUGHILL, ARCHITECT AND CONSULTING ENGINEER INC.

Christopher Tossell and Bruce Caughill have shared a philosophy that recognizes northern Ontario's special geographic, climatic, and social needs. The partners emphasize practicality of design and appropriateness of material as they deal with the extremities of temperature, comparative isolation, and other conditions that make Sault Ste. Marie and the northern centres different from the rest of the province.

Their firm, Tossell and Caughill, Architect and Consulting Engineer

*Tossell and Caughill is committed to serving the special needs of the Sault Ste. Marie community. Two examples of the firm's accomplishments include Central Fire Station (left) and the Home for the Sault Ste. Marie Association for the Mentally Retarded (above).*

Inc., has carried out a wide variety of projects and studies for all levels of government, private corporations, and individuals throughout the North. In Sault Ste. Marie, the projects include Central Fire Station, Water Tower Inn additions, residences for the Association for the Mentally Retarded, District Jail addition, Aurora's Restaurant, and the Creed Fitness Centre. In 1987 Tossell won an Ontario Clay Masonry Design Award for the exterior building design of the city's Second Line Water Treatment Plant.

In addition to designing for the special needs of the north, Tossell and Caughill remains committed to the preservation of the city's architectural heritage. When appropriate and possible, existing buildings have been rehabilitated rather than replaced. Going a step beyond rehabilitation, the

firm has also been involved in the restoration of many of Sault Ste. Marie's heritage structures. These projects have included Precious Blood Cathedral (1875), The Algonquin Hotel (1895), Central United Church (1903), and the St. Marys Paper Inc. general office building (1900).

Tossell began his architectural career in Wales after graduating from the Welsh School of Architecture at the University of Wales Institute of Science and Technology. He obtained experience in assessing heritage buildings by preparing measured drawings for the National Museum of Wales. He emigrated to Canada in 1968, joining the Sault firm of R.V.B. Burgoyne, Architect, as a project architect and later associate partner. Ten years later he established his own businesss, and in 1981 formed a partnership with Caughill to combine

two critical elements in building construction—design and engineering.

Both men are active in many community organizations, service clubs, and professional associations. Tossell is chairman of the Sault Ste. Marie Local Architectural Conservation Advisory Committee and also of Heritage Sault Ste. Marie. He is also a director of the Ontario Heritage Foundation.

Caughill, a Sault native whose father, Norman, was a well-known local builder, is carrying on a family tradition. He began working in construction as a student, received a civil engineering degree from Michigan Technological University in 1969, and worked for a large U.S. contractor as a project engineer on marine and heavy construction projects until 1972, when he returned to the Sault as estimator/design engineer and eventually vice-president of R.M. Elliott Construction Ltd. He set up an independent practice as a professional engineer in 1979, was designated a consulting engineer two years later, and was licensed to practice architecture in 1986.

# TISHMAN REALTY CORP.

Toronto developer Howard Tishman's Sault Ste. Marie office is his car. It is from this location that he does "nine days' worth of work" during his weekly three-day visits to the city.

He has been keeping this hectic pace, which includes rising at 5 a.m. and working 365 days per year, for 14 years, since he first hopped a plane and visited the Sault on a dare.

A drive around the community and a look through the local newspaper told him there was a need he could fill. There were few buildings for rent, and when Tishman saw what was available he believed he could do a better job. He started with an industrial mall on Black Road and "just kept going from there" until he had a dozen projects in the Sault.

These developments include Market Mall, Churchill Downs, renovated Queen Street buildings, and a new shopping centre on the corner of Pim and McNabb streets.

A "great traditionalist" who prefers "to restore something worthy of restoring," he renovated the old Coch-

rane building, constructed in 1912, to house offices. The first major restoration project in the city, it gave new life to a building at the major downtown intersection of Queen and Elgin streets. His Black Road development—an industrial multiple centre built to be sectioned off—also was a first for this city.

Tishman, by a fluke, got into the real estate business in 1967, when he started working for a Toronto developer. It was a quick, intense education, and within a year he had his own company. Initially he was a residential

*A great believer in building restoration, Howard Tishman breathed new life into the old Cochrane building at Queen and Elgin streets, constructed in 1912. This reconditioning was the city's first major renovation project.*

developer, but changed his focus to commercial and industrial development just before he started his work in the Sault.

Tishman's firm operates in a number of communities in Ontario and in the United States. Although he has a house and office in Toronto, he is not involved in developments there, preferring smaller cities.

For a young man born and bred in the big city, it was smallness that attracted him to Halifax and Dalhousie University, where he studied commerce and art. A workaholic, he started working at the age of 11 in his father's dairy business, helping the truck drivers during the summer months. And when he was in university, he was an impresario organizing tours for entertainers along the East Coast. Two weeks out of university he began working in real estate and still embarks on projects that always differ enough to provide him with a challenge.

*The 140,000-square-foot Market Mall, a community shopping centre serving the west end area of the Sault, is one of several projects completed by Tishman.*

# ALGOMA UNIVERSITY COLLEGE

*Algoma University College offers three- and four-year degree-granting programs in the arts, commerce, social work, and science.*

History professor Dr. Ian Brown remembers when rain forced Algoma University College to cancel classes. The pounding sound on the tin roofs of the temporary buildings, housing the institution on the campus it shared with the community college (now Sault College) in the late 1960s, made it impossible to teach.

But by 1971 AUC had moved to its own site at Shingwauk Hall, a former Indian residential school it later purchased from the Anglican Church, on Queen Street East. From these humble beginnings it has grown into a small liberal arts university with a $4-million annual operating budget.

Algoma's roots go back to the 1950s, when a group of local residents who believed postsecondary education should be available in the Sault, formed a junior college association. However, provincial legislation to establish the institution was not passed until 1961. Algoma College gained affiliation with Sudbury's Laurentian University in 1965, and opened its doors two years later to 100 full-time and 300 part-time students. It offered 14 subjects, one year toward a bachelor of arts degree.

When the college was relocated to its own campus, a science building,

additional classroom and office buildings, and a music conservatory were added. A new library wing, which housed 80,000 volumes, was constructed in 1973.

A second year was added to the academic program in 1971, and then a third year in 1972. Seventy-six students graduated in the first class in 1973, and since that time more than 1,500 people, most of them Sault residents, have earned degrees. Fifteen

years later Algoma's enrolment stood at 300 full-time and 850 part-time students, and president Dr. Douglas Lawson estimates the college could grow to 1,000 students by 1992. With 31 full-time faculty and more than 40 sessional instructors, the college offers three- and four-year degree-granting programs in the arts, commerce, social work, and science.

Shingwauk Hall, the college's main building, underwent a $400,000 renovation in 1987, and construction of a new $3.1-million library, approximately 26,000 square feet in area, is to be completed in May 1989. Future expansion plans call for construction of student residences and other buildings to house athletic facilities, classrooms, a student centre, labs, a cafeteria, and faculty offices.

Algoma University College plays a major role in the Sault's academic, intellectual, and cultural lives. City residents make active use of the library's collections and services. The college offers concerts, lectures, a film series, and programs for gifted children. Faculty, students, and staff participate in many community organizations and groups.

*A student works on a computer at the college. Since the first 76 students graduated in 1973, more than 1,500 students, mostly from the Sault area, have earned degrees.*

# GROUP HEALTH CENTRE

Group Health Centre, often referred to as the Ministry of Health's "flagship" of the Health Service Organizations (HSO) system, celebrated 25 years of service to residents of Sault Ste. Marie and the surrounding area in 1988.

The growth and importance of the Group Health Centre is due in large measure to its unique past. The hard work of those in union organizations during the late 1950s laid down the foundation to build a health centre with these principles: community sponsorship through a board representing the people who use the centre, medical group practice, non-fee-for-service payment, and partnership between the association as a user of service and the medical group as a provider of service. The driving force behind the Group Health Centre was John Barker, an area supervisor and national staff representative with the United Steelworkers of America. (USWA).

When local steelworkers decided they wanted improvements in obtaining their health care and a prepaid group practice structure seemed to be the answer, Barker was given the assignment by the USWA to take the idea of a health centre and make it a reality. Group Health Centre's momentum began under the guidance of the labor organizers, including a canvassing committee of 50 individuals who carried the idea to the workplace and to the community. It was not an easy task, and one that required an extra degree of commitment since the canvass took place in the winter of

1960 in 20-degrees-below-zero weather. This dedicated group of visionaries convinced 5,000 citizens to give $135 each for a total of $675,000 to build the Group Health Centre facility.

In 1963 the centre opened with 13 physicians, a support staff of 50, and plans to provide care for 12,000 patients. Dr. Thompson A. Ferrier was named the centre's first medical director.

With the introduction of provincial health plans by the Ontario government in October 1969, the Group Health Centre stood at great risk of being swept away. The board of directors and administrative leadership played a central role in advancing the Group Health Centre as a vital part of the provincial health care system. Through years of hard work the Ministry has recognized the centre as a legitimate and constructive element in the provision of health services.

The centre has grown tremendously in the past 25 years. In 1974 a million-dollar expansion in the form of a second wing doubled the physical size of the centre. A comprehensive range of health and health-related services has developed over the years, and is available to residents of the city and district 24 hours a day. Medical services are family medicine and numerous specialties, including internal

*Group Health Centre founder John Barker, turning the first sod in September 1962. A portrait of Barker is prominently displayed in Group Health Centre, acknowledging the efforts of all the individuals and groups involved in establishing the facility and its philosophy of care.*

medicine, obstetrics and gynecology, surgery, cardiology, pediatrics, emergency medicine, psychiatry, and others. Services include diagnostic imaging, laboratory, physical therapy, vision and eye care, counselling, nutrition consultation, and others. Some 43 physicians and associates and a staff of 200 provide services for an enrolled patient population of approximately one-half of the city's residents.

Group Health Centre continues to expand services. In late 1987 a Women's Health Centre was opened in a separate building at the Group Health Centre McNabb Street location, and a satellite centre with two family physicians and support staff, Group Health Centre West, opened in a west end mall.

Group Health Centre is a living testament that dedicated people, sharing common concerns and working together to solve important public issues, can bring about constructive change.

*In 1963 Group Health Centre was located in Tarentorous Township and was considered to be on the outskirts of Sault Ste. Marie. Today McNabb is the busiest street in Sault Ste. Marie, with a thriving commercial and residential area surrounding the centre.*

# JAMES STREET HARDWARE AND FURNITURE CO. LTD.

When Alfio Spadoni was a boy, lines of workers from the nearby Algoma Steel Corp. were a common sight at his father's James Street store. There were no banks in the west end of Sault Ste. Marie; Adolpho Spadoni provided a cheque-cashing service at his hardware and furniture store. This was typical of the philosophy of properly serving the public that he built his business on, and that belief was shared by his son. "If you did something right and well, the public in turn reimbursed you," Alfio Spadoni explains.

Adolpho Spadoni was 17 years old when he emigrated from Italy to Canada in 1910. He worked at the steel plant until 1918, when he and a partner opened a bicycle shop next door to James Street Hardware and Furniture Co. Ltd.'s present location. In 1922, when the partner returned to Italy, Spadoni bought him out and continued on his own. He expanded, adding hardware and furniture, and eventually moved to adjacent premises.

Spadoni was known for the assis-

tance he provided Italian and other immigrants who settled in the Sault. In the 1950s, when Algoma Steel brought in a large contingent of British tradesmen, the federal immigration department, which knew that only $900 was available elsewhere for furniture, sent them to Spadoni's store. James Street would allow them to purchase up to $2,000 on credit.

Years later many are "still attached to this place and have never forgotten the original treatment they received from James Street Furniture," Alfio Spadoni says.

In 1958 a highline bridge connecting the James Street business area to the Bayview-Buckley sections of the Sault was closed and demolished. Within a few years the once-flourishing business area had declined, and many stores had closed. A major rejuvenation project began in

*Adolpho Spadoni started in business with a bicycle shop on James Street, adjacent to James Street Furniture. Spadoni was known for his support of the Sault's Italians and other immigrants.*

*The third generation of the Spadoni family is involved with operating James Street Furniture: (left to right) Stephen Spadoni, Chris Zalewski, Deborah Van Scoy, and Alan Spadoni.*

the mid-1970s, and James Street Furniture became a main anchor in the James Street shopping mall that was created as part of the urban-renewal scheme.

Alfio got involved with the business at the age of 12. His job was to remove the putty from windows in the store's glass repair area. After graduating with an engineering degree from the University of Toronto, he joined the family business full time in 1953. His father continued with the store until his death in 1971.

Seventy years after the store first opened its doors a third generation of the family—three of Alfio's children and a son-in-law—is coming up through the ranks to continue the James Street Hardware and Furniture Co. Ltd. traditions.

# GENERAL HOSPITAL

In response to an 1896 typhoid epidemic that ravaged Sault Ste. Marie (then without public health care), two French-speaking Grey Nuns of the Cross arrived in the Sault from Ottawa in 1898 to establish a hospital. The cornerstone of the Queen Street East building was laid by Mayor Edward Biggings on September 21, 1898. The four-storey, 80-bed hospital, opened in July 1899, was for two decades the Sault's only hospital.

In 1908 a girl who lived near the hospital stopped to chat with Sister Mary Dorothea, and told her she wished to become a nurse. There was no training school connected with the hospital, but the Sister, who was a nurse, agreed to tutor her. "Come back tomorrow morning and we'll start a school of nursing," Sister Mary Dorothea said. Three years later the girl, Ivy Reynolds, became the first graduate of the St. Mary's School of Nursing. The school graduated more than 500 nurses before the program was transferred to the community's Sault College of Applied Arts and Technology.

In 1926 the hospital's building and property were transferred to the Grey Sisters of the Immaculate Conception, an English-speaking community that continues to operate it today.

Several expansions and renova-

*By 1926 General Hospital's buildings and property—which included a nurses' home (left), administration building (centre), and medical wing (right)—were transferred to the Grey Sisters of the Immaculate Conception, an English-speaking community that continues to operate the facility today.*

tions took place over the next 80 years, and the hospital grew to a modern 254-bed facility with 475 full-time employees and 361 part-time workers. Some 140 doctors and 32 dentists have privileges at the hospital, which has medical and surgical, pediatric, intensive care, coronary care, maternity, and chronic care units.

General Hospital has modern, up-to-date laboratory and radiology departments, and a $2-million CAT (computerized axial tomography) scanner, purchased with money donated by local residents, will be housed at the hospital. There are also qualified staff and state-of-the-art equipment for pulmonary function, electrocardiology (EKG), electroencephalography (EEG), and ophthalmology testing. The Rehabilitation Department includes physiotherapists, occupational therapists, and speech pathologists and audiologists, complemented by the appropriate facilities and equipment.

The Neonatal Intensive Care

Unit, which provides regional service to sick newborns, is classified as Modified Level III, and as such, is one of only a few such advanced facilities in all of Ontario.

But General Hospital is more than the latest in modern technology. A Pastoral Care Department and a Palliative Care Service provide spiritual and emotional support to patients, their families, and staff. They, along with a full-time chaplain and beautiful chapel, provide a spiritual backdrop and enhance the tradition of the founding Grey Sisters.

With rationalization, General Hospital's future role will be to provide medical and surgical services to children and adolescents; obstetrics; the specialty services of urology, otolaryngology (ENT), plastic surgery, and oncology; long-term care services; and palliative care services. In addition, some general medical and surgical beds would be retained by General Hospital for the treatment of other illnesses in the adult population, and hospital-based dentistry would be relocated from the Plummer Memorial Hospital to General Hospital.

*A typhoid epidemic that raged through the Sault in 1896 provided the impetus for the establishment of the city's first hospital—the 80-bed General Hospital—built in 1899 through the efforts of the French-speaking Grey Nuns of the Cross.*

# MARY'S RESTAURANT

Ed Kosiba rebuilt his restaurant from the ashes of a fatal December 1983 fire that swept through half a city block, destroying four Queen Street East businesses. Mary's Lunch had no insurance—it had lapsed—and he was forced to start all over again to rebuild the restaurant opened by his parents, Mike and Mary Kosiba, in February 1948.

The Kosibas had moved to Sault Ste. Marie from Toronto, where Mike was a pastry chef at the Royal York Hotel. They purchased the building at 663 Queen Street East, which housed a florist and Evans Lunch Room. They opened a lunch room and bakery in the divided brick building, which was constructed in 1897.

Ed worked there from day one, doing everything from baking to washing dishes. After his father's death in 1971, he continued to help his mother run the restaurant.

The fire, which killed two people in apartments above the businesses,

broke out in the early-morning hours of December 30, 1983. Firefighters battled the blaze for five hours before they were able to get it under control. Mary Kosiba lived in a second-floor apartment above the restaurant, but the 79-year-old woman escaped the fire because she was downstairs with her son when a policeman told them to get out.

The Kosibas lost everything in the blaze, and at the time it seemed they would have to call it quits after 35 years in business at the same loca-

*Mary's Restaurant reopened in December 1984 at the same location after a year of reconstruction, with a new name and an expanded facility.*

tion. "We rescued some equipment—an oven and dough mixer," Ed recalls. But Ed managed to raise the more than $200,000 needed to reestablish the business, and Mary's Restaurant reopened its doors on December 4, 1984.

The new restaurant and tavern is larger, with 48 seats. There is no bake shop, but Kosiba continues to sell bread, meat pies, French pastry, and other baked goods, such as moose tracks (a pastry that looks like the track of a moose).

He works during the night baking 60 to 70 loaves of bread, and with the long hours the restaurant is open, he gets by on snatches of sleep and naps during quiet moments. Mary's has about 15 full- and part-time employees, including four cooks. It is open seven days a week, and on Thursdays, Fridays, and Saturdays the restaurant stays open 24 hours a day.

With its fresh-out-of-the-oven bread and other specialties, Mary's Restaurant continues to be a favorite spot for regulars who have been eating there for years.

*Mary's Lunch opened in 1948 on Queen Street in this brick building constructed in 1897. When it was destroyed by fire in 1983, few thought that the restaurant would ever reopen.*

# MASTER WELDING AND SAFETY EQUIPMENT COMPANY

In the early days when employees of Master Welding wanted to measure 100 feet of cable they had to wait until there was no traffic on Bruce Street. Then they would pull the cable to the middle of the road—a distance of 100 feet—to get the exact length and reel it up.

Twenty-five years later the company is much more sophisticated, and has electrical reeling equipment and counters to measure cable and wire rope products at its Second Line location.

George Masters established the company on January 1, 1963. He had five employees, including himself, at the shop at 232 Bruce Street. As the northern Ontario manager for Canadian Liquid Air, he had seen an opportunity with only one competitor in Sault Ste. Marie to start a liquid air distributorship. Masters persuaded Canadian Liquid Air to grant him the territory, and his Sault firm became one of the first authorized distributors. The format tested in the Sault became the basis of a program that has swelled to 80 distributors across Canada.

The company initially started with cylinder gases and welding supplies from Canadian Liquid Air and products from Esco Corporation such as buckets, bucket teeth, and other steel castings utilized in the construction and mining industries. A 500-ton press was obtained a few years later, enabling the firm to make cable slings and logging chokers, while it continued to diversify as an industrial and safety supply company.

Three years later he opened a branch in Sudbury and by 1967 had moved Master Welding and Safety Equipment Company to 566 Second Line East in the Sault.

In 1979 Masters sold the business to a group headed by Bill Malpass, who became president and general manager. Curt Damignani, an original shareholder, became co-owner in June 1983 and active in the business later that year. While Malpass became sole shareholder in 1988, Damignani remains active with the company.

Since Malpass became involved with the company, a third branch was added in Manitouwadge in 1984 and a fourth branch in Wawa three years later. Master Welding and Safety Equipment Company has a keen interest in the north and is committed to providing first-rate professional service with quality products to the marketplace. The company does this through four branches that employ 35 people, and through 10 depots in smaller centres that help service the vast territory that stretches from the Killarney area south of Sudbury, north and west through Sudbury, Elliot Lake, Sault Ste. Marie, Wawa, Manitouwadge, and Marathon. Master's customers vary from large industries such as Algoma Steel Corp. to the backyard hobbyist who does repairs and likes to tinker in his garage.

Malpass is chairman of the Sault Ste. Marie Police Commission, vice-chairman of Sault College Innovation Centre, a director of the Municipal Police Authorities representing northern Ontario, and a director and past president of the Canadian Liquid Air Distributors Association for Ontario.

*President of Master Welding Bill Malpass (left), with general manager David Watson.*

# GEORGE STONE & SONS
## DIVISION OF 612354 ONTARIO LTD.

The family pride shows as Harry and Rod Stone discuss their construction company heritage. Their grandfather, George, had operated the company in the Sault as a contracting business since 1915, seven years after coming to the community from Manitoulin Island, where he was born in 1889.

He started building and framing houses, erecting additions, and constructing alterations as George Stone Construction. He operated the business from his home at 394 North Street, where his seven children were always aware of and involved with his business.

In 1945 two sons, Edward and William, who had been in the Canadian Armed Forces during World War II, joined him as partners in what then became known as George Stone & Sons. The youngest son, Robert, started with the firm later as a carpenter, working his way up to foreman. Four years after the company was incorporated as George Stone & Sons Limited in 1961, George Stone retired and Bob became a shareholder in the firm. The company moved to its present location at 99 Northern Avenue in 1958.

A third generation became involved in 1966, when Ed's son Harry began an apprenticeship. He worked as a carpenter, foreman, and superintendent, becoming construction manager in 1980. By 1982 Harry was vice-president of George Stone & Sons and president of Kwik Lumber, which was opened by George, Bill, and Ed in 1960. Bill's son Rodney, who is chief estimator and sales manager, started with the firm in 1973. A Sault College construction engineering technician graduate, he worked in the field until 1978, when he moved into the office. Although Bill and Bob are no longer active with the operations of the company, they still serve as president and secretary/treasurer, respectively.

The firm's business moved from primarily residential work under George to commercial and institutional with the involvement of Bill

*George Stone, founder.*

*Ed Stone*

*Bill Stone*

*Bob Stone*

and Ed. In the 1950s and 1960s George Stone & Sons built schools, as well as major additions and alterations, for both Sault school boards. Larger-scale industrial projects followed in the 1970s and 1980s.

The company, which has done work as far west as Sioux Lookout and east to Manitoulin Island, includes among its more memorable projects the East Street Medical Arts Building, General Hospital's Obstetrical and CAT Scanner areas, Salvation Army Citadel, the United Baptist

Church, the Memorial Gardens Roof Replacement, Sir James Dunn School, Wawa, the $7-million Marathon High School, a $4.5-million Manitoulin Health Centre, several projects at Algoma Steel Corp., and many Sault families are living in homes built by the Stones.

In 1988 George Stone & Sons were listed in the *Canadian Construction Record*'s list of Top 200 Contractors in Canada for the first time—quite an achievement in an industry that ranks as one of the largest in the country.

# CHAMBERS AND MILLER LTD.

*J.B. Chambers and Associates in 1964. Since the firm was founded in 1950, it has provided a variety of legal and engineering surveys to public and government agencies. In 1971 the firm was incorporated as Chambers and Miller Ltd.*

A subdivision on remote James Bay Island and some of Sault Ste. Marie's largest residential areas share a common factor. The survey work was done by Chambers and Miller Ltd., Ontario Land Surveyors.

The Sault-based firm provides a wide variety of legal and engineering surveys to public and government agencies. And while the majority of its work is in the Sault and Algoma District, it has done surveys as far away as Moose Factory Island in James Bay.

J.B. "Bert" Chambers established the company in 1950. A Rydall Bank native, he began working with the survey firm of C.R. Kenny after graduation from Sault Collegiate Institute. He received his commission as a registered Ontario Land Surveyor in 1941. From 1942 to 1945 Bert served as a navigator with the RCAF, and after World War II resumed his career as a land surveyor, doing work throughout northeastern Ontario with the Department of Highways, Ontario Hydro, and Canadian National Railway. He acquired Kenny's practice in 1950 and performed surveys in the Algoma District under the firm name of J.B. Chambers and Associates.

In 1963 Larry Miller received his commission as a registered Ontario Land Surveyor after six years of training and work with the Department of Highways on new road surveys in northern Ontario. Born and educated in Thunder Bay, he joined the firm in 1963, and eight years later it was incorporated as Chambers and Miller Ltd. with Chambers as president.

Sault native F.E. "Ted" Wall, who joined the firm in 1968, received his commission in 1974. He had worked with survey and engineering firms in southwestern Ontario and at Algoma Steel Corp.

Following the death of Chambers in 1984, Miller assumed the presidency. Wall became a partner in 1988.

That same year, to gain access to the technology involved in the rapidly expanding field of digital information and data-base systems, the firm joined a consortium of surveyors from major Ontario communities. Known as the LanData Group, the consortium is capable of providing geographically based information systems, and specializes in computerized mapping and data conversion for initial information management systems.

Chambers and Miller Ltd. has survey records from Sault Ste. Marie dating back to the turn of the century. From 1950 to 1970 the firm obtained the records, plans, and documents of well-known firms such as E.M. MacQuarrie and Lang and Ross.

*From left: Larry Miller, Ted Wall, and Lloyd Hotchkiss.*

# DUBREUIL BROTHERS LIMITED

Dubreuil Brothers Limited's operations, 180 miles north of Sault Ste. Marie, have grown into a modern mill that can produce 110 million board feet of lumber annually, of which 95 percent is shipped to the United States, as well as hardwood, softwood chips, and by-products.

Since the Dubreuil brothers left the family home in Taschereau, Quebec, to work in Ontario they have carved out an industry and privately owned community in the dense northern bush. Four hundred and twenty-five workers are employed in the lumber operations, and 1,200 people live in the town of Dubreuilville, 42 miles north of Wawa.

They spoke limited English when they came to Ontario to begin logging and sawmilling operations, salvaging timber in a burned-over area between Thessalon and Chapleau. They established a mill to harvest the burnt pine and built a community at Mountain Ash Lake in 1948. The best way to attract good men, they decided, was to have their families there, so they built a school and hired a teacher to attract loggers from Quebec.

Napoleon and his brothers— Joachim "George," Augustin, and Marcel—moved their operations to Algoma Central Railway land, north of the Sault, and established the first Dubreuilville at Magpie in 1951. Ten years later they relocated to the present site, where the community grew and prospered, owing to the innovative logging methods and sawmilling practices pioneered by the Dubreuils.

Since 1961 the operation has changed and more machines are in the mill. New technology has maximized recovery so that more is taken from a tree more precisely and requiring less people per unit production. The sawmill production in one shift is more than what was produced annually in their father's sawmill in Quebec in the 1940s.

In 1954 Dubreuil Lumber was opened on Cathcart Street in Sault Ste. Marie to sell jackpine lumber and one-inch boards, which were difficult to market. A retail yard was estab-

*Pictured from left are Nap, George, Augustin, and Marcel Dubreuil with their mother, Cecile. The Dubreuils established a mill and a community in the dense northern bush.*

*The town of Dubreuilville, 42 miles north of Wawa, is home to 1,200 people. Dubreuil Brothers Limited built the community at the site of its lumber operations, which employs 425 workers.*

lished in 1984 on Great Northern Road, but difficult times in the construction industry convinced the Dubreuils to sell to a competitor.

Napoleon retired from the business in 1972, and his youngest brother, Marcel, took over as president. Several other family members, including the third generation, are involved with the company.

As the sole employer in Dubreuilville, the firm has contributed largely in building a school, a church, and a modern arena, and been involved in all aspects of life in the close-knit French-speaking community. The family named the Church Ste. Cecile in honor of their mother, and the School St. Joseph in honor of their father.

And so it goes that 40 years after its initial start-up and 17 years in Dubreuilville, the firm continues to change and to grow in order to ascertain development of its operation.

On May 16, 1988, Jean-Paul, son of Napoleon, took the company. In line with his predecessors, Jean-Paul is determined to keep Dubreuil Brothers Limited an avant-garde business.

# GUGULA/SMEDLEY/MEZZOMO—ARCHITECTS INC.

A log cabin in Sylvan Valley, houseboats on the St. Mary's River, and the multidome St. Mary's Ukrainian Catholic Church speak to the diversity of the architectural firm of Gugula/Smedley/Mezzomo.

The firm does not specialize in any particular field of architecture or planning, but rather has undertaken a variety of projects in diverse fields. This diversity has significantly involved the partners in revitalization of Sault Ste. Marie's downtown core and waterfront, and in many institutional, educational, commercial, industrial, and recreation projects over the years.

An addition to the Centennial Library, the Lions' Senior Citizens building and the multimillion-dollar Ontario government office complex are among recent projects. The multiuse government building will house the Ontario Lottery Corp. head office and computer centre, Forest Resources Group and Aviation and Fire Management Centre for the Ministry of Natural Resources, and a forensic science laboratory for the Ministry of the Solicitor General.

Projects in the district include

*The Sault Ste. Marie Civic Centre.*

housing units in Bruce Mines, the new Blind River hospital, and the Energy, Mines, and Resources Laboratory in Elliot Lake.

The firm became an independent entity in 1974, but its roots go back to 1952, when Joe Gugula established an office for the firm of Rounthwaite and Fairfield at the Plummer Memorial Hospital expansion site. In 1959 he became a partner in Rounthwaite and Associates, and continued to op-

erate the Sault office. Gordon Smedley joined the firm in 1962 after working in England for two years.

Major projects during that period included the rebuilding of St. Luke's Cathedral, additions to the F.J. Davey Home for the Aged, and the original air terminal building at the federal airport.

An independent practice was formed in 1974, Gordon Mezzomo became a partner five years later, and the name Gugula/Smedley/Mezzomo—Architects was adopted in 1986.

*A model of the multimillion-dollar Ontario government office complex, a recent project of Gugula/Smedley/Mezzomo.*

*The East Street medical building.*

# COOPER'S CRANE RENTAL LIMITED

When Cooper's Crane Rental Limited started business in Sault Ste. Marie in 1960, a 35-ton crane was considered large. Nearly 30 years later the industry has made such tremendous strides that there are cranes with a 1,000-ton capacity, and Cooper's has 20 cranes with more than a 100-ton capacity.

Cooper's has expanded to become the largest crane rental outfit in Ontario and the third largest in the country. It has grown under president Mert Wright from a local operation with two 35-ton cranes and four employees to a company with 140 cranes, 20 tractor-float units and other miscellaneous equipment, and up to 125 employees during peak construction periods. Cooper's has branch offices in Sudbury, North Bay, Oshawa, Toronto, Brantford, and Hamilton.

A Kirkland Lake native, Wright was a structural design engineer with Dominion Bridge Company in the Sault for four years before starting his own consulting engineering firm in 1961. He became involved with Cooper's as a minority shareholder in 1960, and within a couple of years he was the principal shareholder. Wright opened a branch office in Sudbury in 1965 and purchased a North Bay hoist rental firm in 1978.

Cooper's general manager, Ken Gregg, a minority shareholder in the business, is a former bank manager who joined the company in 1972.

In the early 1980s, when the recession brought a slump in industrial and

*Cooper's off loads an 800-ton German crane from a ship docked in Oshawa, Ontario.*

general construction, Cooper's decided to expand into markets in southern Ontario. It bought a small crane company in Oshawa, and in 1986 constructed a new building there. That same year Cooper's doubled its size by buying out its largest competitor, Nadrofsky Corp. in Brantford.

Cooper's has constantly expanded its fleet. Its latest acquisition is a 450-ton mobile hydraulic crane.

A heavily unionized company, Cooper's Crane Rental Limited's employees are members of the Operating Engineers of Ontario. In 1987 a crane operator earned $23.13 per hour, compared to the hourly wage of $2.60, 28 years earlier.

The Olympic Stadium in Montreal, James Bay Hydro project in northern Quebec, Toronto's new SkyDome stadium, and the Hemlo gold fields in northwestern Ontario are among the many construction sites Cooper's has worked on.

In addition, Cooper's Crane Rental Limited has its own plane, a six-passenger, twin-engine Cessna-310, that Wright pilots.

Wright has served as a director of the Ontario Northland Economic Development Corporation. Gregg is a director of the Crane Rental Association of Ontario.

*Cooper's general manager Ken Gregg and president Mert Wright, shown with the company airplane, piloted by Wright.*

# PRINGLE & MARTIN INC.

*Sam Pringle's first office building at 369 McNabb Street.*

Sam Pringle and Reg Martin, formerly carpenters, went from building homes to selling real estate to developing some of Sault Ste. Marie's major buildings and complexes. Now partners in Pringle & Martin Inc., they have been working together for more than 20 years.

In 1967 Pringle, a Sault native, opened his own real estate firm at 369 McNabb Street, at which time Martin, who moved to the city from Hamilton in 1960, started as a salesman. Then, in 1970, Martin received his broker's licence and became a partner, at the same time Pringle and a competitor, Lambert, merged their companies to specialize in commercial development.

The firm, called Lambert, Pringle & Martin Ltd., operated for five years from 85 Great Northern Road, and was responsible for many developments, including the Elgin Tower, Children's Aid Society on Willow Avenue, Professional Place, the Elliot Lake municipal building, and the city's first chain donut shop, Country Style Donuts, on Great Northern Road.

In the early 1970s the principals saw a need for serviced land and formed a land development company that developed a number of residential subdivisions locally. They also formed a construction company in 1973 (Penwood Properties Ltd.) that

built residential, commercial, and industrial projects, as well as having a complete designing and drafting department.

In 1975 Pringle & Martin branched out on its own again and built a new office at 15 Great Northern Road, under the name of Pringle & Martin Inc. The firm has since moved to 205 McNabb Street for larger accommodations, into an office building it had built in 1979 for the Co-Operators Insurance Co.

Pringle & Martin Inc. has grown

to include another partner, Steve McGuire, who manages a resale department with nine salespeople. There are now four divisions—land development, general real estate and appraisals, property management, and building development.

Both men have been active with local and provincial realty-related organizations. Pringle is a past president of the local real estate board and was regional vice-president of the Ontario Real Estate Association for northern Ontario. He was also a director and executive member of the Ontario Real Estate Association.

Martin is a past president of the Homebuilders' Association and was an executive member of the Ontario Homebuilders' Association (representing northern Ontario). He was appointed in 1977 to the Commercial Registration Appeal Tribunal representing the homebuilding industry in the province, and is presently on the board of governors of the Fair Rental Policy Organization of Ontario.

*The present offices of Pringle & Martin Inc. are in this building at 205 McNabb Street, which the firm built in 1979 for Co-Operators Insurance Co.*

# McMASTER OIL

McMaster Oil Co. started in the fuel business selling coal but grew to be one of the leading fuel oil distributors in Sault Ste. Marie. James McMaster has been associated with the fuel business since 1935; he became the head of his own company in 1953.

District Services Ltd. had been distributing British American (BA) products for 21 years in the Sault, Blind River, and Bruce Mines area when it was sold to The British American Oil Co. Ltd. in 1953. The petroleum distribution was retained by BA, and the coal business operated by District Services was sold to McMaster, the former general manager. McMaster soon branched out from the coal business, adding propane and fuel oil.

In 1958 he relocated McMaster Fuels from Pim Street to Gouin and Bay streets. In newspaper reports

to distribute to Sault homes and businesses for the cold winter months.

McMaster later entered a lease agreement with Sun Oil Co. for its waterfront tanks, and in the early 1960s the multinational oil company purchased the locally owned McMaster. McMaster Oil, a division of Sunoco

*McMaster Oil offers complete fuel distribution services—both residential and commercial.*

Inc. of Suncor Inc., continues to be operated under the McMaster name.

In 1975 McMaster Oil moved off the waterfront, as other oil companies had done, to a new petroleum storage tank farm and office site at 815 McNabb Street.

A fuel distributor, it operates a terminal for diesel, gasoline, and heating oils and services residential, commercial, and truck fleet customers. McMaster also has a home oil heating group with a service department. It covers an area that stretches from White River to the north and east to Espanola. McMaster Oil also operates and supplies all Sunoco service stations, has five tanks at its east end location, and employs 13 people. Products include industrial lubricants, petroleum for heating, and transportation and energy-control systems.

*(Above and at right): In 1975 McMaster Oil moved to this petroleum storage tank farm and office site at 815 McNabb Street.*

about the move, McMaster, who also was president of Sault Dock Company, said he was pleased with the new location because it offered better dock facilities.

By 1962 the firm had an annual capacity of 9 million gallons of fuel oil

# SEARS CANADA INC.

*Simpsons-Sears opened a new store on the corner of Queen and Elgin streets in 1959. Courtesy, The Sault Star*

Sears Canada Inc.'s roots in Sault Ste. Marie go back to 1940, when The Robert Simpson Co. Ltd. sold major and small appliances, sewing machines, and household furnishings at 368 Queen Street East. The retail and mail-order store operated there until 1951, when it moved to nearby premises at 374-376 Queen Street.

When Simpson-Sears Ltd., a new Canadian catalogue order and retail company, was formed in 1952 by a partnership between Simpsons Ltd. of Canada and Sears, Roebuck and Co. of the United States, the Sault store became a Simpsons-Sears outlet. Ray Clattenburg was named the full-time manager in 1955 and held the position until 1978.

The store had a catalogue sales office, furniture, appliances, radios, televisions, small appliances, carpets, a small credit department, and a staff of 27 people.

A modern, up-to-date store was built in 1959 on the corner of Queen and Elgin streets. With the new three-storey building, Simpson-Sears was able to expand its merchandise to include sporting goods, hardware, plumbing and heating supplies, paint, and an auto accessory department

with a five-car service station. The number of employees more than doubled to reach 65 people.

In 1973 Algocen Realty Holdings Ltd. built the Station Mall, a giant shopping centre on Sault Ste. Marie's waterfront, and Simpson-Sears formed the main anchor for the complex. The two-storey building with more than 400 employees was now in the chain's largest class of retail out-

lets and offered a complete line of all types of merchandise.

In 1971 Simpsons-Sears Ltd. adopted a modified logo in which only the name Sears appeared to prevent confusion between Simpsons and Simpsons-Sears Ltd.

In December 1978 the Hudson's Bay Co. acquired Simpsons Ltd. and gained 35 percent of the outstanding shares of Simpsons-Sears Ltd. As a result of this acquisition, the federal government required Simpson-Sears Ltd. and Simpsons Ltd. to operate as two separate companies and that all shared facilities and services be discontinued.

In 1983 Sears, Roebuck and Co. increased its majority ownership of its Canadian affiliate, and a year later the name change to Sears Canada Inc. was approved.

The Sears store in Sault Ste. Marie is part of a national merchandising organization with more than 80 department stores, more than 1,500 catalogue sales units, and 16 clearance centres. Its staff is active in city projects, the chamber of commerce, the Bon Soo Winter Carnival, the United Way, the employee charitable fund, as well as retail organizations.

*Sault residents arrived en masse for the October 1973 opening of Sears' new store in the Station Mall.*

# THE BANK OF NOVA SCOTIA

The opening in 1949 of Scotiabank's first branch in Sault Ste. Marie accomplished a perfect fit of community and corporate objectives. The full-service downtown banking facility filled a long-standing local need, while marking another advance by Scotiabank toward truly national stature.

Four decades later the bank is solidly established in the city, with three branches responding to a broad range of commercial and personal financial requirements. Across Canada and beyond Canadian coastlines, Scotiabank stands today as a major global financial institution.

One of the country's largest and oldest banking institutions was courted by the Central Business Men's Club of Sault Ste. Marie as early as 1919 in a letter citing the absence of a downtown bank. At the time the bank politely declined and

*Scotiabank's interior, shortly after its opening. Manager A.R. Toreveihe and five staff members served customers from all sectors of the bustling city.*

*Scotiabank's first branch in Sault Ste. Marie, opened in 1949, occupied the ground floor of the Chipley Block at the northwest corner of Queen and Spring streets.*

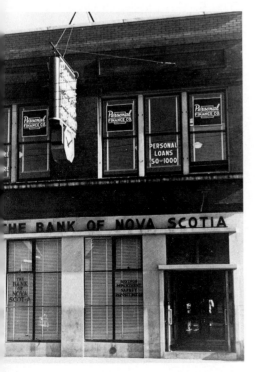

subsequently shelved expansion plans through the Great Depression and World War II.

By the mid-1940s, with economic recovery well under way, Scotiabank embarked on an aggressive expansion program nationwide. One of 28 branches opened in 1949—and part of a 65-branch extension at home and abroad between 1947 and 1949—was the bank's first branch in Sault Ste. Marie, on the ground floor of the Chipley Block at the northwest corner of Queen and Spring streets. There, on July 4, 1949, manager A.R. Toreveihe and five staff members commenced signing up the first customers from the retail sector; the traditional shipping, steel, and lumber industries; and a diversity of enterprises, putting down roots in the bustling city. All of the elements of progress were in place—rising population, improved transportation and communication, and a burgeoning tourist trade—leading a bank officer to observe: "It is almost impossible for one to stay in the Sault for even a day without becoming imbued with

the city's general optimism about its future."

Scotiabank shared in these prosperous times, so much so that plans for further expansion were soon in the works. In 1964 the bank relocated its main branch to more spacious quarters at 500 Queen Street, and opened a second branch at 252 Northern Avenue East and Highway 17. On November 1, 1973, the main branch was moved to Station Mall, while 500 Queen remained open as a branch, completing Scotiabank's alignment in the city today.

Founded in 1832 in Halifax, The Bank of Nova Scotia is one of North America's foremost financial institutions with assets exceeding $71 billion. More than 26,000 dedicated employees, including 47 in Sault Ste. Marie, work in more than 1,000 Scotiabank branches and specialized offices in 44 countries.

# MANITOULIN TRANSPORT

*Manitoulin's present terminal on John Street in Sault Ste. Marie.*

Manitoulin Transport has been "pulling for the North" since 1960, when the first truck pulled out of the firm's Manitoulin Island facility bound for Sudbury. In those days the fleet consisted of two trucks, three tractors, and four trailers.

Twenty-eight years later the company has grown to a regional carrier with a network of 18 terminal locations. It serves most of northern Ontario to and from the Toronto-Hamilton region, Montreal, and northwestern Quebec (Rouyn-Noranda, Val D'Or, Amos, and Lasarre). The firm also directly serves all points on Highway 17 from Sault Ste. Marie to Ottawa, and on Highway 11 from Hearst to Barrie. It hauls a wide range of commodities.

Manitoulin Transport established its Sault Ste. Marie terminal in 1974 in the old fire hall building at 81 Wallace Terrace. Five years later the company purchased an Algoma Central Railway warehouse on the corner of John Street and Second Line West, and relocated its trucking operations to this site. The facility has been modernized twice since 1979 to meet growing service needs in the Sault Ste. Marie area.

In 1980 Manitoulin created and tested the first Super Truck. Developed especially for northern Ontario freight needs, the unique vehicle consists of a modified conventional tractor equipped with a dromedary box behind the cab. Sporting 18-foot boxes, the Super Truck offers Manitoulin Transport considerable flexibility in providing freight services.

The firm's head office is located in Gore Bay on Manitoulin Island and houses all the corporate services, including financial, data processing, central dispatch, and administrative.

Manitoulin Transport, headed by president D.A. Smith and vice-president W. Cumming, has established a solid reputation in the trucking business for its fast service to and from the North.

*Manitoulin Transport created the first Super Truck especially for northern Ontario's needs.*

# ALGONQUIN HOTEL

*In 1983 the Algonquin was designated as a municipal landmark; its exterior was re-bricked and the original tower was reconstructed. One hundred years after its construction, its porches and balconies are the only link to its early façade.*

William H. Plummer built the Algonquin Hotel in 1888 to stave off what he believed was a threat to his business interests during a boom time in Sault Ste. Marie's history.

His commercial interests centred on his general store, hardware, and grocery on Plummer's Corner, at Pim and Queen streets, and a debate was raging as to where the centre of town should be located. Plummer, a leading citizen, was fighting for his corner, while others argued for the more westerly Bruce and Queen streets.

Plummer, who served as mayor for nine terms between 1892 and 1905, initially sold stock in the hotel, but he later gained complete control.

The Algonquin, with its triple-deck porches, was a favorite with both local residents and travellers. Industrialist Francis H. Clergue stayed there in September 1894, when he made the first deal that launched his empire in the Sault. Queen Victoria's son, Prince Arthur, the Duke of Connaught, and his wife, the Duchess, were guests of honor at an August 29, 1912, luncheon in the dining room.

After Plummer's death, the hotel had various owners, until it was purchased in 1966 by Remo and Edith Stanghetta. In 1979 the hotel was sold to Remo's son David and his wife, Diane.

In 1980 major interior renovations took place; seven rooms on the third floor were converted into a family dwelling. This apartment has an overview of what was once Plummer's Corner.

In 1983 the Algonquin was designated under the Ontario Heritage Act as a municipal landmark, and the exterior underwent a $275,000 facelift that included re-bricking and reconstruction of the original tower on the roof.

The hotel has 30 rooms, two apartments, a dining room, and two bars that feature country and western music in a local corner bar atmosphere. It employs 24 people and, as Stanghetta puts it, the Algonquin is "strictly into serving the public with music and comfortable surroundings."

The year 1988 marks the Algonquin Hotel's 100th anniversary. The hotel is a very family-oriented business—proprietors David and Diane and their children, Amy and James, live on the premises.

*Built in 1888, the Algonquin Hotel, with its triple-deck porches and key location, has been frequented by celebrities and is a favorite with travellers and Sault residents alike. Photo circa 1920*

# ALGOMA CONTRACTORS LTD.

When Antonio DiPietro, Alfonso Petrocco, and Antonio Luzzi founded their scrap-recovery business, the workers picked scrap by hand. Fifty years later Algoma Contractors Ltd., which has become an integral part of the steelmaking process at Algoma Steel Corp., uses cranes and devices to do the work.

Algoma Contractors reclaims steel scrap, which involves recovering the metals, processing them, and selling them back to ASC, Canada's third-largest integrated steel producer. It also processes slag to recover iron and services the steelmaker's basic oxygen furnaces and blast furnaces. Algoma Contractors, which has 130 employees, also operates a separation and crushing plant.

Situated on the western reaches of Algoma Steel property, on Base Line off Goulais Avenue, Algoma Contractors' first office was on Queen Street West. It was later moved to Wallace Terrace, at the corner of the steel company's tube division, and in the early 1950s to its present site.

When it was established in 1937, Algoma Contractors' total rolling stock was one Model A truck. In 1939 the company was reorganized,

*Algoma Contractors Ltd. equipment operators pose for a group picture in front of one of the 30-ton rubber-tire earth movers used at the time (winter 1960).*

and a steam shovel dubbed "Martha" was added to the growing company's equipment. By 1942 another steam shovel was acquired.

The three founders' sons followed in their father's footsteps and were shareholders in the company until it was sold to Ogden Metals in 1970. With the sale Algoma Contractors became a subsidiary of Luria Brothers (Cleveland, Ohio), a subsidiary of Ogden. It later came under the

control of Avondale Industries Inc., and then, in 1987, Boston-based Connell Partnerships Ltd., where it remains a subsidiary of Luria Brothers.

Jim DiPietro, who has been with the company since 1974 and is a grandson of one of the founders, is Algoma Contractors Ltd.'s vice-president/operations.

Presently Algoma Contractors employs 130 people to operate its scrap-recovery and crushing plant, as well as to segregate and haul various materials used in steel and ironmaking. A variety of 38 pieces of heavy equipment—hoists, front-end loaders, trucks, slag pot haulers, and gradalls—are used to meet present production requirements—a far cry from its unpretentious beginnings.

Over the years Algoma Contractors Ltd. has been an active supporter of the community and one of the longest constant sponsors of organized sport, particularly minor hockey teams, in Sault Ste. Marie and northern Ontario.

In June 1988 Algoma Contractors Ltd. ceased to exist when Algoma Steel Corp. took over the work done by the American-owned company.

*A series of conveyors that are part of the metallic separating plant used in the processing of B.O.F. Slag (spring 1978).*

# WISHART, NOBLE

The law firm of Wishart, Noble can trace its beginnings to the day in 1901 when the McFadden brothers hung out their shingle.

Moses and Uriah McFadden set up office at the intersection of Brock and Queen streets, and practised together until Moses was appointed to the bench in 1915. Ernest McMillan, a young lawyer from Prince Edward Island, then joined the firm, and when Uriah McFadden was appointed a judge in 1931, Ernest brought his younger brother, Gordon, to the city of Sault Ste. Marie to join him in the practice of law. The firm was known as McMillan and McMillan until 1939, when Arthur Wishart, a New Brunswick-born lawyer, left his practice in Blind River to come to Sault Ste. Marie. The name of the firm was changed to Wishart and McMillan, and by the end of World War II illness had forced Gordon McMillan to leave the firm.

Wishart recruited two young lawyers, Patrick FitzGerald and Derek Holder, and this enabled the firm to accept an appointment as solicitor for the city of Sault Ste. Marie. Wishart was a former mayor of Blind River, and he later served as alderman in the city of Sault Ste. Marie and in 1963

*The partners of Wishart, Noble (from left): Gordon P. Acton, C. Bruce Noble, Q.C., Orlando M. Rosa, Gerald E. Nori, Q.C., Elaine S. Pitcher, and Ross Reilly, Q.C.*

he was elected as the Progressive Conservative member to the provincial legislature. Arthur was appointed Attorney General of the Province of Ontario by John Robarts, the then Premier, and he served in this position for seven years. After having served in several other cabinet posts, Wishart retired from the provincial legislature in 1971 and thereafter served successively as chairman of the Ontario Criminal Injuries Compensation Board and the Commission on Election Contributions and Expenses. In 1978 Wishart was made a member of the Order of Canada.

In addition to a provincial attorney general, the firm of Wishart, Noble has produced a total of six judges.

When Wishart was elected to the Ontario legislature, he retired from active practice, and the firm was left in the hands of Gerald E. Nori and C. Bruce Noble. Noble, a senior partner, is active with numerous professional and community organizations. He has served as a director of Plummer Memorial Hospital, vice-chairman of the

Algoma University College Board of Trustees, and is a bencher of the Law Society of Upper Canada.

Nori, a senior partner, is a former president of the Progressive Conservative Association of Ontario, and currently serves as chairman of the Community Futures Committee of the City of Sault Ste. Marie and is chairman of Algoma University College Board of Governors.

Ross Reilly, another member of the firm, is a director of the St. Mary's River Bridge Company, serves on the board of directors for Science North in Sudbury, and is northern Ontario president of the Liberal Party of Canada.

Gordon Acton, a former member of Canada's Alpine Ski Team, joined the firm in 1980 and holds membership in several associations, including the Law Society of Upper Canada and the Canadian Bar Association.

Orlando Rosa, who joined the firm in 1985, is a member of various professional associations, including the Canadian-Italian Advocates Society.

Sault Ste. Marie native Elaine Pitcher joined Wishart, Noble in April 1988 and is serving on the executive of the Algoma District Law Association.

Drawing on past experience and from an established practice of delivering the very best legal advice available, the Wishart, Noble team of specialists is composed specifically to meet the needs of its diverse range of clients. Whether the legal services that are required are for a large corporation, a small business, a level of government, an educational institution, or an individual, Wishart, Noble has the knowledgeable people who can help. Proof of performance is provided by its clients who, regardless of their volume of legal work, continue to come back to a highly professional pool of legal advisers.

# MAPLE LEAF HOMES & COTTAGES INC.

Peter and Margaret Tarvudd had three workers—themselves and a truck driver—when they opened a retail lumberyard in Echo Bay in 1979. By 1988 they had built Maple Leaf Homes & Cottages Inc. into a manufacturing and retail operation that employs 51 people, has offices in other parts of the province, and sells products throughout Ontario.

The Tarvudds' business started in Echo Bay, a small North Shore community 15 miles east of Sault Ste. Marie. Peter did renovations, construction work, and built and sold cottages. Piles of lumber and supplies stored at home soon attracted people in search of building supplies, at which time they decided to establish a retail lumberyard at the present location.

The Tarvudds began supplying customers with basic building sup-

plies, such as lumber and plywood, in a 4,000-square-foot building. It was heated by a wood stove and housed a store and small office. Other building materials were added as customer demands grew, and by the early 1980s Maple Leaf began selling pre-cut home and cottage packages.

From that point the company expanded every year, adding storage buildings and showrooms, and expanding office areas until it occupied a 48,000-square-foot complex. In 1984 an office was opened in Sudbury, later expanded to include sales offices and showrooms in southern Ontario to expand into that market.

*Maple Leaf Homes & Cottages Inc. has grown into a manufacturing and retail operation that today employs 51 people.*

*Maple Leaf Lumber opened in Echo Bay in 1979, staffed by owners Peter and Margaret Tarvudd and a truck driver.*

The branches also have window and door centres.

Maple Leaf does the drafting, design, and pre-cutting for the many home and cottage packages it markets. Its first full-color home and cottage catalogue with a variety of designs and floor plans was produced in 1985. This was followed by a second catalogue, designed in house with computerized drafting equipment.

In 1988 a related company, Maple Leaf Forest Products, began manufacturing maintenance-free windows and doors. The quality line is sold through dealers across Ontario, and through Maple Leaf's own offices. The windows and doors were designed by the company and also are supplied in the Maple Leaf home and cottage packages. In addition, Maple Leaf Forest Products wholesales lumber and plywood products to retail stores.

Maple Leaf Homes & Cottages Inc. is one of the major employers in Echo Bay with staff from Sault Ste. Marie and the North Shore area. It also is active in the community, sponsoring area hockey teams.

# MUIO'S RESTAURANT AND TAVERN

The home of Muio's Restaurant and Tavern at one of Sault Ste. Marie's busy intersections once housed an armory, a bank, and a warehouse. Located at the corner of Queen and East streets, the two-storey brick building was constructed in 1889 and was the site of the Canadian Bank of Commerce.

In its early days it was used as an armory, but when Pat and Carmen Muio and their partners purchased the building in 1961, it was being utilized as a warehouse. It took on a new look and life as a restaurant that has been an anchor in the downtown area for more than a quarter-century.

Rocco DiRenzo, one of the Muio brothers' partners when they opened the restaurant, continues to operate it with his wife, Linda. DiRenzo started working with the Muios in 1953 as a dishwasher at the Adanac Dairy Bar, a lunch counter the brothers operated on Queen Street. The 16-year-old had emigrated to the Sault from Italy with his parents and sister that same year. When the Muios moved to a new location at 685 Queen Street East on the East Street corner to open a large restaurant, DiRenzo, along with an-

*The building on the corner of Queen and East streets was constructed in 1889. It housed a bank, an armory, and a warehouse before Muio's Restaurant opened there in 1961.*

other brother, Guy Muio, became partners.

With this facility the Muios were able to expand their short-order menu to include Italian and other specialty foods such as pizza and broasted chicken. They also added a takeout service.

In 1974 Muio's became a restaurant and tavern. Pat and Carmen retired in the early 1970s, but Guy remained with the restaurant until 1983.

*Muio's Restaurant and Tavern is located at a busy downtown intersection, where it is operated by Rocco DiRenzo.*

DiRenzo, who puts in 14-hour days cooking and running the restaurant, is assisted by Linda in operating the family business. Two children, Angela and Robbie, work there, while another son, James, is a chef in Toronto, and daughter Sandy is in the restaurant business in southern Ontario.

Muio's Restaurant and Tavern employs 25 people. The cooks have been with the restaurant since it opened, while many other staff members have been there for more than 20 years.

In 1985 DiRenzo purchased property on the other side of the East Street corner to provide parking space for the restaurant. He operates a confectionery store at this site as well.

A member of the Marconi Society, DiRenzo also coaches minor soccer in his spare time.

# AURORA'S PIZZA AND SPAGHETTI HOUSE

When one former Sault Ste. Marie man had an urge for Aurora's pizza, he didn't let a little thing like the Atlantic Ocean stand in his way. He contracted restaurant owner Chuck Gassi for a takeout order and five pizzas were shipped to him in Germany.

Takeouts are a big part of the business at Aurora's Pizza and Spaghetti House, which sells 1,200 such pizzas in a week. It is not unusual for the McNabb Street restaurant to send them to Florida, British Columbia, and Calgary. Aurora's has been synonymous with this Italian specialty for many years and is recognized as one of the first, if not the first, commercial pizza parlors in the Sault.

Aurora Butkovich opened a restaurant in approximately 1944 at the corner of James and Albert streets in the west end of the city. It was a small grill with four or five tables and a sit-down bar where one could sip on a coffee or milkshake. The menu featured hamburgers, sandwiches, and other lunches, but no pizza.

After about 10 years she decided to move east to a more central location, and found a new site at the corner of Bruce and Grosvenor streets. It was here that Aurora began making pizzas and spaghetti—with the assistance of her sister-in-law, Mary Gassi, who provided the basic recipes still used by the restaurant. Aurora operated at this location for 25 years, building up a clientele of takeout pizza customers.

In 1976—after 32 years of hard work—she decided it was time to retire and sold her business to her nephew, Chuck Gassi, and his parents, Mary and Bruno Gassi.

Four years later they relocated the restaurant to a former grocery store across the street, but it soon outgrew this location. In the summer of 1984 the new Aurora's Pizza and Spaghetti House opened in the former Moose Lodge (once a church) at 384 McNabb Street. The renovated building has a 7,000-square-foot, 240-seat dining room with a mezzanine, the takeout, a banquet room for 85 people, and a patio that can seat 50 people. The restaurant interior is decorated on a musical theme—stained glass, photographs, carousel horses, and a grand piano—because the Gassis and other members of their family are talented musicians and singers.

And as Aurora's Pizza and Spaghetti House has grown to a business employing 85 people so has the menu grown; it offers more than 80 different items.

*Aurora's Pizza and Spaghetti House, located at 384 McNabb, is famous throughout the province for its Italian food.*

# PATRONS

The following individuals, companies, and organizations have made a valuable commitment to the quality of this publication. Windsor Publications and the Sault Ste. Marie Chamber of Commerce gratefully acknowledge their participation in *Sault Ste. Marie: City by the Rapids.*

Algoma Central Railway*
Algoma Contractors Ltd.*
Algoma Steel Corp. Ltd.*
Algoma University College*
Algonquin Hotel*
Arthur Funeral Home*
Aurora's Pizza and Spaghetti House*
The Bank of Nova Scotia*
Boston Motors Ltd.*
Canadian Tire Associate Store*
Chambers and Miller Ltd.*
Chitty Insurance Brokers Ltd.*
City of Sault Ste. Marie*
Cliffe Printing 1979 Limited*
Cooper's Crane Rental Limited*
Dawson and Keenan Insurance Ltd.*
Downtown Insurance and Realty Ltd.*
Dubreuil Brothers Limited*
R.M. Elliott Construction Ltd.*
Fleming and Smith Ltd.*
General Hospital*
Great Lakes Power Limited*
Group Health Centre*
Gugula/Smedley/Mezzome—Architects Inc.*
Holiday Inn*
James Street Hardware and Furniture Co. Ltd.*
Lyons Building Centre Ltd.*
A.B. McLean Ltd.*
McMaster Oil*
Major Contracting (Algoma) Ltd.*
Manitoulin Transport*
Maple Leaf Homes & Cottages Inc.*
Mary's Restaurant*
Master Welding and Safety Equipment Company*
Muio's Restaurant and Tavern*
Northern Credit Union Limited*
J.P. Pierman Construction Ltd.*
Plummer Memorial Public Hospital*
Pringle & Martin Inc.*
The Proctor & Redfern Group*
Proham Ltd.*
St. Marys Paper Inc.*
Sault College*
Sault Ste. Marie Rotary Club*
The Sault Star*
Sears Canada Inc.*

Soo Mill Buildall*
George Stone and Sons*
Tishman Realty Corp.*
Tossell and Caughill, Architect and Consulting Engineer Inc.*
Traders Metal Co. Ltd.*
United Steel Workers of America*
Wishart, Noble*
Wood Gundy Inc.*
YMCA*

*Partners in Progress of *Sault Ste. Marie: City by the Rapids.* The histories of these companies and organizations appear in Chapter 7, beginning on page 147.

# BIBLIOGRAPHY

Published Materials

Aggassiz, Louis. *Lake Superior: Its Physical Character, Vegetation and Animals.* Boston: Kendall and Lincoln, 1850.

Balfour, Archibishop C.W. *One Hundred Years of the Church of England in Sault Ste. Marie.* Sault Ste. Marie: N.p., 1932.

Bayliss, Joseph, and Estelle Bayliss. *River of Destiny.* Detroit: Wayne University Press, 1955.

Beaven, James. *Recreations of a Long Vacation or a Visit to Indian Missions in Upper Canada.* London: James Burns, 1846.

Beckman, Margaret, Stephen Longmead, and John Black. *The Best Gift—A Record of the Carnegie Libraries in Ontario.* Toronto: Dundurn Press, 1984.

Bigsby, John. *The Shoe and the Canoe or Pictures of Travels in the Canadas.* Vol. I. London: N.p., 1850.

Bishop, Charles. *The Northern Ojibway and the Fur Trade: An Historical and Ecological Survey.* Toronto: Holt, Rinehart, 1974.

Burns, Robert H. *Abitibi Pulp and Paper—History of the Sault Mill.* N.P., n.d.

Burrows, Dorothy M. *Central Through the Years—The Story of Our Church.* Sault Ste. Marie: Central United Church, 1975.

Butterfield, C.W. *History of the Discovery of the Northwest by Jean Nicolet in 1634 with a Sketch of his Life.* Cincinnati: Robert Clarke and Company, 1881.

Cameletti, John. *The History of the Separate School Board in Sault Ste. Marie.* Sault Ste. Marie: Private Printing, 1969.

Campbell, Marjorie Wilkins. *The North West Company.* Toronto: MacMillan of Canada, 1957.

"Canuck, A". *Early Pioneer Life in Upper Canada.* Toronto: William Biggs, 1905.

Capp, E.H. *The Story of Bawating Being the Annals of Sault Ste. Marie.* Sault Ste. Marie: Sault Star Presses, 1904.

Carver, Jonathan. *Three Years Travels Throughout the Interior Parts of North America.* Walpole, New Hampshire: Isiah Thomas and Co., 1813.

Chort, Jacques, et Joelle Chort. *Sault Ste. Marie et les Premiers Descouveurs.* Sault Ste. Marie: Board of Education, 1981.

Collins, Aileen H. *Our Town.* Volumes 1 and 2. Sault Ste. Marie: Privately Printed, 1963.

Collins, W.H. *North Shore of Lake Huron.* Ottawa: Department of Mines Canada, 1925.

Colloton, Rev. Fred. *The Anglican Church in Algoma.* N.P., 1925.

Conway, Thor. *Archeology in Northeastern Ontario.* Toronto: Ministry of Culture and Recreation, 1981.

Cowan, Hugh. *Gold and Silver Jubilee Yearbook.* Sault Ste. Marie: N.p., 1937.

Cranston, J.H. *Etienne Brule: Immortal Scoundrel.* Toronto: The Ryerson Press, 1949.

Delafield, Joseph. *The Unfortified Boundary.* Reprint. New York: Privately Printed, 1943.

Disturnell, John. *Trips Through the Lakes and River St. Lawrence.* New York: Privately Printed, 1857.

Eldon, Donald. "The Career of Francis H. Clergue." *Explorations in Entrepreneurial History III.* April 1951: 254-268.

Ess, T.J. *Steel at the Sault—The Story of Algoma Steel.* N.p., n.d.

*Farm Lands in the Clay Belt of New Ontario.* Sault Ste. Marie: Algoma Central Railway, 1913.

Ferris, John. *Algoma's Industrial and Trade Union Development.* Sault Ste. Marie: Privately Printed, 1951.

Firth, Edith G. *Profiles of a Province.* Toronto: Ontario Historical Society, 1967.

Franchere, Gabriel. *Narrative of a Journey.* N.P., 1820.

Fuller, George N. *Geological Reports of Douglas Houghton.* Lansing: The Michigan Historical Society, 1928.

Glazebrook, G.P. deT. *Life in Ontario—A Social History.* Toronto: University of Toronto Press, 1968.

Green, Eda. *Pioneer Work in Algoma.* London: Society for the Propagation of the Gospel in Foreign Parts, 1915.

Hale, Katherine (pseud.). *This is Ontario.* Toronto: Ryerson Press, 1946.

Hallowell, Gerald A. *Prohibition in Ontario.* Toronto: Ontario Historical Society Research Bulletin Number 2, 1972.

Harmon, Daniel. *Journals of Travels.* London: S.A. Barnes, 1903.

Heath, Frances M., et al. *Fifty Years of Labour in Algoma—Essays on Aspects of Algoma's Working Class History.* Sault Ste. Marie: Algoma University College, 1978.

Henry, Alexander. *Travels and Adventures in Canada and the Indian Territories 1760-1766.* Reprint. Toronto: George N. Morag and Company, 1901.

*Historical Sketches of Ontario.* Toronto: Ministry of Culture and Recreation, 1975.

*Historical Sketches of the Algoma Presbytery.* Sault Ste. Marie: Central United Church, 1979.

Hornick, G. Leigh, ed. *The Call of Copper.* Bruce Mines: North Shore Printing, 1969.

*Illustrated Atlas of the Twin Cities, Sault Ste. Marie Michigan and Ontario.* Chicago: William Sauer, 1881.

*Information for Intending Settlers: Farming Lands of Algoma and North Nipissing.* Toronto: Warwick and Sons under instructions from the Commissioner of Crown Lands, 1885.

Jackson, Don, ed. *Shingwauk Hall: A History.* Sault Ste. Marie: Algoma University College, 1980.

Jameson, Anna. *Winter Studies and Summer Rambles in Canada.* Reprint. Toronto: McLelland and Stewart, 1965.

Jones, Robert L. *History of Agriculture in Ontario, 1613-1880.* Toronto: University of Toronto Press, 1946.

*Jesuit Relations and Allied Documents—Travels and Explorations of the Jesuit Missionaries in New France, 1610-1791.* Cleveland: Burrdis Brothers, 1896.

Judson, Clara Ingram. *The Mighty Soo—Five Hundred Years at Sault Ste. Marie.* New York: Follett Publishing, 1955.

Kane, Paul. *Wanderings of an Artist Among the Indians of North America.* Toronto: The Radisson Society of Canada, 1925.

Kellogg, Louise P. *The British Regime in Wisconsin and the Northwest.* Madison: The State Historical Society of Wisconsin, 1925.

Kinietz, W. Vernon. *The Indians of the Western Great Lakes, 1650-1760.* Ann Arbor: University of Michigan Press, 1940.

Konarek, J. "The Algoma Central and Hudson's Bay Railway: Its Beginnings." *Ontario History* LXII (June 1970): 73-80.

Lower, A.R.M. *North American Assault on the Canadian Forest.* New York: Greenwood Press Publishers, 1938.

Lower, A.R.M., and H.A. Innes. *Settlement and the Forest and Mining Frontiers.* Toronto: The MacMillan Company of Canada, 1936.

MacDonald, James E. *Shantymen and Sodbusters.* Sault Ste. Marie: Sault Star Commercial Printing, 1966.

MacDonald, James E. *This Point of Land.* Sault Ste. Marie: Sault Star Commerial Printing, 1977.

McDowell, Duncan. *Steel at the Sault.* Toronto: University of Toronto Press, 1984.

McKenny, Thomas. *Sketches of a Tour to the Lakes.* Reprint. Minneapolis: Ross and Haines, 1959.

McNeice, Gladys. *The Ermatinger Family of Sault Ste. Marie.* Sault Ste. Marie: Sault Ste. Marie Historical Society, 1984.

More, Charles. *The St. Mary's Falls Canal Semicentennial, 1905.* Detroit: Semicentennial Commission, 1907.

Nelles, H.V. *The Politics of Development.* Toronto: MacMillan of Canada, 1974.

Newton, Stanley. *Mackinac Island and Sault Ste. Marie.* Sault Ste. Marie, Michigan: N.P., n.d.

Newton, Stanley. *Sault Ste. Marie and Chippewa County.* Sault Ste. Marie, Michigan: Sault News Printing Service, 1923.

Nock, O.S. *Algoma Central Railway.* London: Adam and Charles Ltd., 1975.

Nute, Grace Lee. *Lake Superior.* Indianapolis: The Bobbs-Merrill Co., 1944.

Nute, Grace Lee. *The Voyageur.* St. Paul: The Minnesota Historical Society, 1966.

Oliver, Peter. "Sir William Hearst and the Collapse of the Conservative Party." *Canadian Historical Review* LIII (March 1972): 21-50.

Osborn, Charles S. *The Soo.* Reprint. Grand Rapids: Black Letter Press, 1983.

Osborne, Brian, S. and Donald Swainson. *The Sault Ste. Marie Canal—A Chapter in the History of Great Lakes Transport.* Ottawa: The Ministry of the Environment, 1986.

Parkman, Francis. *The Jesuits in North America in the Seventeenth Century.* Boston: Little, Brown and Company, 1923.

Plummer, J.O. *Canadian Pioneers—The History of the Plummer Family.* Privately Printed, 1958.

Reid, Marjorie. "The Quebec Fur Traders and Western Policy." *Canadian Historical Review* VI (March 1925).

Richardson, Linda. *By the Rapids.* Sault Ste. Marie: The *Sault Star,* 1979.

Ross, Eric. *Beyond the River and the Bay.* Toronto: University of Toronto Press, 1970.

Ross, J.W. LeB. "Transportation in the Early Days." Sault Ste. Marie Historical Society *Annual Report,* 1920-1921.

"Sault Ste. Marie Health Center." *Canadian Labour,* December, 1964.

*Salt Ste. Marie Michigan and Ontario International Bridge.* Sault Ste. Marie, Michigan: International Bridge Authority, 1962.

Sawer, Alvah H. *The Northern Peninsula of Mich-*

*igan and Its People.* Chicago: The Western Historical Company, 1883.

Schoolcraft, Henry R. *Information Respecting the History, Condition and Prospects of the Indians of the United States.* Vol. II. Philadelphia: Lippincott, Grambo and Co., 1853.

Schoolcraft, Henry R. *Personal Memoirs of a Residence of Thirty Years with the Indian Tribes.* Philadelphia: Lippincott, Grambo and Co., 1851.

Schull, Joseph. *Ontario Since 1867.* Toronto: McClelland and Stewart, 1968.

Shortt, Adam, and Arthur G. Doughty. *Canada and Its Provinces.* Volume 18—Ontario. Toronto: Publishers Association of Canada, 1914.

*Souvenir of the Soldiers' Reunion and Discovery Week Celebration.* Sault Ste. Marie: N.p., 1923.

Tennyson, Brian D. "The Ontario Election of 1919." *Journal of Canadian Studies* IV (February 1969): 26-36.

Van Every, Margaret. "Francis Hector Clergue and the Rise of Sault Ste. Marie as an Industrial Centre." *Ontario History* LVI (September 1964): 191-202.

*Voyages of Pierre Esprit Radisson.* Boston: Prince Society, 1885.

Whitaker, Russell. "Sault Ste. Marie Michigan and Ontario: A Study in Comparative Geography." Geographical Society of Philadelphia, *Bulletin,* Volume 32, 1934.

Wilson, Dale. *Tracks of the Black Bear.* Toronto: Green Tree Publishing, 1974.

*Wooded Lands in Ontario—A Description of Land for Settlement in Algoma and Western Ontario.* Montreal: Canadian Pacific Railway, 1888.

Young, A.E. *The Two Soos: American and Canadian.* Grand Rapids: James Bayne Co., n.d.

Zaslow, Morris. *The Opening of the Canadian North, 1870-1914.* Toronto: McClelland and Stewart, 1971

Unpublished Materials, Archival

Madison, Wisconsin. State Historical Society of Wisconsin. Grignon, Law and Proirlier Papers

Ottawa, Ontario. Public Archives of Canada. North West Company Papers. Hudson's Bay Company Papers.

St. Paul, Minnesota. Minnesota Historical Society. Beaver Club Minutes. Cadotte Papers. Gabriel Franchere Papers. North West Company Papers.

Sault Ste. Marie, Michigan. Baylis Public Library. Judge Joseph Steere Collection.

Sault Ste. Marie, Ontario. Algoma University College. Gladys McNeice Papers.

Sault Ste. Marie, Ontario. City of Sault Ste. Marie. Municipal Records.

Sault Ste. Marie, Ontario. Sault Ste. Marie & 49th Field Regiment Historical Society. Archival Collection.

Toronto, Ontario. Archives of Ontario. Bailey Papers. Crown Land Reports. Douglas Family Papers—Correspondence. Irving Papers. Miscellaneous Collection. Pamphlet Collection. Reports of the Immigration Department. Robinson Papers. Strachan Papers. Treasury Department. Vidal Papers. Walker Collection.

Unpublished Materials, Other

Clergue, Francis H. "An Instance of Industrial Evolution in Northern Ontario, Dominion of Canada." Address delivered at a General Meeting of the Board of Trade of the City of Toronto, April 2, 1900.

Clergue, Francis H. Untitled address presented by Clergue at a banquet given in his honour by the citizens of Sault Ste. Marie, February 15, 1901.

Knight, Alan. "Mica Bay, Allen MacDonnell, and the Pointe aux Mines-Mica Bay Affair." Unpublished Ph.D. Research Paper, 1982.

MacDonald, Graham A. "The Saulteur Fishery at Sault Ste. Marie." Unpublished Master's Essay, 1972.

Machum, Donald. *The History of Algoma Steel.* Unpublished three volume typescript. C. 1965.

Newspapers

*Algoma Pioneer,* Sault Ste. Marie, Ontario.
*Saturday Night,* Toronto, Ontario.
*Sault Evening News,* Sault Ste. Marie, Michigan.
*Sault Ste. Marie (Daily) Star,* Sault Ste. Marie, Ontario.
*Steelton News,* Steelton, Ontario.

# INDEX